The Jews among the Greeks and Romans

The Jews among the Greeks and Romans

A Diasporan Sourcebook

Edited by
Margaret Williams

The Johns Hopkins University Press
Baltimore, Maryland

The Johns Hopkins University Press
2715 North Charles Street
Baltimore, Maryland 21218-4363

Library of Congress Cataloging-in-Publication Data

The Jews among the Greeks and Romans : a diasporan sourcebook /
edited [and translated] by Margaret Williams.
    p.   cm.
    Includes bibliographical references and indexes.
    ISBN 0-8018-5937-9 (alk. paper). – ISBN 0-8018-5938-7 (pbk.:
alk. paper.)
    1. Jews–History–589 B.C.–70 A.D.–Sources. 2. Jews-
-History–70-638–Sources. 3. Jews—Rome–History–Sources.
4. Hellenism–Sources. 5. Jews–Diaspora–History–Sources.
6. Judaism–History–Post-exilic period, 586 B.C.–210 A.D.–Sources.
7. Judaism–History–Talmudic period, 10-425–Sources.
I. Williams, Margaret, 1947–.
DS122.J49 1998
909′.04924–dc21   97-32880
                                                             CIP

A catalog record for this book is available from the British Library.

Contents

To the memory of my daughter, Jocelyn
25 Oct. 1977 – 15 Feb. 1978
ἐν εἰρήνῃ ἡ κοίμησίς σου

Preface

The Jews remained an object of fascination throughout antiquity, mainly because they were one of the few ethnic groups in the Graeco-Roman world to resist the powerful pressures of cultural homogenisation. Their ubiquity meant that they were widely known about, even if not well known. Greek and Roman writers devoted much space to them but few bothered to concern themselves with real Jews. What we mainly meet with in their works are stereotypes, and those largely unflattering. Witness many of the entries in Menahem Stern's massive *Greek and Latin Authors on Jews and Judaism* (3 vols, Jerusalem, 1974-84). But evidence does exist, in abundance, to show what real Jews were like in antiquity and how they interacted with the Greeks and Romans, both pagan and Christian. To date, however, no handy (and easily affordable) compendium of it has been made, as anyone who has tried to teach the subject to university students will know. Hence this collection of texts, each one freshly translated, which is heavily, and deliberately, biased towards documentary, and especially epigraphic, source material.

In making this compilation, I have been forced largely through the volume of evidence available to impose certain limits. With few exceptions, each one justified ad loc., all the entries in this book fall within the seven hundred and fifty year span marked by the death of Alexander the Great in 323 BCE and the demise of the Jewish Patriarchate around the 420s CE. This period, which saw, first, the rapid opening up of opportunities to the Jews and, then, in the century after Constantine, the gradual but inexorable erection of barriers against them, forms a natural unity. To have stopped at Constantine himself, my initial intention, would have made little sense: as the epigraphic evidence in particular makes clear, the world did not change overnight for the Jews simply because he had extended official recognition to Christianity and begun to issue hostile enactments against them. Within my chosen period, I have selected material that relates to Diasporan, rather than Palestinian, Jewry. Apart from passage **V.20**, which has been included for a special reason, the handful of Judaean/Palestinian texts that have been admitted have a clear Diasporan dimension. Talmudic evidence has been cited only very sparingly, as I lack the expertise to handle adequately this difficult, ahistoric material.

The very success of the Jews in adapting to life in a foreign environment poses problems for the would-be compiler of a Jewish sourcebook. Greek was the dominant language of Diasporan Jews and their personal names were mainly Greek or Latin. Unless texts emanate from an identifiably Jewish context, such as a Jewish cemetery, or possess unambiguously Jewish features, such as the term *Ioudaios* (a Jew), doubt can arise over attribution. In making my selection of texts, I have admitted only those which are indisputably Jewish or generally argued to be so by scholars. The latter, only a few documents in any case, have been included mainly to illustrate cultural ambiguity. In translating each of my chosen texts, I have aimed at accuracy rather than elegance. With regard to their presentation, the following conventions are to be noted:

(i) All words enclosed in brackets are editorial, those within square brackets being proposed restorations and those within curved parentheses explanatory or amplificatory matter. Angle brackets enclose words and letters assumed to have been carved in error.

(ii) Numerals have been given in the form in which they appear in the original text – i.e. either in figures or in words.

(iii) All names borne by Jews, apart from Ptolemy and Alexander, which have been anglicised throughout, are in transcription. My reason for rejecting the common practice of Latinisation is to draw attention to the linguistic variations and different degrees of acculturation that existed within Diasporan Jewry. Names which, in consequence, may prove hard to identify, are marked in the text with an asterisk and glossed in Appendix 4.

Acknowledgements

Four people have been of signal assistance in the production of this book: Joan Booth, who helped with the translation of certain Latin passages, my daughter Helen, who provided the textual illustrations in chapters II, IV and V, John Crook, who read and offered valuable comments on my manuscript and my husband, Peredur, who, besides giving much-needed technical assistance, has been unstinting in his encouragement and support. I thank them all most warmly.

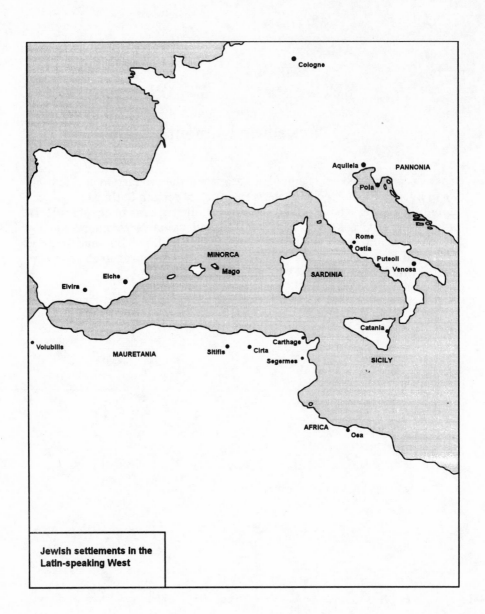

Cologne

Aquileia
Pola
PANNONIA

Elvira
Elche

MINORCA
Mago

Rome
Ostia
Puteoli
Venosa

SARDINIA

Volubilis

MAURETANIA

Sitifis
Cirta
Carthage
Segermes

Catania

SICILY

AFRICA
Oea

**Jewish settlements in the
Latin-speaking West**

Jewish settlements in the
Greek-speaking East

I

The Jewish Diaspora in the Hellenistic and Roman imperial periods

INTRODUCTION

With Alexander the Great's death in 323 BCE, the Hellenistic world, as the area over which he had ruled was later to be called, was torn apart. Rival war-lords, such as Ptolemy and Seleukos, fought to carve out mini-empires for themselves. In the turmoil, which lasted in an acute form for at least fifty years and in a milder one for very much longer, population movement on a quite unprecedented scale took place throughout that area. Conspicuous among the people 'on the move', whether as prisoners of war, refugees, settlers in the new Hellenistic cities or entrepreneurs, were the Jews of Judaea, for their country lay on one of the major fault-lines of the Hellenistic world, the boundary between the Ptolemaic and Seleucid empires, and was frequently the scene of violent disturbance. The impact of these developments upon the Jews is revealed in **I.3** below: by the end of the 2nd century, if not before, Jewish settlements were to be found throughout the eastern half of the Mediterranean.

What Hellenistic warring started, the *Pax Romana* and political instability in Judaea enabled to continue. While peaceful conditions in the eastern provinces, allied to good communications, led to the greater diffusion of Jews already domiciled outside Judaea, many of those still living in Judaea itself were emboldened to leave the homeland, with all its troubles and restricted economic opportunities, and seek peace and material advancement elsewhere. A fair idea of the extent of the Jewish Diaspora by the middle of the 1st century CE is given in **I.5** and **I.6**: these passages show that it stretched from Mesopotamia to Rome. Actually, Jewish settlement then was even further-flung than that. Well before the end of the Julio-Claudian period (68 CE), the Jews had almost certainly reached Spain (an inference from the *Epistle of Paul to the Romans* 15.24) and there is good epigraphic evidence from the 1st century CE for well-established Jewish communities in the Crimea (see, for instance, **I.106**). Christian writers, in a not entirely friendly spirit, later applied the term *diaspora* (dispersion or scattering) to this process of diffusion, which they viewed as a divine punishment. There is no reason to think that the Jews on the whole viewed it in that way. **I.1**, **I.2** and **I.5**, all by Jewish authors, reveal an entirely positive attitude towards the Jewish colonisation of the *oikoumene*, the inhabited world.

1. ITS EXTENT IN PROPHECY AND ACTUALITY

In Alexandrian-Jewish prophecy

Although the Alexandrian-Jewish authorship of this passage is generally accepted, its date is disputed, both the 2nd and 1st century BCE having been suggested as possibilities. See *HJPAJC* III, p. 4 (1st century) and J.J. Collins, *The*

Sibylline Oracles of Egyptian Judaism (Missoula, Montana, 1972), p. 33 (mid-2nd century)

(**I.1**) Every land and every sea shall be filled with you. (*Sibylline Oracles* 3.271)

According to Josephus' version of the prophecy of Balaam

The first prophecy of Balaam (*Numbers* 23.7-10) is here entirely recast by Josephus to reflect the nature of Jewish settlement in his own day – i.e. the late 1st century CE.

(**I.2**) The land to which He himself has sent you, you shall possess; it shall be subject to your children forever and every land and sea shall be filled with their glory; you shall be sufficiently numerous to supply the world and every land with inhabitants from your stock ... now you are few and the land of Canaan shall accommodate you but know that the inhabitable world lies before you as an eternal dwelling place and the majority of you shall live on the islands and continent, your number greater than the stars in the sky. (Josephus, *Jewish Antiquities* 4.115-16)

In the first quarter of the 1st century BCE

Note that both the date and authenticity of **I.3** are disputed. Even if it is not a genuine Roman document from the reign of Simon (143/2-135/4 BCE), the picture it gives of the Diaspora in the first decades of the 1st century BCE, the period when 1 *Maccabees* is thought to have been written, is entirely consistent with other evidence for the extent of the Diaspora at that time. See E.M. Smallwood, *The Jews under Roman Rule from Pompey to Diocletian* (Leiden, 1976), pp. 8-9, n. 15 and 121, n. 5.

(**I.3**) And Noumenios and his fellow-envoys came from Rome, bearing letters for the kings and the countries in which the following were written: Lucius, consul of the Romans to King Ptolemy, greetings. The envoys of the Jews have come to us, since they are our friends and allies, to renew the original friendship and alliance, having been sent by Simon the High Priest and the Jewish people. They have brought a golden shield valued at 1000 minas. It has pleased us, therefore, to write to the kings and countries so that they do not seek to harm them or make war on them, their cities and their territories, or ally themselves with those warring against them. It has seemed right to us to accept the shield from them. If any wrongdoers have fled from their territory to you, hand them over to Simon the High Priest so that he may proceed against them in accordance with their laws. And he wrote these things to Demetrios the king and Attalos and Arathes and Arsakes (the rulers of Syria, Pergamum, Kappadokia and Parthia respectively) and to all the lands and to Sampsakes (name uncertain) and the Spartans and to Delos and to Myndos and to

Sikyon and to Karia and to Samos and to Pamphylia and Lykia and to Halikarnassos and to Rhodes and to Phaselis and to Kos and to Side and to Arad and Gortyn and Knidos and Cyprus and Cyrene. A copy of these things he wrote to Simon the High Priest.(1 *Maccabees* 15.16-24)

(I.4) This same Strabo testifies in another passage that at the time when Sulla crossed over to Greece to make war on Mithridates and had sent Lucullus to deal with the unrest in Cyrene (*c.* 86 BCE), the inhabitable world was full our people. This is what he says – 'There were four status groups in the state of Cyrene – the first comprised of citizens, the second of farmers, the third of resident aliens and the fourth of Jews. This group has already made its way into every city and it is not easy[1] to find a place in the inhabitable world which has not received this people and felt the weight of its influence.'[2] (Strabo, as cited in Josephus, *Jewish Antiquities* 14.114-15 = Stern I no. 105)

In the mid-1st century CE

The speaker in **I.5** is Agrippa I, king of Judaea, and he is addressing the Emperor Gaius/Caligula in 40 CE. Although the speech is probably largely, if not wholly, Philo's invention, the situation it describes is entirely plausible and supported, inter alia, by **I.6**. For discussion, see E.M. Smallwood, *Philonis Alexandrini Legatio ad Gaium* (Leiden, 1961), p. 294.

(I.5) 'Concerning the Holy City, there are points to be made that relate to me. It is, as I have said, my native city and the mother city of not just one country, Judaea, but the majority, because of the colonies[3] it has sent out from time to time both to the neighbouring lands of Egypt, Phoenicia and Syria – the so-called Coele Syria as well as the rest – and to the distant countries of Pamphylia, Cilicia, most of Asia up to Bithynia and the depths of Pontus, and in the same way also to Europe, to Thessaly, Boeotia, Macedonia, Aetolia, Attica, Argos, Corinth and most of the best parts of the Peloponnese. It is not only the continents that are full of Jewish colonies but the most renowned of the islands, Euboea, Cyprus, Crete. Concerning the lands across the Euphrates, I keep silent. Except for a small part ..., they all have Jewish settlers.' (Philo, *Legatio ad Gaium* 281-2)

(I.6) There were living in Jerusalem Jews,[4] devout men, (drawn) from every nation under heaven. At this sound, they all came together and were confounded because each one of them heard his own language being spoken. They were all amazed and they marvelled, saying – 'Look, are not these men who are speaking all Galilaeans? How is that each one of us hears his native language? Parthians and Medes and Elamites, and those who inhabit Mesopotamia, Judaea and Cappadocia, Pontus and Asia (Minor), Phrygia and Pamphylia, Egypt and the parts of Libya around

Cyrene, visitors from Rome, both Jews and proselytes, Cretans and Arabs, we hear them telling in our own tongues the mighty works of God.' (*Acts of the Apostles* 2.5-11)

2. REASONS FOR THE DIFFUSION OF THE JEWS

These are not easy to illustrate. The great dispersion, whose extent was illustrated in the previous section, was not, on the whole, the result of grand public initiatives but the consequence of thousands upon thousands of private decisions made by little people, and our sources rarely concern themselves with such matters. Amongst the papyri, there are no private letters of relevance. Inscriptions, whether funerary or evergetist, are essentially public documents. The focus of much of the literary material is on war and politics. The passages in this section reflect the bias and inadequacies of our sources. Only rarely do we catch a glimpse of Jews emigrating for positive personal reasons. Those portrayed here are mostly victims of matters beyond their control – e.g. war, high political intrigue, and the military demands of the Seleucids and Ptolemies. Such a picture is highly misleading. Jews, after all, continued to move around the Mediterranean basin in great numbers long after the era of dynastic wars and military colonisation had ended and political stability had returned to Judaea itself. Although the reasons for this on-going, voluntary migration are rarely given in our sources, they can easily be inferred from the kinds of places in which dense Jewish settlement took place – rich farming areas, such as the Fayum in Egypt, and commercial centres, such as Alexandria, Antioch, Delos and Rhodes.

(a) Jewish prisoners of war

(i) As a consequence of the Ptolemaic conquest of Palestine in the late 4th century BCE

(I.7) The moment, I thought, had come to raise (with Ptolemy II Philadelphos) the matter concerning which I had often petitioned Sosibios of Tarentum and Andreas, the Chiefs of the Bodyguard, namely the release of those who had been brought out of Judaea by the king's father (*sc.* Ptolemy, son of Lagos). For he, exploiting his luck and bravery, had overrun the whole of Coele Syria and Phoenicia, transplanted some (of the inhabitants), taken others prisoner, and terrorised all into submission. It was on that occasion too that he had transported into Egypt from the country of the Jews around one hundred thousand people. Of these, he armed about thirty thousand picked men and settled them in the country in garrisons. Even before that, many had entered (the country) along with the Persians and, yet earlier again, others had been despatched as auxiliaries to fight with Psammetichos against the king of the Ethiopians. These, however, were not so many in number as the people transported by Ptolemy, son of Lagos. Having, as I said above, selected and armed the best in terms of age and fitness, the remaining mass, which consisted of the old and the young, and even women, he reduced to slavery, not out of personal preference, but because he was overborne by his soldiers. (*Letter of Aristeas* 12-14)

(ii) As a consequence of the Jewish revolt against the Seleucids?

The Jewish slaves mentioned in the two manumission documents below are usually assumed (as, for instance, in *HJPAJC* III, p. 65) to have been Seleucid prisoners of war, who had been enslaved and taken to Greece during the troubles in Judaea in the early Maccabaean period. The first document definitely dates from that time and the second quite possibly so.

(I.8) In the archonship of Emmenidas, the son of Kallias, in the month of Apellaios, Kleon, son of Kleudamos, with the consent of Xenophaneia, the mother of Kleudamos, has sold to Apollo Pythios a male person, by name Ioudaios, a Jew by race, for the sum of four silver minas on these conditions, namely, that he is to be free and not claimed as a slave by anyone throughout his whole life. Inasmuch as Ioudaios has entrusted the sale to the god, he may do whatever he wishes. Guarantors in accordance with the law of the city: Xenon, son of Glaukos; Aristion, son of Agon. Witnesses: Amyntas (and) Tarantinos, the priests of Apollo, and the archons, Aristion, Asandros (and) Aristomachos. Laymen: Sodamidas, Theuphrastos, Teison, Glaukos, son of Xenon, Menes. (*CIJ* I² no. 710 – Delphi; 162 BCE)

(I.9) In the archonship of Archon, son of Kallias, in the month of Endyspoitropios, Atisidas, son of Orthaios, has sold to Apollo Pythios three females called Antigona, a Jewess by race, and her two daughters, Theodora and Dorothea, for the sum of seven silver minas, and he is in possession of the full price. Guarantor according to the law of the city: Eudokos, son of Praxias, a Delphian. Antigona and Theodora and Dorothea have entrusted the sale to the god, on the condition that they be free and not claimed as slaves by anyone throughout their lives. If anyone seizes them for the purpose of enslavement, let the vendor Atisidas and the guarantor Eudokos provide confirmation (of the sale). If the vendor and guarantor do not provide confirmation of the sale to the god, let them be liable to a financial penalty in accordance with the law. Similarly, let whoever comes across them have the authority to rescue them, since they are freedwomen, without incurring any penalty and without becoming liable to any charge or financial penalty. Witnesses: Amyntas, the priest of Apollo and the archons Nikarchos; Kleon, son of Demosthenes; Hagion, son of Ekephylos. Laymen: Archon, son of Nikoboulos; Eudoros, son of Amyntas. (*CIJ* I² no. 709 – Delphi; 170-157/6 BCE)

(iii) As a consequence of the Roman conquest of Judaea

(I.10) Besides the pirate-chiefs, the prisoners of war led in (Pompey's) triumph included the son of Tigranes the Armenian, with his wife and daughter, Zosime, the wife of King Tigranes himself, Aristoboulos (II), King of the Jews,[5] a sister and five children of Mithridates ... (Plutarch, *Life of Pompey* 45.5 = Stern I no. 262)

(**I.11**) Most of them (the Jews of Transtiberine Rome) were Roman freedmen. For they had been brought to Italy as prisoners of war[6] and then freed by their owners and they had not been compelled to debase any of their native customs. (Philo, *Legatio ad Gaium* 155)

(iv) As a consequence of revolt against Rome

The aftermath of the fall of Jerusalem in 70 CE

(**I.12**) Since the soldiers were by now becoming weary of slaughtering, even though large numbers of survivors were still coming to light, Caesar (*sc.* Titus) gave orders to kill only those who were armed or offering resistance. The remainder they were to take prisoner. In addition to those specified in their instructions, they liquidated the old and the weak. Those in their prime, and potentially useful, they herded into the Temple and confined in the Court of the Women. As guard, Caesar set over them one of his freedmen. Fronto, one of his friends, was to determine the appropriate fate for each. He executed all the revolutionaries and the brigands. They had laid information against each other. Of the young, he selected the tallest and finest and kept them back for the triumph. Of the remainder, those over seventeen he bound and despatched to the quarries in Egypt.[7] Most of them, however, he made over to the provinces for destruction in the theatre by the sword or wild beasts. Those under seventeen years were sold. (Josephus, *Jewish War* 6.414-18)

(**I.13**) 'Thus saith the Lord; a voice was heard in Ramah, lamentation and bitter weeping ... ' (an extended commentary on the phrase follows). Some of the Jews interpret this passage thus, because, after the capture of Jerusalem in Vespasian's time, countless thousands of captives were sent via this route, Gaza and Alexandria, to Rome. (Jerome, *In Ieremiam* 31.15 = *CCL* 74, 307)

(**I.14**) Claudia Aster*, a captive from Jerusalem.[8] Tiberius Claudius [Mas?]culus, a freedman of the Emperor, has taken care (to have this funerary monument erected). I ask you to make every effort to see to it that no one, in contravention of the law, casts down my epitaph. She lived 25 years. (*CIJ* I² no. 556 = Noy I no. 26 – possibly Naples; 1st century CE)

Aftermath of the Second Jewish War (135 CE)

(**I.15**) During the consulship of these men,[9] the Jews staged an insurrection. Hadrian went to Jerusalem and took the Jews prisoner. He then went down to the place called Terebinthos (Hebron), where he set up a market and sold them off, each one at the price of a horse. Those who were left over he took to Gaza. There too he set up a market and sold them. To this very day that market is called Hadrian's. (*Chronikon Paschale* I, ed. Dindorf, p. 474)

(I.16) Let us read the old histories and the traditions of the wailing Jews because in the Tabernacle of Abraham, where now a famous market is held every year, thousands of men were put on sale after their final defeat at the hands of Hadrian. Those who could not be sold, perished on transportation to Egypt, as much through shipwreck and hunger as through deliberate genocide. (Jerome, *In Zachariam* 11.4-5 = *CCL* 76a, 851)

(b) Jews as military colonists

In Ptolemaic Egypt and Cyrene

(I.17) Ptolemy son of Lagos held the same opinion of the Jews who dwelt in Alexandria as Alexander, for he entrusted to them the fortresses throughout Egypt, in the belief that they would be faithful and excellent guards. And when he wanted to exert firm control over Cyrene and the other cities of Libya, he sent a detachment of Jews to them to act as military colonists. (Josephus, *Contra Apionem* 2.44)

In Seleucid Asia Minor

Note that the authenticity of the following letter of Antiochus III the Great to his satrap in Lydia, generally dated to around 210-201 BCE, has been challenged (*HJPAJC* III, p. 17, n. 33). The majority opinion, accepted here, is that it is substantially genuine.

(I.18) King Antiochos to Zeuxis, his father, greeting. If you are well, that is good. I too am in sound health. Having learned that the people in Lydia and Phrygia are in revolt, I have come to the conclusion that this requires serious attention on my part. Having consulted with my Friends as to what I should do, I have decided to transport, with their effects, two thousand Jewish families from Mesopotamia and Babylonia to the fortresses and most important places (of Lydia and Phrygia). For I am persuaded that they will be loyal guardians of our interests because of their piety to their god, and I know that they have had the testimony of my forefathers to their good faith and zeal in doing what they are asked. I wish, therefore, to transport them, even though the enterprise is difficult, and I have promised (them) that they may use their own laws. When you bring them to the places mentioned above, you shall give each of them a site for house construction and land for cultivation and planting with vines and exempt them from payment of taxes on the produce of the land for ten years. Also, let grain be measured out for feeding their servants, until they acquire produce from the land. Let there be given also to those in our service (meaning of text not quite clear here) sufficient for their needs so that by meeting with kind treatment from us they may show themselves the more zealous in our cause. Take as much thought as possible for their nation, that it be not harassed by anyone. (Josephus, *Jewish Antiquities* 12.148-53)

Babylonian Jews as colonists of Herod the Great

(I.19) At that time, Herod, wishing to secure himself against the Trachonites (they lived to the north-east of his kingdom), decided to create a village the size of a city between them and the Jews ... Learning that a Jew from Babylonia had crossed the Euphrates with five hundred horsemen, all of them mounted archers, and as many as a hundred kinsmen, and that by chance he was staying at Antioch near Daphne in Syria, since Saturninus,[10] the governor of Syria at that time (*c.* 9-6 BCE), had given him a place called Oulatha to dwell in, he summoned him with his band of followers and promised to provide him with land in the toparchy called Batanea which bordered on Trachonitis. Wishing to have the settlement as a bulwark, he announced that the land would be tax-free and they would be exempt from all the customary levies ... Persuaded by this offer, the Babylonian came.[11] Having acquired the land, he built fortresses and a village, to which he gave the name Bathyra. (Josephus, *Jewish Antiquities* 17.23-6)

(c) Jewish refugees

(I.20) At the time when Antiochos, surnamed Epiphanes, was disputing the suzerainty of Syria with Ptolemy the Sixth (in the so-called Sixth Syrian War, 170-168 BCE), faction-fighting broke out among the Jewish aristocracy. The rivalry was over supreme power, since no individual of high rank would brook subjection to his peers. Onias, one of the chief priests, having gained the upper hand, expelled from the city the sons of Tobias. Taking refuge with Antiochos, they beseeched him to use them as guides and invade Judaea. The king, who had long set his heart on this design, was won over. Setting out with a large army, he took the city by force and liquidated a large number of Ptolemy's supporters. To his soldiers he gave unrestricted licence to pillage and he himself plundered the Temple and caused the regular course of daily sacrifices to cease for three years and six months. The chief priest Onias, having escaped to Ptolemy and received from him a site in the nome of Heliopolis, built a small town modelled on Jerusalem and founded a temple like the one there.[12] (Josephus, *Jewish War* 1.31-3)

(I.21) After this, Paul departed from Athens and came to Corinth. There he came across a Jew called Aquila, a native of Pontus, and his wife

Priscilla. He had recently arrived from Italy (*c.* 49 CE), because of Claudius' order that all the Jews should depart from Rome.[13] (*Acts of the Apostles* 18.1-2)

(**I.22**) After Masada had been captured in this way, the general (L. Flavius Silva) left a garrison in the fortress and himself retired with his army to Caesarea, for not a single enemy was left in the country. The whole of it had already been subdued in the course of the long war, which had impinged upon and threatened with disorder many of those who lived even in the remotest parts. Even at Alexandria in Egypt, it came about that many Jews subsequently perished. For certain of the faction of the Sicarii succeeded in escaping there ...[14] (Josephus, *Jewish War* 7.407-10)

(**I.23**) From there (Alexandria) I (the speaker is Josephus) was sent with Titus to the siege of Jerusalem. Frequently my life was in danger from both the Jews who, for the sake of revenge, were eager to get their hands on me, and the Romans who attributed every defeat they suffered to treachery on my part ... When the city of Jerusalem was on the point of being forcibly taken, Titus Caesar repeatedly tried to persuade me to grab whatever I wanted from the wreckage of my native city ... When he was about to set sail for Rome, he took me as his fellow-passenger and gave me every mark of respect. When we arrived in Rome, I met with great consideration from Vespasian.[15] (Josephus, *Vita* 416-23)

(d) Jewish civilian settlers

(**I.24**) They (the Jews) also received honour from the kings of Asia, after serving them in war. For example, Seleukos Nikator (305-281 BCE) deemed them worthy of citizenship[16] in the cities he founded in Asia, Lower Syria and in his very capital, Antioch, and declared them to be of equal status with the Macedonians and Greeks who had settled there, so that these rights remain even now. (Josephus, *Jewish Antiquities* 12.119)

(e) A Jewish merchant from Asia Minor at Rome

Both the Greek term for grave (*soros*), as well as the language of the curse formula in the following inscription, indicate that the merchant was a native of Asia Minor, possibly from Phrygia. (See J.H.M. Strubbe, 'Curses against the violation of the grave' in *SEJE*, pp. 126-7.) The advance purchase of this family tomb suggests that he was probably an immigrant to Rome rather than a casual visitor.

(**I.25**) ... I, [K]atilia Eutychi ... have made [in advance?] ... This grave contains Hermione, beloved 4 year old foster-child of Hermias. I, Pouplis* Katilis Hermias, a merchant, aged 35, lie here. If anyone opens this grave (*soros*) and puts in another body, he shall pay to the treasury 5,000 denarii.

If anyone buys this tomb or damages its lettering, the wrath of God will destroy his whole family. (Noy II no. 360 – Rome; 2nd-3rd century CE(?))

(f) Moving for the purpose of matrimony

(I.26) At this period (i.e. after Josephus had settled permanently in Rome) I divorced my wife in displeasure at her ways, even though she was the mother of three sons of mine ... Afterwards I married a woman who had settled in Crete but was a Jewess by birth. Her parents were well-born, indeed the most notable people in that place. (Josephus, *Vita* 426-7)

(I.27) An Antiochene from the land of [Karia?],[17] from ancestors who won many (civic) honours, by name Debbora, I was given to Pamphylos of Sillyon, a famous man and lover of children, and to fleecy Phrygia. I have received (this tomb) as a mark of gratitude from him for my virgin marriage. (*CIJ* II no. 772, now superseded by *MAMA* IV no. 202 – Apollonia in Phrygia; 2nd-3rd century CE)

3. EVIDENCE FOR JEWISH MOBILITY WITHIN THE GRAECO-ROMAN WORLD

In the previous section the focus was on permanent displacement. Here we present a sample of the abundant evidence for Jewish movement around the Graeco-Roman world. (For visits by Diasporan Jews to Judaea, see **III.1-6**.) That these texts all date from the Roman imperial period is not a coincidence. It was the *Pax Romana* which enabled people to travel with unprecedented ease from one part of the Mediterranean to another.

(a) A Jewish adventurer, *c.* 5 BCE

(I.28) At this time, a certain young man, Jewish by birth but reared at Sidon by a Roman freedman, passing himself off on the strength of his physical resemblance as Alexander, (the Hasmonaean son) whom Herod had liquidated, came to Rome in the expectation of escaping detection. Collaborating with him was a fellow Jew who knew everything that went on in the kingdom (of Herod). Under this man's instruction, he put it about that the men who had been sent to liquidate both him and Aristoboulos (his brother) had, out of pity, smuggled them away and substituted bodies that resembled theirs. Having thoroughly taken in the Jews of Crete with these claims and been lavishly kitted out by them for his journey, he sailed across to Melos. There, through his extreme plausibility, he collected much more and even persuaded his hosts to sail with him to Rome. Landing at Dikaiarchia,[18] he received from the Jews there vast numbers of gifts and was escorted on his way like a king by his (supposed) father's friends. The physical likeness was so convincing that those who had seen Alexander and known him well swore that it was he. The whole of Roman Jewry poured forth to view him and vast was the crowd in the narrow streets through which he was carried. For the Melians had become so deranged that they transported him in a litter and provided at their own expense a royal retinue. (Josephus, *Jewish War* 2.101-5)

(b) Early Christian evidence for Jewish mobility

(I.29) Those who had been scattered after the persecution that arose over Stephen made their way as far as Phoenicia and Cyprus and Antioch. They spoke the word (i.e. gave the Christian message) to no one except the Jews. Some among them were from Cyprus and Cyrene. Coming to Antioch, they started to speak to the Greeks too, telling them the good news about the Lord Jesus. (*Acts of the Apostles* 11.19-20)

(I.30) There were at Antioch, in the (Christian) congregation there, certain prophets and teachers: Barnabas, Symeon called Niger, Lucius of Cyrene, Manaen, who had been brought up with Herod the tetrarch and Saul.[19] (*Acts of the Apostles* 13.1)

(I.31) So these two (Paul and Barnabas), having been sent out by the Holy Spirit, went down (from Antioch) to Seleucia and from there sailed to Cyprus. Arriving at Salamis, they preached the word of God in the synagogues of the Jews. They had John with them as their helper as well. They passed through the whole island as far as Paphos ... Leaving Paphos, Paul and his party came to Perge in Pamphylia. John left them and returned to Jerusalem but they continued on from Perge and came to Antioch in Pisidia. Entering the synagogue on the day of the Sabbath, they sat down ... But the Jews stirred up the women of quality who were worshipping and the leading men of the city. They started up a persecution against Paul and Barnabas and drove them out of their district. Shaking the dust from their feet in protest against them, they went to Iconium ... At Iconium similarly they entered the synagogue of the Jews and spoke in such a way that a large number of Jews and Greeks became believers ... But when a move was made by the Gentiles and the Jews and the rulers (*archons*) of the latter to assault them and stone them, they got wind of it and fled to the cities of Lykaonia, namely Lystra and Derbe, and the surrounding countryside. There they continued their evangelisation ... After evangelising in that town (Derbe) and gaining a good number of converts, they returned to Lystra and Iconium and Antioch ... Then they journeyed through Pisidia and came to Pamphylia. When they had preached the word at Perge, they went down to Attalia. From there they sailed to Antioch where they had originally been commended to the grace of God for the task which they had now completed. (*Acts of the Apostles* 13.4-6; 13-14; 50-1 and 14.1-2; 5-7; 21; 24-6)

(I.32) A certain Jew called Apollos, who by birth was an Alexandrian, arrived in Ephesos. He was a learned man and skilled in the Scriptures. (*Acts of the Apostles* 18.24)

(c) Epigraphic evidence for mobility

(i) Inscriptions from the Aegean, Greece and the Black Sea

(I.33) Zosas of Paros to the Most High God, (in fulfilment of) a vow. (*CIJ* I² no. 727 = *DF* no. 4 – from the synagogue at Delos)

(I.34) Menippos, from Jerusalem;[20] five hundred (drachmas?). (*IG* XII.1, no. 11 – line from a fragmentary donor list from Rhodes)

(I.35) Ammia, a Jerusalemite. (*CIJ* I² no. 715a – Athens; 1st century CE)

(I.36) Ioustos, son of Andromache, of Tiberias (in Galilee). (*CIJ* I² no. 721a – Taenarum in Laconia; undated)

(I.37) [Iak]ob and Le[onti]os, grandsons of [I]akobo[s], of Caesarea (Maritima?). (*CIJ* I no. 715 – Greece, probably Athens; undated)

(I.38) Matthaia of Antioch, farewell. (*CIJ* I² no. 715d – Athens; date uncertain)

(I.39) Matthaia, daughter of Philon, from Arad, wife of Sokrates of Sidon. (*CIJ* I² no. 715f – Athens; first century CE)

(I.40) Memorial of Eusebios, an Alexandrian, and Theodora his wife. God is watching. Farewell to the (chosen) people. (*CIJ* I² no. 696 = HN no. 144 – from Phthiotic Thebes in Thessaly; date uncertain)

(ii) Inscriptions from Rome and the western Mediterranean

All the inscriptions listed here, except the last, are from Rome and tentatively dated to the 3rd-4th century CE.

(I.41) Maximos, from Thabraca (in Numidia). (*SEG* 26 (1976-7) no. 1167 = Noy II no. 508)

(I.42) Here lies Ioustos, son of Amachios, of Katania (in Sicily), aged 22 years. In peace his sleep. (*SEG* 26 (1976-7) no. 1173 = Noy II no. 515)

(I.43) Here lies Oursakia, daughter of Oursakios from Aquileia (in north Italy), a *gerousiarch*. In peace her sleep. (*CIJ* I no. 147 = Noy II no. 238)

(I.44) Here lies (name lost) from Achaea (Greece). In peace (his/her sleep). (*SEG* 26 (1976-7) no. 1163 = Noy II no. 503)

(I.45) Here lies Ammias, a Jewess from Laodicea,[21] who lived 85 years. Peace (*Shalom*)! (*CIJ* I[2] no. 296 = Noy II no. 183)

(I.46) Here lies Symmachos, *gerousiarch*, from Tripolis,[22] aged 80 years. In peace his sleep. (*CIJ* I[2] no. 408 = Noy II no. 113)

(I.47) Here lies Eusebis, wife of Gelasios of Caesarea (Maritima?),[23] aged 35 years. Blessing upon all. (*CIJ* I[2] no. 25 = Noy II no. 459)

(I.48) Ionios, also called Akone (= Aconios?), from Sepphoris (in Galilee). (*CIJ* I[2] no. 362 = Noy II no. 60)

(I.49) Alypis* from Tiberias and his sons, Ioustos and Alypis, Hebrews, lie here with their father. (*CIJ* I no. 502 = Noy II no. 561)

(I.50) Asiatikos, son of Marinos, from Tiberias. (Le Bohec, no. 28 – Carthage;[24] 2nd-3rd century CE)

4. STATISTICAL INFORMATION ABOUT DIASPORAN JEWS

Ancient writers, Jewish and Gentile, make much of the numerousness of the Jews of the Graeco-Roman world. Modern writers tend to be more specific: figures like six, seven and eight million have been proposed. Baron has even gone so far as to assert that in the Roman Empire as a whole one person in ten was Jewish and in its eastern half one in five. (S. Baron, *Social and Religious History of the Jews* I[2] (Columbia, 1952), p. 171.) Such claims, based in large part on a Medieval datum of dubious authority (Bar-Hebraeus' figure of 6,944,000 for world Jewry during the time of Claudius), cannot be substantiated by contemporary evidence. The statistical data available to us are few, relate only to the Jewish communities of Egypt, Cyrene and Rome, and to those only at isolated moments in their history.

(a) Egyptian Jewry in the first century CE

Philo's rhetorical purpose in the *In Flaccum* required exaggeration of the size of the Jewish population of Egypt. Hence the huge round number given in the extract below. It is highly unlikely that any accurate statistical data were available to him. Until the imposition of the Jewish tax by Rome in 71/2 CE, probably no precise count of Jews was made. See V. Tcherikover, *Corpus Papyrorum Judaicarum* I (Cambridge, Mass., 1957) *Prolegomena*, p. 4, who views as equally unreliable the figure of 100,000 given in the *Letter of Aristeas* 12-14 **(I.7)** for the number of Jewish captives transported to Egypt by Ptolemy I Soter.

(I.51) What, then, did the governor of the country do (in response to the proposal of the Alexandrian Greeks to instal images of Caesar in the synagogues of Alexandria)? Knowing that both the city (Alexandria) and all Egypt have two categories of inhabitants, us (the Jews) and them (the Greeks), and that the Jews dwelling in Alexandria and the country from Katabathmos by Libya to the borders with Ethiopia are not less than a million, that the attack was against all of them and that it was not profitable to disturb ancestral customs, he disregarded all these factors and permitted the installation of the statues ... (Philo, *In Flaccum* 43)

(b) The Jewish community of Rome

Although frequent attempts have been made to establish the size of the Roman Jewish community in antiquity on the basis of the numerical data given in the three passages below (estimates range from twenty to sixty thousand persons),[25] they are doomed to failure, as the figures we have relate (in all probability) only to adult Jewish males and to those only around the start of the Common Era.

Roman Jewry, c. 4 BCE

(I.52) But at Rome, Archelaus[26] was faced with another hearing, this time against Jews who, with Varus'[27] permission, had set out (from Judaea) before the revolt in order to petition for the independence of their nation. There were fifty of them present and they were supported by more than eight thousand of the Jews of Rome. (Josephus, *Jewish War* 2.80; cf. *Jewish Antiquities* 17.300)

Roman Jewry in 19 CE

(I.53) And Tiberius[28] ... ordered the entire Jewish community to leave Rome. The consuls conscripted four thousand of them and sent them to the island of Sardinia. Most, though, they punished, for refusing to serve on account of their adherence to their native laws. (Josephus, *Jewish Antiquities* 18.83-4)

(I.54) Another debate (by the Roman Senate) concerned the expulsion of Egyptian and Jewish rites and a decree of the Senate was passed to the effect that four thousand suitably aged men of freedman stock who had been infected by that superstition, should be transported to the island of Sardinia, in order to suppress brigandage there. If they died on account of the harshness of the climate, the loss would be cheap. If the rest had not given up their profane rites before a certain day, they should leave Italy. (Tacitus, *Annals* 2.85.5 = Stern II no. 284)

(c) Cyrene in 70 CE

(I.55) After them, Catullus (the Roman governor of Cyrene) liquidated all the Jewish males of conspicuous wealth, three thousand persons altogether. He thought he could do this with impunity, since he was confiscating their property for the imperial coffers. (Josephus, *Jewish War* 7.445)

5. LOCATION OF JEWISH COMMUNITIES

The ghetto was not a feature of Graeco-Roman Jewry. Apart from a few months during the race-riots of 38 CE when the Alexandrian Jews were temporarily penned up in one section of the city, Jews in general were not confined to living in any particular area. Evidence for Jewish quarters, however, does exist – at Sardis, Apollinopolis Magna/Edfu and in the three *megalopoleis* of the Graeco-Roman world, Alexandria, Rome and Antioch. Some of these quarters were, as at Sardis, officially designated in response to Jewish petitioning (**II.16** and **122**). But often, as at Rome and perhaps Apollinopolis Magna/Edfu, Jewish quarters sprang up spontaneously, presumably as a response to the common human need for the comfort of one's own kind in a foreign and sometimes hostile environment. But although such areas existed, there was no question of anyone being compelled to reside in them and many Jews did not. At the time of Philo, Jews lived all over the city of Alexandria. The material evidence from Rome suggests that by no means all the Jews there lived in the three main Jewish quarters of the city, namely those located in the Transtiberinum, the Subura and the area around the start of the Appian Way (S. Collon, 'Remarques sur les quartiers juifs de la Rome antique', *Mélanges d'Archéologie et d'Histoire de l'École Française de Rome* 57 (1940), 72-94). And at Antioch, the mansion of the Jewish city councillor, Asabinos, for which see **V.9**, was located well away from the city's main Jewish quarter in the Kerateion.

(a) Alexandria

(**I.56**) There are five sections to the city, named after the first letters of the alphabet. Two of these are called Jewish because the majority of their inhabitants are Jews. But very many dwell in the other sections, scattered here and there. What then did the Greeks do? From four of these sections, they evicted the Jews and they drove them into a very small section of one (the so-called Delta section, for which, see next note and passage). On account of their numbers, they poured out onto the beaches,[29] rubbish-dumps and tombs, deprived of all their property. (Philo, *In Flaccum* 55-6)

(**I.57**) Seeing that the Jews would not stop rioting until they had been made to pay heavily, he (*sc.* Tiberius Julius Alexander, the governor of Egypt at that time – i.e. 66 CE) let loose upon them the two Roman legions stationed in the city, as well as two thousand soldiers from Libya who by chance were on hand to complete the ruin of the Jews. He gave permission not only to kill them but to plunder their property and burn down their dwellings. Dashing into the so-called Delta district, where the Jews were concentrated,[30] they carried out his orders but not without injury to themselves. (Josephus, *Jewish War* 2.494-5)

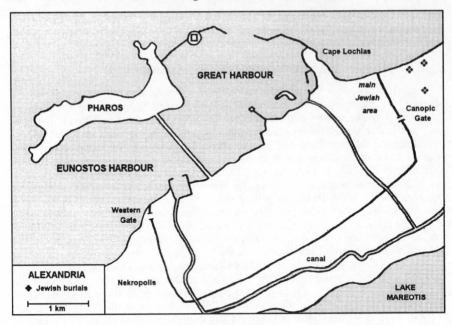

(b) Apollinopolis Magna/Edfu in Upper Egypt

Excavations at Apollinopolis Magna/Edfu indicate that the 4th District, mentioned in both the text below and many other Jewish tax receipts, was the town's
Jewish quarter. Tcherikover (*CPJ* II, pp. 108-9) suggests that the Jews may have
started to congregate there voluntarily in the period after 70 CE, mainly in
response to the increasing hostility shown to Jews in the Flavian period. Although
Jews are known in the town in the Ptolemaic period (see **II.8**), there is no sign of
a Jewish quarter at that time.

(I.58) 4th District. Akakias, son of Herakleides, for the Jewish tax for the
10th year of our lord Trajan, 4 drachmas. Year 10. Epeiph 5. (*CPJ* II no.
209 – 107 CE)

(c) Rome

(i) Transtiberinum

This, the only area of Jewish occupation mentioned by Philo, was probably the only
one in existence in his day. For the later (3rd-4th century?) Jewish inscriptions
from the area, see Noy II nos. 1-202.

(I.59) Augustus knew that the large section of Rome beyond the river
Tiber was owned and inhabited by the Jews. (Philo, *Legatio ad Gaium* 155)

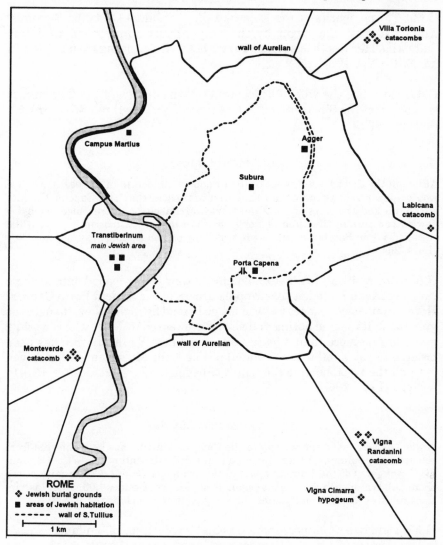

(ii) Subura

That Jews had begun to settle in the Subura at least from the early 2nd century
CE is indicated by the term *proseuche* (prayer-house) in the next text, a pagan
inscription whose estimated date is the 1st-2nd century CE. (The Agger or rampart,
near which the prayer-house was located, was the name given to the Servian Wall
in the vicinity of the Subura.) How dense the settlement was then, we do not know.
By the 3rd century the number of Suburan Jews must have considerable – several
large Jewish cemeteries of that date have been found in the area, most notably the
two beneath the Villa Torlonia. For the epitaphs from these, see Noy II nos.
410-529.

(I.60) To the Spirits of the Departed. For P(ublius) Corfidius Signinus, fruit vendor at the Agger by the prayer-house (*proseuche*). Q(uintus) Sallustius Hermes (has set this up) for his well-deserving friend ... (*CIJ* I no. 531 = Noy II no. 602)

(I.61) Here lies the wife of Eulogetos (?),[31] the *archon* of the Community (*synagoge*) of the Sibouresians.[32] (*CIJ* I² no. 22 = Noy II no. 451 – 3rd-4th century CE(?))

(iii) Porta Capena

Although the Jewish settlement contemptuously alluded to in the passage below would appear to be no more than a squatter camp near the Porta Capena, the gate which marked the start of the Appian Way, archaeology has revealed extensive Jewish remains in this area of Rome. For the numerous inscriptions from the so-called Vigna Randanini catacomb, which lay off the Appian Way, see now Noy II nos. 204-401.

(I.62) But while all his household effects were being loaded onto a single cart, my friend halted at the dripping arches of the ancient Porta Capena. Here, Numa used to meet up with his girlfriend by night. Now, though, the grove with its sacred spring and shrine are rented to Jews, whose worldly goods are no more than a basket and some hay. For every tree has been ordered to pay a toll to the (Roman) people,[33] the Muses have been driven out and the wood become the haunt of beggars. (Juvenal, *Satires* 3.10-16 = Stern II no. 296)

(iv) The Campus Martius

Jewish settlement in the vicinity of the Campus Martius has been inferred from references in epitaphs, generally dated to the 3rd-4th century CE, to the Community (*synagoge*) of the Campesians and the *synagoga Campi* (Community of the Campus). When such settlement began, is not known. Besides **I.63**, other inscriptions in this collection mentioning this congregation are **II.68** and **VII.30**.

(I.63) Here lies Annianos, *archon*, a child (*nepios*), son of Ioulianos, Father of the Community of the Campesians. Aged 8 years, 2 months. In peace his sleep. (*CIJ* I no. 88 = Noy II no. 288 – Rome; 3rd-4th century CE(?))

(d) Antioch

Jewish settlements are known in two parts of Antioch in antiquity, one within and the other outside the city walls. The former was in the Kerateion, an area in the south of the city between the Cherubim Gate and the western flank of Mt Silpius (G. Downey, *A History of Antioch in Syria* (Princeton, 1961) p. 544, n. 179 and p. 620) and the latter in the south-western suburb of Daphne.

(I.64) After him, Demetrianos (I Soter), son of Seleukos, reigned for eight years (162-150 BCE). There came to Antioch the Great a certain man, Judas by name, a Jew by race, who begged and entreated Demetrianos the king. He made over to him the Temple and the remains of the Maccabees. They buried them in Antioch the Great in the district known as the Kerateion, for there was a Jewish synagogue there. (John Malalas, *Chronographia* 206 = *PG* 97, col. 324)

(I.65) Titus founded the theatre of Daphne and inscribed on it: 'From the spoils of Judaea.' The site of the same theatre was formerly a synagogue of the Jews. Out of contempt for them he pulled down their synagogue and built a theatre, placing there a marble statue of himself, which stands to the present day. (John Malalas, *Chronographia* 261 = *PG* 97, col. 396)

(I.66) While books do have a holiness of their own, they do not impart it to a place if those who frequent it are defiled. You should think about the synagogue in the same way. Even if there is no idol there, demons inhabit the place. And I say this not only about the synagogue here in the city (i.e. Antioch itself) but also about the one in Daphne. (John Chrysostom, *Adversus Iudaeos* 1.6 = *PG* 48, cols. 851-2)

6. OCCUPATIONS OF DIASPORAN JEWS

Josephus claims (*Contra Apionem* 1.60) that the Jews were primarily a race of farmers and commerce held very little attraction for them. Conceivably that may have been true for the Jews of Judaea but it certainly was not the case with those who lived outside. Although Jewish agricultural workers and pastoralists are to be found among them, most notably in Ptolemaic Egypt, our sources abound in references to Jewish craftsmen, traders and retailers. In modifying Josephus, however, we should not be led into over-estimating the involvement of the Jews of the Graeco-Roman world in commercial activities or thinking that they had a 'monopoly' in money-lending. Specifically Jewish activities did not exist in antiquity. What the evidence demonstrates quite clearly is that the occupations of the Jews were very much like those of their Gentile neighbours.

(Jews in the service of the Ptolemies and Romans are discussed in Chapter IV below.)

(a) In Ptolemaic Egypt

Jewish shepherds / dealers in wool

(I.67) Zenon to Krotos, greetings. As soon as you get this letter, get from Pasis the Jew wool to the value of 25 minas and give it to Artemidoros so that he may make a mattress, long enough for a double seat or a little bigger, and covered on both sides, for it is needed for Pisikles. As soon as you have done this, send it to Artemidoros at Memphis and try to get the job done within 15 days. We have written to Pasis too (and told him) to give you the wool. Farewell. Year 33, Epeiph 28. (*CPJ* I no. 9a – 253 BCE)

(I.68) Harmeusis, a wool merchant, an inhabitant of the town of Krokodilopolis, to King Ptolemy (IV), greetings. I am being wronged by Seos, a Jew who lives at Alabanthis. He sold me at 4 drachmas, 5 obols and 2 chalkoi each, the fleece of 118 cross-bred sheep, which I bought for Amyntas so that (text lost) from the king's *parabole* (meaning of this phrase unclear). He received from me a deposit of 76 drachmas, on the condition that I pay the remainder to him when I sheared the sheep. Seos, however, coming upon the flock washed and (text lost) and sheared it and removed the wool for himself. Despite a request from me, he refuses to give it back. I entreat you, therefore, O King, if it seems right to you, to instruct Diophanes the *strategos* to write to the *epistates*, (telling him) to send Seos to Diophanes the *strategos*, so that if it appears that he did sell the wool and take the deposit, he may compel him to give me the wool. If this happens, I shall not be wronged and Amyntas, for whom I have carried out other purchases also, (will be enabled to pay) the taxes which he owes at Alexandria. (Thus) we, having appealed to you, O King, the common saviour of all, shall obtain justice. (*CPJ* I no. 38 – 218 BCE)

A Jewish farmer

(I.69) To Zopyros, *epimeletes* (a financial official), from Ioudas, son of Dositheos, a Jew. I farm around Philadelpheia 3 arouras of dry ground at the pre-existing annual rent of 4 artabas of wheat per aroura. At much hardship and expense I have worked (this land) and without complaint paid the annual rent up to the 23rd year. Now Marres, the village scribe, contrary to what is right, has entered me for $5\frac{2}{3}$ artabas per aroura over and above the rent, even though I have never paid that amount. Wherefore, appealing to your sense of fairness, I request you, if it seems right to you, to write to whom it may concern for the hard facts of the case to be sent to you, so that if they are as I write, you may see to it that I shall not be forced to make any improper payment and may meet with justice. Farewell. (*CPJ* I no. 43 – 2nd century BCE)

A Jewish vine-dresser

(I.70) Year 6, Tybi 17. Declaration to Andromachos, chief of police at Philadelpheia, by Samoelis* and Alexander, vine-dressers who have been contracted to tend the vineyard of Zenon and Sostratos. On the night before the 16th, there vanished from the vineyard of Zenon and Sostratos thirty thousand reed canes. On the 16th, we reported this to you and to (name lost), one of the men who had been sent out from those under the control of Agenor the *strategos*, and to Theopompos the policeman. There were others present too in the vineyard of Keleesis. We value them (i.e. the reed canes) at 14 copper drachmas per ten thousand, making a total of 42 copper drachmas ... (*CPJ* I no. 14 – 241 BCE)

Two Jewish potters

(I.71) Sabbataios, the son of Horos and his son Dosas*, Jewish potters from the Syrian village, to Petesouchos and his sons, Nepheros and Nechthanoupis, greetings. We agree that we share with you, from Tybi 25th of Year 7 to Mesore 30th of the same year, the pottery near Neilopolis which at present belongs to Paous, the son of Sabbataios, according to the division of a fourth part to me and a quarter (interpretation of text here is disputed) for my son too. We shall pay the tax together, each according to his portion. If there is any loss or profits, let them be in common and divided up. Nor let it be possible for us to leave the pottery until the aforesaid year is out or for you to throw us out of the pottery. And if we do not act in accordance with what has been written, we shall pay into the royal treasury 40 silver drachmas. Let this contract be valid everywhere. Chairemon, the son of Kallikrates, has written this on their behalf and at their request, since they say that they are illiterate. Year 7, Tybi 25. Witnesses: Sabaidon, son of Nikon; Nikodromos, son of Philippos. (*CPJ* I no. 46 – 2nd or 1st century BCE)

A Jewish weaver

(I.72) Pachon 27. Measured into the granary at ... for the 8th year by Iapheas,[34] son of Dositheos, weaver, ten and seven-twelfths. Total: $10\frac{7}{12}$ artabas of wheat. (*CPJ* I no. 95 – Apollinopolis Magna/Edfu (?); 2nd century BCE)

A Jewish musician

The following text consists of the last three entries in a list drawn up by a village scribe at Samareia in the Fayum of cattle grazing in his village.

(I.73) Ioannes, son of Antipater: 30 cattle; 15 sheep; 1 she-goat; 2 kids. Stratippos, son of Stratippos: 17 cattle; 10 sheep; 1 she-goat. The flute player,[35] Iakoubis*, son of Iakoubis*: 13 cattle; 7 sheep; 1 she-goat. (*CPJ* I no. 28 – mid-2nd century BCE)

(b) In Roman Egypt

A Jewish financier

Father of Tiberius Julius Alexander **(IV.30-4)** and brother of Philo, Alexander the alabarch was not only a conspicuous benefactor of the Temple in Jerusalem **(III.15)** but, as this passage shows, a major figure on the financial scene, whose clientele included royalty and whose business operations extended as far as western Italy. On the office of *alabarch*, see note at **IV.35**.

(I.74) At that time (*c*. 36 CE), Agrippa pretended that he was going to obey the orders (to remain in Judaea because of unpaid debts to the Roman treasury) but at nightfall he cut the mooring cables and sailed away to Alexandria. There he asked Alexander the *alabarch* to make him a loan of two hundred thousand drachmas. The latter said he would not make it available it to *him* but he did not refuse it to Cypros (Agrippa's wife), by whose love of her husband and general virtuousness he had been impressed. On her promise (to repay the money), Alexander gave five talents to them in Alexandria and announced that he would make the remainder available to them once they had arrived at Dikaiarchia (Puteoli). For he feared Agrippa's spendthrift ways. (Josephus, *Jewish Antiquities* 18.159-60)

A stereotypical Alexandrian money-lender?

Although Philo is rather unspecific here, his words have been taken by some scholars, most recently L.H. Feldman, *Jew and Gentile in the Ancient World* (Princeton, 1993), p. 76, as an allusion to the activities of Jewish money-lenders in 1st century CE Alexandria.

(**I.75**) 'I would say to you, Mr Money-Lender, why do you disguise your unco-operative ways by (a show of) co-operation? Why do you pretend to be kindly and charitable but display in your actions inhumanity and a dreadful deviousness, exacting more than you have lent, sometimes double, and making the the pauper even poorer?' (Philo, *The Special Laws* 2.75)

Jewish money-lending in Alexandria in 41 CE?

Although some scholars deny that Jewish money-lenders are referred to in the next document (e.g. J. Mélèze Modrzejewski in *The Jews of Egypt from Rameses II to Emperor Hadrian*, translated from the French by R. Cornman (Edinburgh, 1995), p. 180), Tcherikover (*CPJ*, comm ad loc.) was surely right to conclude that its general contents imply that. For the upsurge in inter-communal violence at Alexandria which may have led to a heightened suspicion of the Jews at that time, see Smallwood, *Jews under Roman Rule*, p. 245.

(**I.76**) Sarapion to our Herakleides, greetings. I have sent you two other letters, one through Nedymos, the other through Kronios, the policeman. Well, I got the letter from the Arab and I read it and was distressed. Stay close to Ptollarion all the time. Perhaps he can sort you out. Say to him: 'It's one thing for me and another for everyone else. I'm just a slave. I have sold you my wares for a talent too little. I don't know what my master (lit. patron) will do to me. We have lots of creditors. Don't ruin us.' Ask him every day. Perhaps he'll pity you. If not, you be wary, like everyone else, of the Jews ... (*CPJ* II no. 152 – 4th August 41 CE)

Alexandrian Jewish traders in 38 CE

(I.77) Another group (of Greeks) positioned themselves by the harbours of the river (Nile), in order to seize the Jews who put in there and the merchandise they were carrying. They boarded the ships and carried off the cargo under the eyes of its owners. The owners themselves they pinioned by the arms and burned alive, using for kindling rudders, tillers, poles and deck-planking.[36] (Philo, *Legatio ad Gaium* 129)

A Jew with business interests in the Red Sea area

(I.78) Antiochos, son of Satornilos through Poplios Mamilios Andromachos, to Nikanor, son of Panes, greetings. I have received (from you) in Myos Hormos (a Red Sea port), on the account of Markos Ioulios Alexander[37] eight and a half artabas of wheat, artabas $8\frac{1}{2}$.[38] Year 4 of the Emperor Tiberius Claudius Caesar Augustus Germanicus ... (*CPJ* II no. 419d – 43/4 CE)

Alexandrian Jewish artisans

The ransacking of Jewish workshops in June 38 CE during the official mourning for the Emperor Gaius' favourite sister, Drusilla, is graphically described here.

(I.79) Having overrun the abandoned houses (of the Jews), the Greeks turned to plundering and distributed the contents like booty from a war. Since no one stopped them, they broke into the workshops of the Jews which had been shut because of the official mourning for Drusilla. All that they found – and there was a lot of it – they carted off. They carried it through the middle of the market-place, treating other people's property as if it was their own. A worse evil than the plundering was the enforced inactivity. For the businessmen had lost their deposits and no one, whether farmer, shipper, trader or artisan, was allowed to ply his customary trade ... (Philo, *In Flaccum* 56-7)

The important place believed to have been occupied by artisans within the Jewish community of Alexandria emerges clearly from this late (c. 6th century CE), probably apocryphal, description of the Great Synagogue there.

(I.80) They moreover did not occupy the seats indiscriminately, but goldsmiths sat separately, silversmiths separately, blacksmiths separately, metalworkers separately and weavers separately, so that when a poor man entered the place he recognised the members of his craft and on applying to that quarter obtained a livelihood for himself and the members of his family. (bT, *Sukkah* 51b)

A Jewish farmer at Apollinopolis Magna / Edfu

(I.81) Tryphas, son of Nikon,[39] has measured as tax on behalf of the upper highland area from the crop of the 10th year in the month of Mesore two-thirds (of an artaba) and an eighth of an artaba of wheat. Total of wheat: $\frac{2}{3}$ and $\frac{1}{8}$ artabas. Year 10. Mesore 28. (*CPJ* II no. 272 – 78 CE)

A Jew engaged in overland transport

(I.82) Philippos,[40] son of Thedetos*, on behalf of the tax for donkey-driving for the 8th year of Domitian, 4 drachmas. Year 8, Epeiph ... (*CPJ* II no. 282 – Apollinopolis Magna/Edfu; 89 CE)

(c) In Mesopotamia and Syria

Jewish weavers at Nearda in Babylonia, 1st century CE

(I.83) There were two brothers, Asinaios and Anilaios, who were natives of Nearda. Since their father was dead, their mother apprenticed them to learn the weaving trade, for it is not thought unseemly by the people of that country for men to spin wool. (Josephus, *Jewish Antiquities* 18.314)

A doctor and a retailer at Constantine (Tella) in Mespotamia

(I.84) Isaakes, doctor; Kaioumas, retailer. (*CIJ* II no. 1419 – undated)

A Jewish banker from Palmyra

(I.85) We (are the sons) of Leontios from Palmyra, a banker. (*CIJ* II no. 1010 = *BS* II no. 92 – Beth She'arim; 3rd century CE)

Peasant farmers on the estate of Libanius near Antioch

(I.86) Some Jews – of that famous people – who have worked our land for a long time, four generations, set their hearts upon being no longer what they had been. Casting off the old yoke they took it upon themselves to define how we were to employ them. Refusing to tolerate that, we took them to court. (Libanius, *Orationes* 47.13 = Stern II no. 495a)

A Jewish advocate at Apamea

(I.87) Euthalis, an advocate (*scholastikos*),[41] has made (i.e. paid for the mosaicking of) 140 feet (of the synagogue floor). (*CIJ* II no. 814 = *IGLS* IV no. 1330 = *DF* no. 49 – 391-2 CE)

A Jewish silk-mercer at Beirut

(I.88) Tomb belonging to Samouelos*, son of Samouelos, silk-mercer ...[42] (*CIJ* II no. 873 – Beirut; undated)

(d) In Asia Minor, the Black Sea area and Greece

A perfumer at Korykos

(I.89) Tomb of Eusambatios, a Jew, an Elder (*presbyteros*) (and) a perfumer. (*CIJ* II no. 790 = *MAMA* III no. 344 – Korykos; 4th-5th century CE)

A doctor at Ephesos

(I.90) [This is the tomb] of Io[ulios?] (rest of name lost), chief doctor (*archiatros*)[43] [and] his wife Ioulia [...]e and their children. [It was erected] during their lifetime. This tomb is in the care of the Jews at Ephesos. (*CIJ* II no. 745 = *IK* Ephesos V no. 1677 – 2nd-3rd century CE)

Goldsmiths in the synagogue at Sardis

Besides the Jewish goldsmiths listed here, see also **IV.39** (Palmyra), **VII.12** (Aphrodisias) and P. Trebilco, *Jewish Communities in Asia Minor* (Cambridge, 1991), p. 209, n. 33 (mentioning two further cases from Sardis still awaiting publication).

(I.91) I, Aurelios Hermogenes, citizen of Sardis, councillor, goldsmith, have fulfilled my vow. (*DF* no. 23 – 3rd or 4th century CE)

(I.92) I, [name lost], councillor, goldsmith, together with my wife Eu[...], have given (this). (*DF* no. 22 – 3rd or 4th century CE)

A Jewish sculptor at Sardis?

The solitary personal name of which the next inscription consists, is carved on an elaborate marble menorah found in the synagogue at Sardis. Although it has been claimed that Sokrates made the menorah himself (see G. Hanfmann, *Sardis from Pre-historic to Roman Times* (Cambridge, Mass. and London, 1983), caption to fig. 268), he could just as easily have been its donor. Evidence of Jewish marble-working in Asia Minor has, however, recently come to light. Jews engaged in marble-quarrying have been attested at both Docimeium and Amorium. See S. Mitchell, *Anatolia, Land, Men, and Gods in Asia Minor* (Oxford, 1993) II, p. 35.

(I.93) Sokrates. (Hanfmann, *Sardis*, fig. 268)

Tent-makers from Cilicia and Pontus at Corinth

The fellow tent-makers of the apostle Paul, who are alluded to in this passage, are Aquila, a Jew of Pontus (for whom see **I.21**) and his wife, Priscilla.

(I.94) Because they shared the same trade, Paul stayed with them and they plied their craft together. For they were tent-makers by trade. (*Acts of the Apostles* 18.3)

A Jewish advocate at Larissa in Thessaly

(I.95) (Tomb of) Alexander, advocate (*scholastikos*) and *prostates* (probably president of the synagogue).[44] (*SEG* 29 (1979) no. 537 – Larissa; 1st century CE)

A Jewish wine-merchant at Tomis on the Black Sea

It is from the iconography on this stone (a palm and a star) that scholars have classified the following text as Jewish.

(I.96) … son of Seppon, wine merchant from Alexandria. (*CIJ* I², no. 681b = *New Docs*. II, no. 114 – Tomis on the Black Sea; undated)

(e) At Rome

Besides the cases listed here, see also **I.25** (a merchant); **II.84** and **V.42** (teachers of the Torah); **VI.20** (an actor).

(I.97) Alexander, a butcher from the market, who lived for 30 years, a good soul and a friend to all. May your sleep be among the righteous. (*CIJ* I² no. 210 = Noy II no. 343 and Plate XVI – 3rd-4th century CE(?))

(I.98) Here lies Eudoxios, a painter from nature (*zographos*).[45] In peace (his sleep). (*CIJ* I no. 109 = Noy II no. 277 – 3rd-4th century CE(?))

(I.99) Here lies Aper, *archon* of the Calcaresians (lime-burners?).[46] In peace [his] sleep. Iouleios set up (this memorial) to his (son?). (*CIJ* I no. 304 = Noy II no. 69 – 3rd-4th century CE(?))

(f) A Jewish pearl-setter of unknown provenance

(I.100) On behalf of a vow: Iacob, leader of the congregation, setter of pearls. (*CIJ* I² no. 731g = *SEG* 41 (1991) no. 1738 – dates assigned range from the 2nd to the 8th century CE!)

7. TERMINOLOGY FOR DIASPORAN COMMUNITIES

Jewish communities that had been deliberately planted by the Ptolemies and Seleucids for military purposes presumably possessed from the outset some official designation. Late evidence from Phrygia, where Antiochus III had once carried out an extensive programme of Jewish colonisation (**I.18**), suggests that, in Seleucid territories at least, they were termed *katoikiai*. Most Jewish communities, however, were not premeditated creations but the outcome of gradual immigration. Initially, there was no formal term for them, for the simple reason that it took time for sophisticated organisational structures, and hence the vocabulary for them, to develop. The phrases we meet with regularly in Jewish inscriptions from early Ptolemaic Egypt are 'the Jews in/of such and such a place'. But as communities took root, formal structures did evolve and a formal terminology came largely to replace the old generalisations. What were these new terms? Since it is stated in all the standard works on the Graeco-Roman Diaspora that in Greek-speaking areas the official term for a Jewish community was *politeuma* and in Latin-speaking ones *collegium*, it may occasion surprise that neither features in the list below. But *collegium* is nowhere attested as a Jewish organisational title and while *politeuma* is so (only at Alexandria and Cyrene, however), it is far from certain that it refers to the *entire* community in an administrative/constitutional sense. Recently it has been argued that it may designate no more than a small group *within* the Jewish community made up of the better-off. (See C. Zuckermann, 'Hellenistic politeumata and the Jews: a reconsideration', *SCI* 8-9 (1985-8), pp. 171-85 and G. Lüderitz, 'What is the politeuma?' in *SEJE*, pp. 183-225.) Given this uncertainty, the passages in which the term appears are not discussed collectively here under the heading *politeuma* but dealt with individually in other contexts.

But if Jewish communities were not called *politeumata* and *collegia*, how did they formally characterise themselves? Three terms, in particular, are to be noted: *plethos*, *synagoge* and (from the 3rd century CE only) *laos*. (For the epigraphically rare and ambiguous *ethnos*, see **VI.37**.) These crop up again and again and it is easy to see why they should have been so favoured. *Plethos* (a multitude), besides being used by the Greeks themselves as a term for the *whole* community in an administrative/constitutional sense, was the broad equivalent of a Hebrew organisational term, *ha-rabim*. *Synagoge*, likewise, was common among the Greeks. They used it loosely in the sense of a meeting or gathering and as a formal term for a religious association. And *laos*, the Greek word for people, had a special significance for the Jews: from the time when the Hebrew Bible had been translated into Greek for them it had meant 'the chosen people'. Of the three, *synagoge* is by far the most frequently attested and most widely diffused. Even in the Latin-speaking west it is the standard word for Jewish community. By the 1st century CE its meaning had even become extended. We find it being used (as, for instance, in **I.107**) to designate not simply the individual congregation but its meeting place too – whence our word synagogue. Formerly that had been called the *proseuche* – i.e. the *prayer-house*.

It will have been noticed that no Latin terms figure in the discussion above. The reason is that they do not seem to have been used. Only once do we find a Latin word employed to describe a Jewish Diasporan community – *universitas* in **I.113**. However, it is not a formal *Jewish* term. Indeed, in this document it is probably not even a technical term at all. See discussion ad loc.

(a) *katoikia* (military settlement)

(I.101) This sarcophagus and the area around it (belong to) Aurelia Augusta, daughter of Zotikos. In it she will be buried and her husband Glykonianos, also called Apros, and their children. If anyone else buries (another in it), he shall pay to the community (*katoikia*) of the Jews dwelling at Hierapolis a fine of (amount lost) denarii and two thousand denarii to the one who has sought recompense. A copy has been placed in the record-office of the Jews.[47] (*CIJ* II no. 775 – Hierapolis in Phrygia; 2nd-3rd century CE)

(b) *hoi Ioudaioi* (the Jews)

These two inscriptions date, respectively, from the reigns of Ptolemy III Euergetes I (246-222 BCE) and Ptolemy VIII Euergetes II Physkon (145-116 BCE).

(I.102) On behalf of King Ptolemy, the son of Ptolemy, and Queen Berenike, his wife and sister, and their children, the Jews in Krokodilopolis (have dedicated) the prayer-house[48] and (text lost). (*CPJ* III no. 1532a = HN no. 117, with further editing by Horsley in *Jewish Studies Quarterly* 2 (1995), 94)

(I.103) On behalf of King Ptolemy and Queen Kleopatra his sister and Queen Kleopatra his wife, (all three) Benefactors, the Jews in Nitriai (near Alexandria have dedicated) the prayer-house and the adjacent buildings.[49] (*CIJ* II no. 1442 = HN no. 25)

(c) *plethos* (multitude)

Presentation of the Septuagint to the Alexandrian Jewish community (plethos)

The events described below are alleged to have taken place during the reign of Ptolemy II Philadelphos (282-246 BCE). For the validation legend of the translation of the Septuagint, see **V.40-41.**

(I.104) When it (the Greek translation of the Hebrew scriptures) had been completed, Demetrios assembled the community (*plethos*) of the Jews[50] at the place where the work of translation had been completed and read it out to all of them. The translators too were present and they received a great reception from the community (*plethos*), in that they had been the cause of a great service. To Demetrios also they gave a similar reception and they called upon him to have the whole Law transcribed and handed over to their leaders. When the scrolls had been read, the priests and the elders of the translators and of those belonging to the *politeuma*[51] and the leaders of the community (*plethos*) stood up and said, 'Since the translation has been done well and piously and accurately in every respect, it is

fitting that it should stay as it is and that no revision should ever be made.'
(*Letter of Aristeas* 308-10)

Decree of a Jewish plethos in Egypt

The words 'decided' and 'gold crown' show that this is an honorary decree (cf.
V.35-7), the enacting body of which is probably the *plethos* mentioned earlier in
the document. Although the exact provenance of this Egyptian inscription is
unknown, the name Chelkias indicates a Jewish origin. For other epigraphic
examples of *plethos*, see **III.84** (Apamea) and **VII.11** (Aphrodisias).

(I.105) (son) of Chelkias, general (?) ... of the *plethos* of those in the sacred
precinct ... to those who were honoured ... to him on account of ... it was
decided ... general ... with a gold crown ... by the kings (?). (*CIJ* II no. 1450
= HN no. 129)

(d) *synagoge* – assembled community

Only a small number of the many *synagoge* inscriptions in existence are listed
here. Among the other examples included in this collection, **II.14**, **V.37**, **VI.6**,
VII.10 and **17** are particularly worthy of note.

A manumission document from the Bosporan kingdom

(I.106) In the reign of king Kotys, Year 348 (of the Bosporan era), Month
of Xandikos 1. Psycharion and his sons Sogos (and) Anos. Karsandanos
and Karagos and Metroteimos, are manumitted to the prayer-house,
unassailable (and) unhindered, except that they serve and respect the
prayer-house. And they are manumitted also under the guardianship of
the Jewish community (*synagoge*). (*Bulletin of Judaeo-Greek Studies* 13
(Winter, 1993), p. 27 – Phanagoria; 51 CE)

A donor list from Berenice (Benghazi, Libya)

Note the use in this important document of the word *synagoge* in two different
senses: firstly to denote the *community* passing the decree and secondly the
building it used for its meetings.

(I.107) In the 2nd year of the emperor Nero Claudius Caesar Drusus
Germanicus (55 CE), Choiak 16, the community (*synagoge*) of the Jews in
Berenice has decided to inscribe on a stele of Parian marble (the names of)
those who have contributed to the repair of the synagogue (*synagoge*):

(First column)
Zenion, son of Zoilos – 10 drachmas
Eisidoros, son of Doseitheos, *archon* – 10 drachmas
Doseitheos, son of Ammonios, *archon* – 10 drachmas

Pratis, son of Ionathas*, *archon* – 10 drachmas
Karnedas, son of Kornelios, *archon* – 10 drachmas
Herakleides, son of Heraklides (*sic*), *archon* – 10 drachmas
Thaliarchos, son of Dositheos, *archon* – 10 drachmas
Sosibios, son of Iason, *archon* – 10 drachmas
Pratomedes, son of Sokrates, *archon* – 10 drachmas
Antigon(o)s, son of Straton, *archon* – 10 drachmas
Kartisthenes, son of Archias, priest – 10 drachmas
Lysanias, son of Lysanias – 25 drachmas
Zenodoros, son of Theuphilos* – 28 drachmas
Marion, son of [...] – 25 drachmas

(Second column)
Alexander, son of Euphranor – 5 drachmas
Eisidora, daughter of Serap(i)on – 5 drachmas
Zosime, daughter of Terpolios – 5 drachmas
Polon, son of Dositheos – 5 drachmas
(*DF* no. 100 = *CJZC* no. 72)

The Jewish community (synagoge) at Nikomedia in Bithynia

(**I.108**) I have set up the tomb and the altar for my sweetest mother, Oulpia Kapitylla and I want no one else to disturb it. Otherwise, he will have to face the judgement (of God)[52] and pay to the (Jewish) community (*synagoge*) 1,000 denarii and to the treasury 500. Farewell. (*TAM* IV.1, no. 376 – 3rd century CE(?))

(e) *laos* (people)

Besides the cases listed here, note also **II.74; 100-1; 104**.

(**I.109**) Loukios Lollios Iousstos (*sic*), *grammateus* of the *laos* at Smyrna, has set up this tomb for himself and his own family. (*IK* Smyrna no. 296 = *Hellenica* 11-12 (1960) 260 – Smyrna; not dated)

(**I.110**) This tomb and the base on which it rests [and] the site (belong to) Aurelia Glykones, daughter of Ammianos, and her husband, M(arkos) Aur(elios) Alexander, son of Theophilos, also called [..]aph[..]os, Jews.[53] It is for their burial. No one else shall be allowed to bury anyone else in it. Otherwise, he shall pay to the *laos*[54] of the Jews by way of a fine one thousand denarii. A faithful copy of this inscription has been deposited in the record office. (*CIJ* II no. 776 – Hierapolis; 3rd century CE)

(**I.111**) Menander, son of Apollonides has made (this). He has constructed the place (i.e. the synagogue) from the east-facing inscription[55] for the community (*laos*) and the cultic association (*synodos*)[56] of which Dositheos, son of Theogenes, is head. (*DF* no. 31 – Nysa in Caria; 3rd-4th century CE)

(I.112) Prayer-house of the people (*laou*). (*CIJ* I² no. 662 = Noy I no. 180 – mosaic inscription from Elche, Spain; 4th (?) century CE)

(f) *universitas* – the whole; a number of persons associated in one body

Probably *universitas* in this rescript of the emperor Caracalla (198-217 CE) to the Roman jurist Tryphoninus is not a technical term for the Jewish community of Antioch but a translation of an imprecise Greek phrase meaning 'all the Jews who live in Antioch'. For discussion, see Linder, comm. ad loc.

(I.113) The Emperor Antoninus Augustus to Claudius Tryphoninus. That which Cornelia Salvia has left as a legacy to the community of the Jews who dwell in the city of the Antiochenes cannot be claimed in court. Given on the day before the Kalends of July in the 4th consulship of Antoninus Augustus and the (1st) consulship of Balbinus. (*Codex Iustinianus* 1.9.1 = Linder no. 3 – 30 June, 213 CE)

II

Life inside the Jewish Diasporan community

1. THE SYNAGOGUE AS THE FOCAL POINT OF COMMUNITY LIFE

Wherever Jews settled in any numbers outside Judaea, the focal point of their communal life was the synagogue – basically a prayer-hall, to which various ancillary structures, such as dining and guest rooms, might be attached. The complex had many functions. Besides being the locus for the teaching of the Law, most notably on the Sabbath, and the venue for the worship of God, it also operated as the community's social, administrative and legal centre. The commoner words for it reflect its principal usages – *proseuche* (lit. prayer) stresses its function as a prayer-house and *synagoge* (lit. assembly) its rôle as the community's gathering-place. *Hagios topos* (holy place), a term found in inscriptions of the 3rd century and later (cf. **III.81-3**), points to the increased liturgical significance of the synagogue in the era after the destruction of the Temple.

(a) As a place for teaching the Law

Sabbath instruction

(II.1) On each seventh day there stand wide open in every city countless places for teaching practical wisdom and sound judgement and courage and justice and the other virtues. In these the students sit in order quietly, their ears alert ... while one of special experience stands up and expounds what is best and profitable and capable of improving the quality of the whole of life. (Philo, *The Special Laws* 2.62)

A Teacher of Wisdom in the synagogue at Sardis

Found in the heart of the Sardis synagogue, the next text has been included, even though it is rather late (its approximate date is 500 CE), as it is the best inscriptional evidence available for the synagogue's traditional educational function. Samoes' school will probably have met around the platform in whose immediate vicinity this inscription was found. (See A.T. Kraabel in Hanfmann, *Sardis*, p. 189.) For other teachers and students of the Law, see **II.84-9**.

(II.2) Vow of Samoes*, priest and *sophodidaskalos* (teacher of wisdom). (*BASOR* 187 (1967) 29)

(b) As a place of worship

(II.3) Travelling by way of Amphipolis and Apollonia, Paul and Silas came to Thessalonica, where there was a synagogue of the Jews. In accordance with his usual practice, Paul attended their meetings. Three Sabbaths in a row he discoursed on the Scriptures, expounding them and applying them to show that the Messiah had to suffer and rise from the dead. (*Acts of the Apostles* 17.1-3)

(II.4) Aur(elios) Ethe[l]asios, son of Makedonios the Lector,[1] and Aur(elia) Thamar have put this sarcophagus in place during their lifetime. Blessing upon all. (*CIJ* II no. 798 = *TAM* IV.1, no. 374 – Nicomedia, Bithynia; 3rd (?) century CE)

(II.5) Here lies Gaianos, secretary (*grammateus*), singer of psalms (*psalmoidos*),[2] lover of the Law (*philonomos*). In peace his sleep. (*SEG* 26 (1976-7) no. 1162 = Noy II no. 502 – Rome, probably 3rd century CE)

(c) As a social centre

The synagogue as a venue for meetings

The following (1st century BCE(?)) papyrus fragment from Egypt constitutes our only surviving record of an actual meeting in a Diasporan synagogue. It seems to have been held by the members of a Jewish burial club (*taphiastai*), whose president was the *syntaphiastes* mentioned at the end of our extract.

(II.6) ... At the meeting held in the prayer-house. To Demetrios of the first friends and the door-keepers (?) and the ushers and the chief officials ... secretary ... to the association ... the corporation of Burial Workers (*taphiastai*) ... the *syntaphiastes* ... (*CPJ* I no. 138)

Construction of a synagogal dining room at Stobi, Macedonia

(II.7) [Klaudios] Tiberios Polycharmos, also called Achyrios, the Father of the Community at Stobi, who has conducted his whole life in accordance with Judaism, in fulfilment of a vow (has constructed), out of his own resources, without touching in any way the sacred monies, the rooms attached to the holy place (i.e. the synagogue) and the dining room (*triclinium*)[3] with its colonnade. I, Klaudios Tiberios Polycharmos and my heirs, retain life-ownership and complete control over the entire upper storey. Anyone who wishes to overturn any of my decisions shall pay to the Patriarch[4] two hundred and fifty thousand denarii. As for the maintenance of the roof of the upper storey, I have decided that that shall be the responsibility of me and my heirs. (*CIJ* I² no. 694 = *DF* no. 10 – late 3rd century CE)

Communal dining in the Diaspora

Fragment from the records of a Jewish dining club at Apollinopolis Magna/Edfu in Upper Egypt (probably 1st century BCE).

(II.8) 15th. Third Feast: Theuxo[...]; Lysimachos, a scholar (?); Sephthais ...; Iosepos*, a priest; (total) 1,000. 16th. Fourth Feast: Themas ...; Iosepos, a priest ...; Teuphilos* ...; the contributions ... (*CPJ* I no. 139)

Roman authorisation of Jewish communal dining

(II.9) Julius Gaius,[5] Supreme Commander (i.e. Consul) of the Romans, to the magistrates, council and people of Parium (in the Troad),[6] greeting. The Jews in Delos and some of the neighbouring Jews, some of your envoys also being present, have appealed to me and made it plain that you are preventing them by decree from observing their national customs and sacred rites. Now it does not please me that such decrees should be made against our friends and allies and that they should be prevented from living in accordance with their customs and contributing money to common meals and sacred rites, for this they are not prevented from doing even at Rome. For Gaius Caesar (i.e. Julius Caesar), our Supreme Commander, in his edict preventing religious societies from meeting in the city (i.e. Rome), these people alone (*sc.* the Jews) did not prevent from either contributing money or holding common meals. Likewise I, (while) forbidding the other religious societies, these people alone permit to assemble and feast in accordance with their native customs and ordinances. If you have passed any decree against our friends and allies, you therefore will do well to revoke it because of their worthy deeds on our behalf and their goodwill towards us. (Josephus, *Jewish Antiquities* 14.213-16)

(d) As the locus for charitable giving

(II.10) Of these (the vulgar expressions of Epicurus), some, one may say, hail from the brothel, others are like things said at festivals of Demeter by women celebrating the Thesmophoria, and others (come) from the middle of the prayer-house and those begging in its courtyards.[7] (Cleomedes, *On the circular motion of celestial bodies* 2.1.91 = Stern II no. 333)

(II.11) (The hoodlum) confronts me and orders me to stop.[8] You must obey. For what can you do, when force is applied by someone who is both mad and stronger than you. 'Where do you come from?', he yells. 'By whose vinegar and beans are you blown up? What cobbler has been eating chopped leeks and boiled wether's lips with you? You've nothing to say? Speak or I'll kick you. Tell me where you place your pitch (for begging). In what prayer-house shall I find you?' (Juvenal, *Satires* 3.290-6 = Stern II no. 297)

(e) As a collection point for dues and taxes

(**II.12**) Augustus, therefore, knew that they (the Jews of Rome) had prayer-houses and met in them, especially on the holy seventh day, when publicly they undergo instruction in their ancestral philosophy. He also knew that they collected sacred money from the first-fruits and sent them to Jerusalem by means of envoys who would offer sacrifices (on their behalf). Nonetheless, he neither expelled them from Rome nor deprived them of their Roman rights because they were mindful of their Jewish ones. Nor did he introduce any changes into their prayer-houses or prevent them from assembling for the exposition of the Law or obstruct their offering of the first-fruits. (Philo, *Legatio ad Gaium* 156-7)

(**II.13**) And Agrippa himself wrote on the Jews' behalf in the following manner: 'Agrippa to the magistrates, council and people of Ephesos, greetings. It is my wish that the Jews in Asia, in accordance with their ancestral customs, have care and custody over the sacred monies that have been put by for the Temple in Jerusalem. It is my wish that those who steal the sacred monies of the Jews and take refuge in places of asylum shall be dragged from them and handed over to the Jews under the same law by which temple-robbers[9] are dragged away (from asylum) ...' (Josephus, *Jewish Antiquities* 16.167-8)

(f) As the locus for legal transactions

(**II.14**) In the reign of King Tiberios Ioulios Rheskouporis, the Friend of Kaisar and the Friend of Rome, the Pious, in the year 377 (of the Bosporan era), on the 12th of the month Pereitios, I, Chreste, formerly wife of Drousos, manumit once and for all, at the prayer-house in accordance with my vow, my home-bred slave Heraklas, (on condition that he be) unassailable and unmolested by all my heirs. He is to go wherever he wants without hindrance, as I have vowed, except that he respect and serve the prayer-house. With the agreement of my heirs, Herakleides and Helikonias, and with the Jewish community (*synagoge*) acting as guardian. (*CIJ* I^2 no. 683 = *CIRB* no. 70 – Panticapaeum in the Cimmerian Bosporus; 80 CE)

(**II.15**) Let me tell you this, not from guesswork but from my own experience. Three days ago – believe me, I am not lying – I saw a free woman of good bearing, modest, and a believer. A brutal, unfeeling man, reputed to be a Christian – for I would not call a person who would dare to do such a thing a sincere Christian – was forcing her to enter the shrine of the Hebrews (i.e. the synagogue) and to swear there an oath about some matters under dispute with him. She came up to me and asked for help; she begged me to prevent this lawless violence – for it was forbidden her, who had shared in the divine mysteries (i.e. the Mass) to enter the place

... After I had talked with him at great length and had driven the folly of error from his soul, I asked him why he rejected the Church and dragged the woman to the place where the Hebrews assembled. He answered that many people had told him that oaths sworn there were more to be feared. (John Chrysostom, *Adversus Iudaeos* 1.3 = *PG* 48, cols. 847-8)

(g) As a court of law

(II.16) Lucius Antonius, son of Marcus, proquaestor and propraetor, to the magistrates, council and people of Sardis, greetings. Jewish citizens of ours have come to me and pointed out to me that from earliest times they have had, in accordance with their native laws, a private association (*synodos*) and a place of their own,[10] in which they manage their affairs and settle the disputes they have with each other. Upon their request that they be permitted to do these things, I have decided to allow them to retain (these privileges). (Josephus, *Jewish Antiquities* 14.235)

(II.17) Five times the Jews have given me (it is the Apostle Paul who is speaking) thirty-nine strokes;[11] three times I have been beaten with rods;[12] once I was stoned ... (2 *Corinthians* 11.24-5)

(II.18) ... synagogues of the Jews, sources of persecutions, in which the Apostles were forced to endure the scourge.[13] (Tertullian, *Scorpiace* 10)

2. OFFICIALS AND DIGNITARIES

(a) Synagogal officers and dignitaries

Diasporan synagogues, whatever their date and precise location, seem to have been run in broadly the same way. While matters such as the upkeep of the premises and the provision of water for ritual purposes were generally handled by the executive officers of the council (*gerousia*), liturgical affairs appear to have been the province of entirely different officials – the *archisynagogos* and his assistant. Many minor local variations, however, are to be noted – e.g. in the terminology for several of the synagogue's officers (see below under the President of the Council and the synagogal assistant) and the composition of its council: *gerousiai* at 3rd to 4th century Rome, for instance, regularly lack the *presbyteroi* (Elders) then common in the synagogues of Asia Minor. Bestowing largely honorific titles upon the richer members of the congregation (and, therefore, upon its benefactors, actual or potential) was also a common practice in the Diasporan synagogue but here, too, considerable local variation is to be noted. While *archisynagogissai* and their close analogues, for instance, are found only in Diasporan communities of the eastern Mediterranean (see **V.32-3**), Fathers/Mothers of the Community and child magistrates (for the latter, see **VI.26-30**) are restricted largely to Rome and places where Roman cultural influence was paramount. It may cause surprise that rabbis do not appear in the list below. The reason is that the precise significance of the term 'rabbi' in our period is unknown. (See S.J.D. Cohen, 'Epigraphical Rabbis', *JQR* 72 (1981), pp. 1-17.) What it does indicate, is

Palestinian influence over the Diaspora. Hence it is treated in the context of Diasporan-Palestinian relations (**III.87-9**).

(i) The President of the Council

Notwithstanding the small and geographically confined sample of texts presented here (for additional examples, see, **I.43** and **46**; **V.63**; **VI.33** and **36**), *gerousiarch* is the most frequently and widely attested term for the president of the synagogal council, with *prostates*, a common Greek word for president, coming only a distant second. Two other widely attested terms in the Greek world for presiding officer, *epistates* and *politarchon*, are also found occasionally in Jewish inscriptions but their precise meaning in each case is disputed. About the formal duties of the synagogal president we have no information. What our evidence does show is that the holders of the office tended to be men of mature years. Ages testified for *gerousiarchs* range from fifty-four to eighty.

Gerousiarch (lit. 'ruler of the council of old men')

(**II.19**) Ti(berius) Claudius Philippus, *(archon)* for life[14] and *gerousiarch*, has built the wall. (*CIJ* I no. 561 = Noy I no. 23 – vicinity of Puteoli – 1st century CE(?))

(**II.20**) Here lies Kyntianos*, *gerousiarch* of the Community (*synagoge*) of the Augustesians, who lived for 54 years. In peace his sleep. (*CIJ* I no. 368 = Noy II no. 189 – Rome, 3rd-4th century CE(?))

(**II.21**) Aneis Geneiales*, *gerousiarch*, who lived a good life to the age of 65 years, 5 months. (*CIJ* I no. 9 = Noy II no. 487 – Rome, 3rd-4th century CE(?))

Prostates (lit. 'one who stands before')

(**II.22**) On behalf of King Ptolemy (VIII) and Queen Kleopatra, his sister, and Queen Kleopatra, his wife, the Jews from Xenephyris (have dedicated) the gateway to the prayer-house during the presidency (*prostanton*) of Theodoros and Achillion. (*CIJ* II no. 1441 = HN no. 24 – Xenephyris; 140-116 BCE)

(**II.23**) Here lies Gai(o)s, *prostates*, who lived for 72 years. In peace your sleep. (*CIJ* I² no. 100 = Noy II no. 373 – Rome; 3rd-4th century CE(?))

(**II.24**) Here lies Kaili(o)s, *prostates*[15] of the Agrippesians. In peace let him sleep. (*CIJ* I no. 365 = Noy II no. 170 – Rome; 3rd-4th century CE(?))

Epistates ton palaion (lit. 'one who stands over the ancient ones')

(**II.25**) Here lies Sanbati(o)s, son of Gerontios, *presbyteros* (Elder), *gram-*

mateus (secretary) and *epistates ton palaion*.[16] Peace. (*CIJ* II no. 800 = *IK* Kalchedon no. 75 – Bithynia; undated)

Politarchon (lit. 'ruler of the community')

(II.26) When he had already completed a cycle of fifty-three years, the Tamer of All snatched him away to Hades. O sandy earth, what a body you cover, (that which contained) the soul of the most blessed Abramos. For he was not without honour in the city but was crowned in his wisdom with a communal magistracy over all the people. For you were honoured as community leader (*politarchon*[17]) in two places[18] and handled with grace the double expense ... (*CPJ* III no. 1530a = HN no. 39 – Leontopolis? early imperial?)

(ii) Members of the synagogal council

Archon (lit. 'ruler')

Found throughout the Diaspora, the *archons* are the most frequently attested of all synagogal officers. Although it is known that they were elected at the Jewish New Year, there is very little hard evidence for what they did in their capacity as *archons* and no evidence at all as to how many of them sat on a typical synagogal board. (At Berenice, where they seem, uniquely, to have comprised the whole administration, their numbers steadily increased over time, reflecting perhaps an increase in community numbers.) Nor is it known how long their term of office was. Some *archons* certainly were elected for a fixed term: at Rome, there are examples of men who served twice and even three times in the post. Life-holders of the office, however, are found there too and on occasion the position seems to have been purely honorary – child archons (*archontes nepioi*) and infant *mellarchontes* (archons-elect) can hardly have been functional figures. (For these, see **I.63** and **VI.27-9**.) The same may well have been the case with the archons of all honour (*archontes pases times*). Common sense suggests that the reason for some, if not all, of these differences will have been variant congregational practice but the matter is not susceptible of proof.

Archontal elections

(II.27) The month of September itself they (the Jews) term their New Year. In that month they elect their magistrates, whom they call *archons*. (Pseudo-Chrysostom, *De nativitate S. Ioannis* in *PL* Supp.I, col. 564)

A mellarchon – i.e. an archon-elect

(II.28) To Aelius Primitivus, incomparable husband (and) *mellarchon*, who lived for 38 years (and) with whom I lived for 16 years without a single quarrel. To a most sweet, well-deserving husband, Flavia Maria has set up (this stone). (*CIJ* I no. 457 = Noy II no. 179 – Rome; 3rd-4th century CE(?))

Archons plain and simple

Besides the Roman examples listed here, note also **I.107** (Berenice); **V.31** (Alexandria); **V.35-6** (Berenice); **V.39** (Tlos); **VII.11** (Aphrodisias).

(II.29) Here lies Maron(i)os, also called ... etos, grandson of Alexander, also called Mathios*, *archon* of the Siburesians, aged 24 years and 3 months. In peace (his) sleep. (*CIJ* I no. 140 = Noy II no. 338 – Rome, 3rd-4th century CE(?))

(II.30) Klaudios Ioses, *archon*, (who) lived for 35 years. (*CIJ* I no. 538 = Noy II no. 585 – Rome or Porto; 2nd century CE(?))

(II.31) Zonatha*, (the) *archon*, lies here, aged 19 years. In peace, (his) sleep. (*CIJ* I² no. 277 = Noy II no. 402 – Rome; 3rd century CE(?))

Re-elected archons

Besides the examples listed here, note **II.60** and **107**; **VI.24-5**.

(II.32) Here lies Sabbatis, twice *archon*. He lived for 35 years. In peace his sleep. Peace upon Israel (in Hebrew). (*CIJ* I no. 397 = Noy II no. 193 – Rome; 3rd-4th century CE(?))

(II.33) Here lies Pomponis*, the *archon* twice of the Community (*synagoge*) of the Calcaresians (lime burners?). He lived for 60 years. In peace his sleep. (*CIJ* I² no. 384 = Noy II no. 165 – Rome; 3rd-4th century CE(?))

(II.34) Here lies Prokoulous*, the *archon* twice, and his wife, Euodia. (Also) Ioulia, nine years and nine months, Sabates, nine years, Euodia, two years and nine months. In peace (their sleep). (*CIJ* I² no. 391 = Noy II no. 110 – Rome; 3rd-4th century CE(?))

The dia biou (lit. 'for life') or (archon) for life

The common view that the designation *dia biou*, sometimes written *zabiou* or *dia viu*, stands for *archon* for life and thus indicates a permanent member of the synagogal council is followed here. For discussion, see *HJPAJC* III, p. 99; for further examples of the office, see **II.19**; **VI.34-5**.

(II.35) Here lies Flabia Antonina, wife of Datibos*, the (*archon*) for life of the Community (*synagoge*) of the Augustesians. (*CIJ* I² no. 416 = Noy II no. 194 – Rome; 3rd-4th century CE(?))

(II.36) Here lies Sabeinos, (*archon*) for life of the Bernaclesii.[19] (*CIJ* I no. 398 = Noy II no. 106 – Rome; 3rd-4th century CE(?))

archon pases times (lit. 'archon of all honour')

The significance of this unusual title, found only at Rome and perhaps on Samos (see **II.50**), is elusive. It may be purely honorific or a congregational variant for *archon* for life or (this, at Rome only) indicate membership of a supra-synagogal council (on this, see introductory note at **II.76**). For a text revealing the high status of this type of archonship, see **VI.24**.

(II.37) Alexander, *archon pases times* to his sweetest child, Alexander, *mellarchon*. In peace your sleep. (*CIJ* I no. 85 = Noy II no. 259 – Rome; 3rd-4th century CE(?))

(II.38) Hermogenys*, *archon pases times*, lies here. (*CIJ* I² no. 324 = Noy II no. 121 – Rome; 3rd-4th century CE(?))

Archontal activity

That it was the archons who were responsible for securing the synagogue's ritually essential water-supply emerges from the following text – a brief extract from a document that lists, inter alia, the amounts paid monthly to the municipality of Arsinoe in Egypt for the supply of public water.

(II.39) From the *archons* of the prayer-house of the Theban Jews, 128 drachmas monthly. (*CPJ* II no. 432 – Arsinoe in Egypt; 113 CE)

Phrontistes (lit. 'manager')

An important, elective post, senior to the archonship, at least at Rome (see **VI.24-5**), whose duties were probably financial and managerial. The small number of *phrontistai* attested suggests that only a minority of congregations (the richest?) had such officers.

(II.40) During Theodoros the Younger's time as *phrontistes*, the decoration (of the synagogue) with mosaics has been carried out at community expense. Blessing upon all who enter. (*CIJ* I² no. 723 = *DF* no. 2 – Aegina; 4th century CE)

(II.41) To Hezekiah, son of Isas*, *phrontistes* of Alexandria. (*CIJ* II no. 918 = HN no. 146; Jaffa; 2nd-4th century CE)

(II.42) ... with ... and Theodo[tos?] and Hillel, *phrontistai*. (Noy I no. 17 – Porto; 4th century CE(?))

Grammateus (lit. 'secretary')

Although some scholars claim that the *grammateus* was a mere employee of the synagogal community, the titular evidence from Rome for *grammateis*, which clearly parallels that for the *archons* there, does not support that view. Like the archonship, the post of *grammateus* could be elective and the title was sometimes given to the young sons of the 'great and good', presumably as a mark of respect (see **VI.26-7**). Whatever the duties of the *grammateus*, the position was clearly prestigious. In some families, it was virtually hereditary. How many *grammateis* there were per synagogal board is not known. The very large number of attestations from Rome (*archon* aside, it is the most frequently occurring title of all) suggests that there may well have been more than one at a time.

A *mellogrammateus* – i.e. a grammateus elect

(II.43) Here lies Ioudas, *mellogrammateus*, who lived for 24 years. In peace your sleep. (*CIJ* I no. 121 = Noy II no. 231 – Rome; 3rd-4th century CE(?))

A *family of grammateis at Rome*

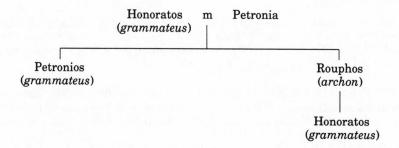

(II.44) Here lies Honoratos, *grammateus*, a pious man who lived for 70 years, 8 months (and) 12 days. Rouphos, (the) *archon*, to the sweetest of fathers. In peace your sleep. (*CIJ* I no. 145 = Noy II no. 257 – Rome; 3rd-4th century CE(?))

(II.45) Honoratos, (the) father, *grammateus*, (and) Petronia, the mother, to their peerless son Petronios, *grammateus*, (who) lived for 24 years, 4 months (and) 15 days. In peace his sleep. (*CIJ* I no. 149 = Noy II no. 223 – Rome; 3rd-4th century CE(?))

(II.46) Here lies Honoratos, *grammateus*, a child, son of Rouphos, (the) *archon*. He lived for 6 years (and) 28 days. In peace your sleep. (*CIJ* I no. 146 = Noy II no. 256 – Rome; 3rd-4th century CE(?))

Some individual grammateis

(II.47) Here lies Zokles*, *grammateus*, aged 50 years. In peace his sleep. (*RivAC* 51 (1975), p. 362 = Noy II no. 575 – Rome; 3rd-4th century CE(?))

(II.48) Elius* Aprilicus, *grammateus*, who lived for 35 years. His wife set (this) up to her well-deserving husband. (*CIJ* I no. 456 = Noy II no. 85 – Rome; 3rd-4th century CE(?))

(II.49) Here lies Oursos*, *grammateous* (*sic*), who lived for 22 years and three months. The memory of the bridegroom-to-be (is for a blessing?).[20] In peace his sleep. (*CIJ* I no. 148 = Noy II no. 253 – Rome; 3rd-4th century CE(?))

Presbyteros (= 'elder' or 'Elder')

An ambiguous word which, when not simply meaning 'elderly man', may denote the ordinary, non-executive members of the synagogal council. In inscriptions, mainly of the fourth century and later, *presbytera* and its analogue *presbyteressa* also appear. Absence of information about the activities of any of the women so designated makes it hard to be certain whether they were functioning members of the synagogal council or simply elderly members of the community. For discussion, see B. Brooten, *Women Leaders in the Ancient Synagogues* (Chico, California, 1982), ch. 3 and R. Kraemer, 'A new inscription from Malta and the question of women elders in the diaspora Jewish communities', *HTR* 78 (1985), pp. 431-8.

Presbyteroi as non-executive council members – i.e. Elders

(II.50) ... and the *presbyteroi* and ... of the Jews of the ... synagogue in [Samos(?)] have honoured Ar[... *presby*]*teros* (restoration and, therefore, meaning uncertain), the [*archon*(?)] of all honour ... for having constructed for us ... (rest unintelligible). (*CIJ* I² no. 731f – Samos; 2nd-3rd century CE)

(II.51) Vow (?) of the *archons* and *presbyteroi*. (*CIJ* I² no. 663 = *DF* no. 101 = Noy I no. 181 – Elche, Spain; 4th century CE (?) – mosaic inscription, probably from the floor of a synagogue)

(II.52) Samouel, son of Eiddeos, *presbyteros* of the Jews, has built (the synagogue). (*CIJ* II no. 829 = *DF* no. 58 – Doura-Europos; mid-3rd century CE)

Female presbyters

(II.53) ... (name lost), *gerousiarch*, lover of the commandments (*philentoli[os]*) and Eulogia, *presbytera*, his wife. (Noy I no. 163 – Rabat, Malta; 4th-5th century CE)

(II.54) Tomb of the blessed Mazauzala, *presbeteresa*. She lived ... Rest. God (is) with the holy and righteous. (*SEG* 27 (1977) no. 1201 = Le Bohec, no. 4 – Oea, Africa; 4th-5th century CE(?))

(II.55) Tomb of Rebeka, *presbytera*, who has fallen asleep. (*CIJ* I² no. 692 – Bizye, Thrace; no earlier than the 4th-5th century CE)

(iii) Officials concerned with cultic matters

Archisynagogos *(lit. 'ruler of the synagogue')*

Although it is sometimes claimed that the duties of *archisynagogoi* were wide-ranging (see, for instance, Leon, *Jews of Rome*, pp. 171-3), there in clear evidence only for their direction of proceedings in the synagogue on the Sabbath. Inscriptions testify to the ubiquity of *archisynagogoi* but the information they yield about the character of the office is so varied that it is impossible to determine what, if anything, was normative. While some congregations appear to have had only one *archisynagogos* at any given time, others had several. And while in some synagogues the office clearly was elective and held by men for a fixed term, in others it was awarded for life or given (as an honour?) to women and little children (see **V.32-3** and **VI.30** and **37** below.) A few texts (e.g. **III.2**) suggest that in some congregations it might have been hereditary. Sometimes the position of *archisynagogos* was held in tandem with other community offices such as the post of *phrontistes*. How common this kind of 'doubling-up' was we cannot say. Nor do we know what the relative statuses were within the Diasporan synagogue of the *archisynagogos* on the one hand and the president of the synagogal council on the other. What does seem to be clear is that the title, at one time used also by Gentiles in their cultic associations, was virtually abandoned by them after the 2nd century CE – presumably because it had come to be regarded as quintessentially Jewish. For good modern discussions of the office, see G.H.R. Horsley, *New Documents Illustrating Early Christianity* IV (MacQuarie University, 1987), pp. 213-20 and T. Rajak and D. Noy, 'Archisynagogoi: office, title and social status in the Greco-Jewish synagogue', *JRS* 83 (1993), pp. 75-93.

The cultic role of the archisynagogos

(II.56) They (Paul and his companions) continued on from Perge and arrived at Antioch in Pisidia. Coming into the synagogue on the day of the Sabbath, they sat down. After the reading of the Law and the prophets, the *archisynagogoi* sent this message to them – 'Brothers, if you have any word of exhortation for the community (*laos*), speak.' (*Acts of the Apostles* 13.14-15)

Some individual archisynagogoi

(II.57) To Plotius Fortunatus, *archisynagogus*. Plotius, Ampliatus, Secundinus and Secunda have set up (this memorial) to their patron (interpretation of the text uncertain here) and Ofilia Basilia to her well-deserving husband. (Noy I no. 14 – Ostia; 1st-2nd century CE)

(II.58) Here lies Poly[me?]ni(o)s, *archisynagogos* of the Community (*synagoge*) of the Vernaculi, aged 53. In peace his sleep. (*CIJ* I no. 383 = Noy II no. 117 – Rome; 3rd-4th century CE(?))

(II.59) Asterius, son of Rusticus, *arcosinagogus* (*sic*) (and) Margarita (wife/daughter?) of Riddeus, have paved part of the portico with mosaics. (Le Bohec, no. 14 – Hammam Lif (Naro); 4th century CE(?))

A re-elected archisynagogos

(II.60) ... of ... *archisynagogos* for the fifth time, the son of Ananias, *archon* twice. (*DF* no. 85 – Salamis, Cyprus; 3rd century CE)

A life archisynagogos

For another example, see **VII.17**.

(II.61) The most illustrious P(oplios) Rout(ilios) Ioses*, the *archisynagogos* for life, along with his wife, Bisinnia Demo, (has built the synagogue) from the foundations up, out of his own resources. (*CIJ* II no. 744 = *DF* no. 16; Teos in Ionia; 3rd century CE)

Multiple archisynagogoi

Besides this example, note **II.56** and **VII.17**.

(II.62) During the office of the most honoured *archisynagogoi* Eusebios, Nemias* and Phineas, and of Theodoros the *gerousiarch*, and the most honoured *presbyteroi* Eisakios* and Saoulos* and others, Ilasios, *archisynagogos* of the Antiochenes, has paved 150 feet of the entryway (of the synagogue) with mosaics. Year 703, Eudyneos 7. Blessing upon all (who enter). (*CIJ* II no. 803 = *IGLS* IV no. 1319 = *DF* no. 38; re-edited by Bingen, *ZPE* 109 (1995), p. 194 – Apamea in Syria; 392 CE)

'Doubling-up' of the offices of archisynagogos and phrontistes

(II.63) I, Theodoros, *archisynagogos*, during my four year stint as *phrontistes*,[21] have built the synagogue from its foundations out of 85 gold coins from the revenues and 105 gold coins from the gifts (bequeathed?) to God. (*CIJ* I² no. 722 = *DF* no. 1 – Aegina; 4th century CE)

The synagogal assistant

Various terms are found desigating this office – *neokoros* and *hyperetes* in documents from the more Hellenised parts of the Diaspora, *hazzan* in areas where semitic influences were stronger (e.g. Cilicia, for which, see **III.76**). Epigraphically there are very few attestations, probably because of the lowliness of the position. For the functions of the assistant, there is no good *Diasporan* evidence. The *hazzan's* activities in the Great Synagogue at Alexandria (for which see **II.67**) will certainly have been atypical (proceedings in small synagogues will hardly have needed such a Master of Ceremonies) and may well be apocryphal.

Terms for the synagogal assistant

Neokoros

(II.64) [To King Ptolemy, greetings from] ... who lives in Alexandrou-Nesos. I am being wronged by [Dorotheos, a Jew who lives in the same] village. In the 5th year, according to the financial calendar, on Phamenoth [... as I was talking?] to my fellow worker, my cloak [which is worth ... drachmas caught Dorotheos' eye and?] he went off with it. When I noticed, he [took refuge?] in the prayer-house of the Jews ... Lezelmis, 100 arourai-holder, arrived on the scene [and gave] the cloak to Nikomachos, the *neokoros*,[22] (for safekeeping) until the trial. Wherefore, I beg of you, O King, to instruct Diophanes [the *strategos* to write to] the *epistates* [telling him] to order Dorotheos and Nikomachos [to hand over] the cloak to him and, if I write the truth, [to make him give to me] either the cloak or its value ... (*CPJ* I no. 129 – 218 BCE)

Hyperetes (lit. servant; attendant)

(II.65) Flabios Ioulianos, *hyperetes*. Flabia Iouliane, (his) daughter, (has set this up) to her father. In peace your sleep. (*CIJ* I no. 172 = Noy II no. 290 – Rome; 3rd-4th century CE(?))

Hazzan

(II.66) When Nemias* was *hazzan* and *diakon* (i.e. deacon), the porch of the sanctuary was paved with mosaics. Year 703, 9th day of Dystros. [...]on did this, in fulfilment of a vow, together with his wife and children. (*CIJ* II no. 805 = *IGLS* IV no. 1321 = *DF* no. 40 – Apamea in Syria; 391-2 CE)

The functions of the synagogal assistant

(II.67) There (was) ... a wooden platform in the middle upon which the attendant of the synagogue (*hazzan*) stood with a napkin in his hand; when the time came to answer Amen he waved his napkin and all the congregation duly responded.[23] (bT, *Sukkah* 51b.)

(iv) Honorific titles

Pater / Mater Synagogae (lit. 'Father / Mother of the Community')

The titles Father and Mother of the Community occur predominantly at Rome itself and in areas where Roman cultural influence was strong. Given the broad patronal connotations of the words *pater / mater* in Roman society, it seems only fair to conclude that the Jewish men and women who bore these titles must have been conspicuous patrons and benefactors of their communities. (For other instances of patronal behaviour among the Jews, see **VI.36-9**.) Analogous titles (probably) are the rare *pater tou laou* and *pater tou stemmatos*. The significance of the bald term *pater*, found in several Jewish inscription of our period (e.g. **VI.36**) is wholly uncertain and accordingly not listed here.

Pater synagogae – Father of the Community

For additional instances of the title, see **I.63**; **II.7**; **VI.17** and **25**.

(II.68) Here lies Eirena, maiden wife of Klodios, brother of Kountos* Klaudios Synesios, Father of the Community (*synagoge*) of the Campesians at Rome. Peace (*Shalom*)! (*CIJ* I no. 319 = Noy II no. 560 – Rome; 3rd-4th century CE(?))

(II.69) Kattia Ammias, daughter of Menophilos, Father of the Community (*synagoge*) of the Calcaresians, who has conducted an upright life in Judaism and lived for thirty-four years with her husband. From her children she saw grandchildren. Here lies Kattia Ammias. (*CIJ* I no. 537 = Noy II no. 584 – Rome; 3rd-4th century CE(?))

(II.70) Avilia Aster*, a Jewess. M(arcus) Avilius Ianuarius, Father of the Community (*sinagoga*), to his sweetest daughter. (Le Bohec, no. 74 – Sitifis, Mauretania; 2nd-3rd century CE)

Mater Synagogae – Mother of the Community

For a Mother of Communities, see **VII.30**.

(II.71) Here lies [...]ia Markella, Mother of the Community (*synagoge*) of the Augustesians. May she be remembered. In peace her sleep. (*CIJ* I no. 496 = Noy II no. 542 – Rome; 3rd century CE(?))

(II.72) Here lies Simp[likia ... Mother] of the Community (and) lover of her husband ... [Father?] of the Community (*synagoge*) [set this up] to his own spouse.[24] (*CIJ* I² no. 166. See also Noy II no. 251 – Rome; 3rd-4th century CE(?))

(II.73) To Coelia Paterna, Mother of the Community (*synagoga*) of the Brescians (i.e. the Jews of Brescia). (*CIJ* I² no. 639 = Noy I no. 5 – Brescia; 4th century CE or earlier)

Pater tou laou (lit. 'Father of the People' – i.e. the Jewish community)[25]

(II.74) Aur(elios) Elpidys, *pater tou laou* for life, (has made) a gift of a vestibule to the synagogue. (*CIJ* I² no. 720 = *DF* no. 9 – Mantinea, Greece – 3rd-4th century CE)

Pater tou stemmatos (Father of the Community)[26]

(II.75) I, Irenopoios, *presbyteros* (Elder) and *pater tou stemmatos*, son of Eiakob*, a *presbyteros* (Elder) too, in fulfilment of a vow made by (my)self and my wife and my lawfully begotten son, have made, and beautifully too, the mosaic of the interior (of the synagogue) and the balustrade. (Cost) – 7 (gold) coins. (*CIJ* II no. 739 = *DF* no. 14 – Smyrna; 4th century CE)

(b) Supra-synagogal bodies and officials

In contrast to most Diasporan communities, which were probably serviced by a single synagogue, the Jews of Alexandria, Antioch and Rome are known to have possessed many. (For a recently published inscription indicating the presence of multiple synagogues at Thessaloniki, see M. Nigdelis, 'Synagoge(n) und Gemeinde der Juden in Thessaloniki: Fragen auf grund einer neuen jüdischen Grabinschrift der Kaiserzeit', *ZPE* 102 (1994), pp. 297-306.) At Alexandria this led to the creation of a supra-synagogal layer of administration, which until 10-11 CE was headed by an *ethnarch* and after that date by a council of Elders (*gerousia*), comprised largely, if not exclusively, of *archons*. (If bT *Sukkah* 51b is to be believed, there were seventy-one of the latter.) What happened at Antioch and Rome is less clear. Although a case has been made out for the existence at each of these places of an Alexandrian-style central council, presided over by (respectively) a *gerousiarch* and an *archgerousiarch*, the evidence is not decisive.

(i) Alexandria

The Jewish ethnarch

(II.76) In Egypt, at any rate, an independent settlement (*katoikia*) of Jews has been set up,[27] and a large part of the city of Alexandria has been marked out for this people. An *ethnarch* stands over them,[28] who administers the community (*ethnos*) and judges lawsuits and takes care of contracts and (government) ordinances, just as if he were the ruler of an independent polity. (Strabo, as quoted in Josephus, *Jewish Antiquities* 14.117)

The supra-synagogal gerousia

The following two passages describe the attack made on this body by Avillius Flaccus, the Roman prefect of Egypt, during the racial unrest of 38 CE.

(II.77) Having smashed up everything like a housebreaker and left no part of Jewish life untouched by a hostility of the highest order, this doer of mighty deeds, this inventor of new iniquities, Flaccus himself, devised a monstrous and unparalleled mode of attack. Our Saviour and Benefactor Augustus had appointed a council of elders (*gerousia*) to take care of Jewish affairs after the death of the *genarch*.[29] He had done this through written instructions to Magius Maximus when the latter was about to take up office for the second time as Prefect of Alexandria and the country (i.e. Egypt). Having arrested thirty-eight members of our council who had been found in their homes, he gave orders that they should be bound immediately. A fine procession he then organized and led through the middle of the market place to the theatre – old men in bonds, their arms pinioned, some with straps, others with iron chains. (Philo, *In Flaccum* 73-4)

(II.78) But none at all of the festal proceedings was being carried out.[30] The *archons*, after their irremediable and unendurable sufferings and injuries, were still in prison[31] and private individuals regarded the misfortunes of those men as being shared by the whole community (*ethnos*) ... (Philo, *In Flaccum* 117)

(ii) Antioch

A supra-synagogal gerousiarch?

The following two passages have sometimes been thought to reveal the existence at Antioch of a supreme, supra-synagogal *gerousiarch*.

(II.79) Tomb of Aidesios, *gerousiarch*, from Antioch. (*BS* II no. 141 – 3rd century CE)

(II.80) A commotion has arisen among our Jews[32] at the prospect of a wicked old man entering into authority over them. When he held the office previously, they expelled him, since he had turned it into a tyranny. They think that the ruler (*archon*)[33] who has power over their own rulers (*archons*) will order this to be done at your behest, for they claim that you accepted the old man's supplications in ignorance of his behaviour, which not even age has been able to amend. In their agitation, they think that this is how things stand. While they have not been able to convince me of this, they have been able to compel me to write. Please pardon both me and them, me for having yielded to so many, them for behaving as crowds do – being easily taken in. (Libanius, *Epistulae* 1251 = Stern II no. 504 – 364 CE)

(iii) Rome

The archgerousiarch

It is possible, but cannot be proved, that this official was the head of all Roman Jewry. The term *archgerousiarch* could be a simple variant of *gerousiarch*. See Horsley, *New Docs.* II, pp. 18-19 and III, p. 64.

(II.81) Here lies Anastasios, *archgerousiarch*, son of Anastasios, aged (?). (*SEG* 26 (1976-7) no. 1178 = Noy II no. 521 – Rome; 3rd-4th century CE)

The archon alti ordinis (lit. archon of high rank)

Certainty is impossible as to the precise position occupied within Roman Jewry by this uniquely titled official. Some argue that he may have sat on a supra-synagogal council (for bibliography, see Leon, *Jews of Rome*, pp. 168-9), others (e.g. Baron, *Social and Religious History of the Jews* II², p. 199) that he played a mainly honorary role within the synagogue. I. Di Stefano Manzella's view that this inscription is not Jewish is not accepted here. For this, see 'L. Maecius Archon, centurio alti ordinis. Nota critica su *CIL* VI.39084 = *CIJ* I, 470', *ZPE* 77 (1989), pp. 103-12.

(II.82) To L(ucius) Maecius Constantius, son of L(ucius) and Maecia Lucianis, daughter of L(ucius) and to L(ucius) Maecius Victorinus and L(ucia) Maecia Sabbatis, his children and Iulia Alexandria his wife, L(ucius) Maecius, son of Lucius(?), *archon alti ordinis*, has set up (this memorial). (*CIJ* I² no. 470 = Noy II no. 618 – Rome; 2nd-3rd century CE(?))

3. COMMUNITY STRUCTURES OTHER THAN THE SYNAGOGUE

(a) The community record-office

Although a record-office probably existed in many (all large?) Jewish communities, the only places where such an institution is attested are Alexandria, as in the document cited here, and Hierapolis in Phrygia, for which, see **I.101**.

(II.83) To Protarchos. From Dionysia, the daughter of Ariston, with her guardian, her mother's brother, Agathinos, the son of Philotas and from Alexander, the son of Neikodemos. Concerning the matter in dispute, Dionysia concedes that she has duly received from Alexander 100 silver drachmas out of the 200 which Theodoros, the deceased brother of Alexander, bequeathed her, in accordance with the will which he deposited in the record-office of the Jews ... (*CPJ* II no. 143 – 13 BCE)

(b) Evidence pointing to the existence of educational institutions

Schools and synagogues were distinct and the Talmud regularly distinguishes between them. However, there was some overlap, since synagogues, as can be seen from **II.1-2**, were often used for study. The evidence set out here, though showing that teaching and learning did go on within Jewish Diasporan communities, does not tell us exactly where.

Teachers

(II.84) Here lies Eusebis* the teacher (*didaskalos*), a student of the Law (*nomomathes*), with his wife Eirene. (*CIJ* I² no. 333 = Noy II no. 68 – Rome; 3rd-4th century CE(?))

(II.85) Beniames*, son of Lachares, assistant schoolmaster (*proscholos*). (*CIJ* I² no. 715b – Athens; 2nd-3rd century CE)

Students, male and female

(II.86) Eusebios ... a student of the Law (*nomomathes*) ... lived ... years (*CIJ* I no. 113 = Noy II no. 374 – Rome; 3rd-4th century CE(?))

(II.87) ... a (female) student (of the Law?) and ... easily taught (*eudidakte*).[34] (*CIJ* I no. 190. See also Noy II no. 390 – Rome; 3rd-4th century CE(?))

(II.88) Sempronious Baseileus (*sic*) to Aurelia Kailereina*, a good wife and a good student (of the Law?), with whom I have lived for 17 (?) years. He has set up (this plaque) to a well-deserving wife. (*CIJ* I² no. 215 = Noy II no. 328 – Rome; 3rd-4th century CE(?))

(II.89) Here lies Mniaseas*, student of the sages (*mathetes sophon*)[35] and Father of Communities (*pater synagogion*). (*CIJ* I² no. 508 = Noy II no. 544 – Rome; 3rd-4th century CE(?))

4. COMMUNITY VALUES

(a) Devotion to the Law (Torah)

The Jews' devotion to their Law, celebrated by Josephus (e.g. **II.103**) and mocked by Juvenal (**VII.20**), is illustrated here by a small selection of material from Rome and its environs. The *aron*, the synagogal cupboard containing the scrolls of the Law, was often depicted on burial plaques in the Jewish catacombs to draw attention to the deceased's diligence in that regard. The funerary epithets *philonomos* (lover of the Law) and *philentolos* (lover of the commandments (*mitzvot*)), served the same purpose.

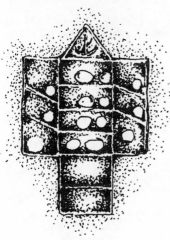

(II.90) (Burial) place of Maran. (Fasola, fig. 11 = Noy II no. 516)

Crudely carved beneath Maran's epitaph is the *aron* depicted to the left with its fourteen scrolls of the Law. On each side of it (not shown) was a seven-branched candlestick (a *menorah*). It is thought that the the lines in the pediment on top of the cupboard may represent another (this time, drawn with five branches).

(II.91) Here lies in peace the blameless and pious (*theosebes*) Roupheinos*, a pupil of the Holy Laws and Wisdom.[36] Aged 21 years (and) 8 days. (He died) at the 10th hour of the night. (Noy I no. 12 – Lorium, near Rome; 2nd-4th century CE(?))

(II.92) Here lies Eukarpos, a child, devout, a lover of the Law (*philonomos*).[37] In peace your sleep. (*CIJ* I² no. 111 = Noy II no. 212 – Rome; 3rd-4th century CE(?))

(II.93) Krispeina*, wife/daughter (?) of Prokopios, zealous, a lover of the commandments (*philentolos*).[38] Here she lies. In peace her sleep. (*CIJ* I no. 132 = Noy II no. 281 – Rome; 3rd-4th century CE(?))

(II.94) Victorina, who lived for about thirty-five years (and) died the day before the Ides of May, while Gallicanus and Symmachus were consuls. Just, devout, a lover of the commandments (*filentolia*).[39] (*CIJ* I² no. 482 = Noy II no. 564 – Rome(?); 14 May, 330 CE)

(b) High regard for priestly ancestry

That the Jews continued to hold the priesthood in high regard even after it lost its chief *raison d'être* with the destruction of the Temple in 70 CE is shown by the long and widespread use of the terms 'priest' (*hiereus*) and 'priestess' (*hierisa*) as status indicators. In recent years the significance of the latter has been much debated. Did the women so designated play an active cultic rôle – i.e. perform the same, rather limited, cultic functions within the synagogue as men of Aaronic descent or was it just a courtesy title bestowed upon the wives and daughters of such men? The recent publication of the epitaph from pre-70 CE Jerusalem of Megiste, the priestess (*SEG* 41 (1991) no.1561) makes the latter view more likely. Since women never played an active part in the rituals of the Temple, she can only have been the wife or daughter of a priest – i.e a *kohenet*. For full discussion of this text, see T. Ilan, 'New ossuary inscriptions from Jerusalem', *SCI* (1991-2), pp. 157-9.

Priests (hiereis)

(II.95) The tomb belongs to Mar(kos) Moussios,[40] priest. (He erected it) during his lifetime. The Jews (of Ephesos) are responsible for it. (*CIJ* II no. 746, now superseded by *IK* Ephesos V no. 1676 – Ephesos; 2nd-3rd century CE)

(II.96) Here lie Ioudas and Ioses*, *archons* and priests and brothers. (*CIJ* I no. 347 = Noy II no. 124 – Rome; 3rd-4th century CE(?))

Priestesses (hierisai)

(II.97) Here lies Gaudentia, priestess, aged 24. In peace her sleep. (*CIJ* I² no. 315 = Noy II no. 11 – Rome; 3rd-4th century CE(?))

(II.98) Sara, daughter of Naimia*, mother of the priestess, the Lady

Mareia, lies here.[41] (*CIJ* II no. 1107 = *BS* II no. 66 – burial of a Palmyrene Jewess at Beth She'arim; 3rd-4th century CE)

(c) Loyalty to the community

(**II.99**) You know how great their (the Roman Jews') numbers are,[42] how they stick together, what weight they carry in public meetings. (Cicero, *Pro Flacco* 28.66 = Stern I no. 68)

(**II.100**) Here lies Pancharios, Father of the Community (*synagoge*) of Elaia, aged one hundred and ten, a lover of the (Jewish) community (*philolaos*),[43] a lover of the commandments (*philentolos*), who lived a good life. In peace his sleep. (*CIJ* I no. 509 = Noy II no. 576 – Rome; 3rd-4th century CE(?))

(**II.101**) Maria, daughter of Iouda(s), wife of Leontiskos. Farewell to the community (*laos*).[44] May you rejoice, wise man, whoever you are. (*CIJ* I² no. 701 – Larissa in Thessaly; 2nd-3rd century CE)

(**II.102**) Here lies Lazar, pious, just, lover of his children, lover of his brothers, lover of his community (*philosynagogos*),[45] aged 31 years. In [peace] his sleep. (*CIJ* I no. 321 = Noy II no. 171 – Rome; 3rd-4th century CE(?))

(d) Devotion to charity

(**II.103**) They (the Greeks and barbarians) attempt to imitate our unanimity and our charitable enterprises and our diligence in our crafts and our endurance when persecuted on account of our laws. (Josephus, *Contra Apionem* 2.283)

(**II.104**) ... lover of the (Jewish) community (*philolaos*), lover of the commandments (*phil[entol]os*), friend of the poor (*philopenes*).[46] [In peace] the sleep of the *archon*(?). (*CIJ* I no. 203. See also Noy II no. 240 – Rome; 3rd-4th century CE(?))

(**II.105**) Establish many hostels in every city so that strangers may derive benefit from our kindness – not just our own people but any others who may be in need ... I have given orders that each year 30,000 modii of corn and 60,000 pints of wine are to be assigned for the whole of Galatia. I declare that one fifth is to be used for the poor who service the (pagan) priests and the rest distributed by us among strangers and beggars. For it is a disgrace that while no Jew ever begs and the impious Galilaeans (i.e. Christians) provide food for both their own and our poor, our people clearly lack support from us. (The emperor Julian, as cited in Sozomenus, *History* 5.16.5 = Stern II no. 482)

(e) Family-centredness

(II.106) Roupheinos*, lover of his parents (*philogoneous* (*sic*)).[47] He lived for 12 years. (*SEG* 26 (1976-7) no. 1183 = Noy II no. 414 – Rome; 3rd-4th century CE)

(II.107) Ious(t)os, *grammateus*, lover of his father (*philopator*) and lover of his brother (*philadelphos*) (lies here). Maron, *archon* for the second time, (has set this up) for his beloved child, aged thirty-seven. (*CIJ* I no. 125 = Noy II no. 344 – Rome; 3rd-4th century CE(?))

(II.108) Here lies Kailia Euodous, devout, just, a lover of her children (*philotaiknos* (*sic*)), a lover of her siblings (*philadelphon* (*sic*)). In peace her sleep. (*CIJ* I^2 no. 363 = Noy II no. 127 – Rome; 3rd-4th century CE(?))

(f) Abhorrence of infanticide

Singular enough to be commented upon by both Greek and Roman writers was the Jews' refusal to expose unwanted infants. In addition to the excerpt from Diodorus Siculus set out here, note Tacitus, *Histories* 5.3 **(VII.2)**. Josephus' sensitivity about this Jewish 'non-practice' comes out in his attempt to justify it.

(II.109) Moses compelled those who lived in the land (of Judaea) to rear their children. And since babies are reared at little expense, the Jewish nation has always been very populous. (Hecataeus, as cited in Diodorus Siculus 40.3.8 = Stern I no. 11)

(II.110) The Law orders that all children be reared and it forbids women to either cause abortion or destroy the foetus ... (Josephus, *Contra Apionem* 2.202)

5. DISTINCTIVE JEWISH PRACTICES

(a) Sabbath observance

This, the most conspicuous of all Diasporan Jewish practices (it was marked by the closure of shops, the cessation of work and the ritual lighting of the lamps on the Sabbath eve), is referred to many times in Graeco-Roman sources. Though often treated with levity and even contempt by poets and moralists, it was, if Josephus is to be believed **(VII.6)**, widely copied in the Gentile world. Among Greeks and Romans, there were many who, though aware of the Sabbath, did not fully understand it – the emperor Augustus, for one, erroneously thought it was a day of fasting. But there was a general appreciation of its importance to Jews – hence the frequent attempts by the maliciously-minded to exploit it to the Jews' disadvantage – e.g. by requiring them either to appear in court on the Sabbath or forfeit their case **(IV.28-9)**.

The Sabbath as a day of rest

A document from Philadelpheia in the Fayum recording the cessation of brick-deliveries on the Sabbath.

(II.111)
5th – I have to hand bricks from Phileas – 920.
6th – 1,000.
7th – Sabbath.
8th – 1,000.
9th – 1,000.
10th – 2,000, of which Demetrios has brought 1,000. Those of Tanis, 1,000.
11th – 936, of which Demetrios has brought 888. Those of Tanis, 48.

(CPJ I no. 10 – 2nd century BCE(?))

The following passage contains one of several allusions in the Augustan poets to the Sabbath as a day on which *not* to do things. Others are to be found at Tibullus, 1.3.18; Horace, *Satires* 9.67-70 and Ovid, *Ars Amatoria* 1.75-6 and 415-16. See Stern I nos. 126; 129 (= **VII.3**) and 141-2.

(II.112) But the less you wish to go, the more be mindful of going. Persist, and force your unwilling feet to run. Don't hope for rain and don't let the foreign Sabbath or the Allia,[48] notorious for ill-luck, delay you. (Ovid, *Remedia Amoris* 217-20 = Stern I no. 143)

(II.113) Among other superstitions of the civil theology, Seneca also criticises the sacred rituals of the Jews, especially the Sabbath. He claims that their practice is inexpedient, because they lose in idleness almost a seventh part of their life by inserting into every seven day cycle one day (of rest) and get hurt by not attending to urgent matters. (Seneca, as cited by Augustine, *City of God* 6.11 = Stern I no. 186)

(II.114) Don't you feel ashamed, don't you blush on account of the Jews, who keep the Sabbath with such diligence and from its very eve abstain from all work? If they see the sun beginning to set on the day of preparation (for it), they break off deals and interrupt purchases. If someone has made a purchase before the evening and comes in the evening bringing the purchase-money, they do not countenance accepting it, nor do they take the money.[49] (John Chrysostom, *Si esurierit inimicus* 161 = *PG* 51, col. 176)

The lighting of the lamps

(II.115) But when the days of Herod come and all along the greasy window-sills[50] the lamps, wreathed in violets, belch forth their fatty clouds and the floating tail of the tuna encircles the earthenware bowl and the white pot swells with wine,[51] then silently you move your lips and grow pale at the Sabbath of the circumcised. (Persius, *Satires* 5.179-84 = Stern I no. 190)

(II.116) It is customary to issue precepts as to how the gods are to be worshipped. Let us forbid anyone to light lamps on the Sabbath, since the gods do not need light and not even men delight in soot. (Seneca, *Epistulae Morales* 95.47 = Stern I no. 188)

Gentile misapprehensions about the Sabbath

(II.117) To quote Augustus again: 'Not even a Jew, my dear Tiberius, fasts as diligently on his Sabbath[52] as I have done today. It was not until after the first hour of the night that I munched a couple of mouthfuls of bread in the bath prior to being oiled.' (Suetonius, *Augustus* 76.2 = Stern II no. 303)

(b) Circumcision

After Sabbath observance, circumcision is the Jewish practice most frequently alluded to by Greek and Roman writers. (Besides the passages cited here, note also **II.115; VII.3** and **20.**) Although in itself circumcision was not exclusively Jewish, the Romans in particular tended to regard it as such. Under the emperor Domitian (81-96 CE), it was regarded as tantamount to proof of Jewishness and hence of liability for the Jewish tax **(IV.66)** and in later legal texts **(II.120-1)** it is specifically referred to as the *ritus Iudaicus* (Jewish rite/custom) or *nota Iudaica* (Jewish mark). In general, the Roman attitude to this 'mutilation of the genitals' was hostile and an attempt was made by the emperor Hadrian to ban it completely (*SHA, Hadrianus* 14.2 = Stern II no. 511). It was not successful, as the legal texts presented here show. Right down to the end of our period, the Jews persisted in circumcising not only their own sons – a concession originally made to them by the emperor Antoninus Pius – but their Gentile slaves as well.

(II.118) 'As a man of letters, Eumolpus must have some ink. With the aid of this, let's dye ourselves from top to toe. Then, like Ethiopian slaves, all smiles at having avoided torture, we'll attend upon you. By changing our colour, let's take in our enemies!' 'And what about circumcising us too', said Giton, 'so that we may look like Jews, or piercing our ears, so that we look like Arabs, or whitening our faces, so that Gaul thinks we're her sons? As if this colour alone could alter our appearance.' (Petronius, *Satyricon* 102.13-14 = Stern I no. 194)

(II.119) Modestinus,[53] in the sixth book of his Rules: it is permitted to the Jews under a rescript of the divine Pius to circumcise their sons alone.[54] If any Jew performs the act upon someone not of the same religion,[55] the penalty for castration shall be inflicted.[56] (*Digest* 48.8.11 = Linder no. 1)

(II.120) Roman citizens who, following Jewish custom (*Iudaico ritu*), allow themselves or their slaves to be circumcised, are to be relegated to an island in perpetuity and their property confiscated. The doctors shall suffer capital punishment. If Jews circumcise purchased slaves of another nation, they are to be either banished or suffer capital punishment.[57] (Paulus, *Sententiae* 5.22.3-4 = Linder, no. 6 – probably late 3rd century CE)

(**II.121**) The same two Augusti (*sc.* the emperors Honorius and Theodosius II) to Aurelian, Praetorian Prefect for the second time ... If he himself (the Patriarch Gamaliel VI) or any other Jew attempts to defile with the Jewish mark (*Iudaica nota*) a Christian or a member of any sect whatsoever, whether a freeman or a slave, he shall be subjected to the severity of the laws. If he also holds anywhere slaves of the Christian faith (lit. sanctity), they are to be handed over to the church in accordance with the law of Constantine. Given on the 13th day before the Kalends of November at Constantinople, during the 10th consulship of Honorius Augustus and the 6th of Theodosius Augustus. (*Codex Theodosianus* 16.8.22 = Linder no. 41 – 20 October, 415 CE)

(c) Food laws

Apart from the taboo on the consumption of pork, which was well known and often commented upon, our sources do not reveal much awareness on the part of the Greeks and Romans of Jewish dietary habits or laws.

(**II.122**) Decree of the people of Sardis. On the motion of the magistrates, the council and people have made the following decision. Whereas the Jews[58] dwelling in our city have always received from the people many great privileges, and have now come before the council and people with the request that, as their laws and freedom have been restored by the Senate and People of Rome, they may, in accordance with their accepted customs, come together and have a communal life and use their own system of justice, and that a place be given them in which they may assemble with their wives and children and offer their ancestral prayers and sacrifices[59] to God, it has been decided by the council and people to allow them to come together on the stated days and perform those acts which are in accordance with their laws, and to have set aside for them by the magistrates for building and habitation a place such as they may consider to be suitable for this purpose and that the market-officials of the city (the *agoranomoi*) shall be responsible for the importation of suitable foodstuffs[60] for them. (Josephus, *Jewish Antiquities* 14.259-61)

(**II.123**) When Augustus heard that among the boys under two years old in Syria whom Herod the king of the Jews had ordered to be killed, his own son also had been slain, he said, 'It is better to be Herod's pig[61] than his son.' (Macrobius, *Saturnalia* 2.4.11 = Stern II no. 543)

(II.124) When Gaius (Caligula) had given some instructions about the buildings, he posed a great and solemn question (to the Jewish delegation)[62] – 'Why do you abstain from the flesh of the pig?' (Philo, *Legatio ad Gaium* 361)

(II.125) Compelled by this teaching (i.e. Pythagoreanism), I began to abstain from (the flesh of) animals and after a year I found the habit not only easy but sweet. I believed that my mind was more active, though whether that really was the case I could not tell you for certain today. You ask why I stopped. My youth coincided with the first part of the principate of Tiberius. At that time action was being taken against foreign rites[63] and among the proofs of interest in those superstitions was abstinence from (the flesh of) certain animals. Therefore, at the request of my father, who did not fear false accusation[64] but hated philosophy, I returned to my former habits. It was not difficult to persuade me to begin to eat better. (Seneca, *Epistulae Morales* 108.22 = Stern I no. 189)

(II.126) Similar behaviour to this is to be found also in respect of food in people's worship of their gods. A Jew or an Egyptian priest would die rather than eat pork ... (Sextus Empiricus[65], *Hypotyposes* 3.222-3 = Stern II no. 334)

(d) The practice of magic

To the Greeks and Romans, Moses was the supreme sorcerer and the Jews themselves skilled and valuable practitioners of the magic arts (see, for instance, Pliny, *Natural History* 30.11 and Apuleius, *Apologia* 90 = Stern I no. 221 and II no. 361). Although many magic texts from antiquity contain clear Jewish elements (e.g. the divine names, Ia, Iao and Sabbaoth and invocations to angels), the extent to which they were actually composed by Jews for Jewish use is usually impossible to determine, as they often possess clear pagan features too. Here we present just two examples, whose Jewish character seems reasonably assured. (See R. Kotansky, 'Two inscribed Jewish Aramaic amulets from Syria', *IEJ* 41 (1991) 267-81.) For other texts illustrating Jewish magical expertise or Jewish influence on the practice of magic, see J. Naveh and S. Shaked, *Amulets and Magic Bowls. Aramaic Incantations of Late Antiquity* (Jerusalem and Leiden, 1985) and **V.98**; **VI.57** and **VII.49-50**.

A Jewish sorcerer on Cyprus in the late 40s CE

(II.127) Traversing the whole island as far as Paphos, Barnabas and Saul came across a certain man who was a sorcerer, a false-prophet and a Jew. His name was Bar-Jesus and he was part of the entourage of the pro-consul,[66] Sergius Paulus, a clever man. (*Acts of the Apostles* 13.6-7)

Jewish exorcists at Ephesus in the 50s CE

(II.128) Certain roving Jewish exorcists tried to use the name of the Lord

Jesus on those who had evil spirits, by saying, 'I adjure you by the Jesus whom Paul proclaims.' Engaged in this activity were the seven sons of Sceva, a Jew of High Priestly extraction. But the evil spirit replied to them (thus), 'Jesus I recognise and Paul I know but who are you?' Springing on them, the man who was possessed by the evil spirit overpowered them and used such force against them that they fled from his house naked and wounded. (*Acts of the Apostles* 19.13-16)

Two magic texts from Syria

(**II.129**) I call upon you Holy Angels to heal Arsinoe from every illness: Prince of the Hosts of Yahweh, Michael, and the man, Gabriel, and Raphael, master of healing, and Anael, who answers the daughters of Eve, Tsadqiel, Uriel, Nahariel, Seraphiel, Barqiel, Yakonel, Tsuriel, Suriel, Rahabiel, Ramiel, Harbiel, Shatqiel, Doliel and Yahobel, Sitriel, Azriel, Sammael, Azazel, Yehezqel, Yaqtiel, Amtsiel and Uzziel, Nuriel and Amatiel and Amoriel and Emuniel and Anaqiel.[67] I pray you, heal Arsinoe from every evil spirit. For Thy loving-kindness and truth. (*IEJ* 41 (1991), p. 275 – Syria; late Roman/early Byzantine period)

(**II.130**) I am writing so that Arsinoe may be healed. In the name of Yeshrumiel and Yeshumel and Nahariel, who is over the rivers of God, and Tahomiel ... rescue and save Arsinoe from all destroyer-demons ... Heal Arsinoe. For Thy loving-kindness. (*IEJ* 41 (1991), 270 – Syria; late Roman/early Byzantine period)

6. JEWISH FESTIVALS

Although the traditional Jewish festivals were celebrated in the Diaspora in the Hellenistic and Roman imperial periods, they have left very little mark on contemporary Graeco-Roman literature. Apart from Plutarch's garbled account in *Moralia* 671D-E (= Stern I no. 258) of the Feast of Tabernacles (as celebrated, however, in the Temple at Jerusalem and so not included here), references are altogether lacking. Allusions in Jewish Diasporan literature are also scanty. (For references to Hanukkah, see **III.64-5**.) However, the frequent depiction on Jewish burial plaques at Rome of the ritual objects that featured prominently in the traditional festivals (e.g. the palm branch that was waved at the Feast of Tabernacles), shows that the latter played an important part in the life of Diasporan Jews. Indeed, in 4th-century Antioch the traditional Jewish festivals were celebrated with such splendour that, to the chagrin of the local bishop, John Chrysostom, they were extremely popular with his Christian flock! (See **V.97**.) Besides the traditional festivals, a few of a purely local character were also celebrated. Alexandrian Jews marked with annual jamborees both the translation of the Septuagint and the miraculous rescue of their ancestors from the trampling elephants of a murderous Ptolemy (probably Physkon).

(a) *Rosh ha-Shanah* – the Jewish New Year Festival

A feature of this festival, which was celebrated in September/October on the 1st of Tishri, was the blowing of the *shofar* – the ram's horn trumpet, whence the festival's other name, the Feast of Trumpets. There are a number of depictions of the *shofar* in the Jewish catacombs at Rome. A sketch of one is presented here, along with the epitaph it decorates.

(**II.131**) Here lies Phaustina. (*CIJ* I² no. 283 = Noy II no. 535 – 3rd century CE)

Carved beneath her epitaph are the symbols shown below: a *shofar, menorah, lulab* (for whose ritual function, see below under *Sukkot*/Feast of Tabernacles) and, in Hebrew, *Shalom* (peace).

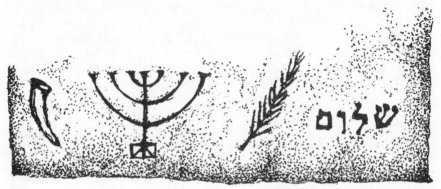

(b) *Yom Kippur* – the Day of Atonement

This, the most sacred day in the Jewish calendar, was celebrated ten days after *Rosh ha-Shanah*. It marked the culmination of a ten-day period of penitence. The whole day was spent in the synagogue in prayer and confession and ended with the blowing of the *shofar*.

(**II.132**) On the tenth day (of Tishri) there is a fast, which is carefully observed by not only those with a zeal for piety and holiness but also those who during the rest of their life perform no religious acts. For all are overcome by the sanctity that surrounds it ... (Philo, *The Special Laws* 1.186)

A prayer for vengeance on Yom Kippur

(**II.133**) I call upon and pray to God the Most High, the Lord of the spirits and of all flesh, (to take action) against those who have treacherously murdered or poisoned the wretched Heraklea, untimely dead, and wickedly poured out her innocent blood, so that the same fate may befall both those who murdered or poisoned her and their children. You, Lord, who see everything and the angels of God, before Whom every soul on this day abases itself with supplications,[68] (please see to it) that you avenge the blood of the innocent and seek payment (for it) as soon as possible. (*CIJ* I no. 725 – Delos; 2nd-1st century BCE)

(c) *Sukkot* – the Feast of Tabernacles

Celebrated five days after *Yom Kippur* on Tishri 15, this jolly, week-long festival (to Greeks such as Plutarch it seemed positively Dionysiac), originally marked the completion of the harvest and vintage. Communal feasting took place under specially erected, straw-covered booths (*sukkot*), whence the festival's Hebrew name. (For its Greek name, *skenopegia* – lit. 'the setting up of tents', see **II.135** and **V.35**.) In the rituals that marked the festival, the *ethrog* (citron) and *lulab* (palm-branch) were carried in procession in the synagogue. Their frequent representation in the Jewish catacombs of Rome shows the attachment of the local community to this festival.

Its non-celebration at Alexandria in 38 CE

(II.134) Such was the unprecedented misfortune that Flaccus suffered.[69] He was captured like an enemy in the country of which he was the governor. It came about, so it seems to me, because of the Jews whom he had, in his hunger for fame, determined to wipe out utterly. A clear proof (of this) is also the time of his arrest, for it was the national Jewish festival of the autumnal equinox, at which it is the Jewish custom to dwell in tents. But none of the festal proceedings at all were being carried out[70] ... (Philo, *In Flaccum* 116)

Its celebration in Egypt in the 2nd century CE

(II.135) 24th. From Ismaelos*, by the hand of Pasias, 100 drachmas. From 23 workers, 3 drachmas, 2 obols. By the hand of Amarantos, on the night festival (*pannuchis*)[71] of the Feast of Tabernacles (*skenopegia*), 100 drachmas. (*CPJ* III no. 452a – possibly from Apollinopolis Magna/Edfu)

Depiction of Sukkot symbols on a Romano-Jewish epitaph

(II.136) Here lies Maria, wife of Saloutios, who lived a good life with her husband. In peace her sleep. (*CIJ* I no. 374 = Noy II no. 56 – 3rd-4th century CE(?))

Beneath the text the symbols shown at the top of p. 62 were carved. They include (second left) an *ethrog* and (far right) a *lulab*.

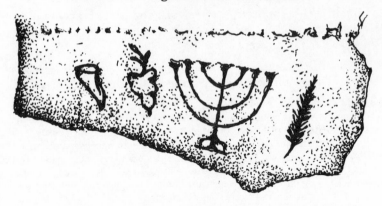

(d) *Pesach* (Passover/the Feast of Unleavened Bread) and Pentecost

Allusions to these festivals, the first celebrated on the 19th of Nisan (March/April), the second seven weeks later, are rare in texts from the Diaspora. Disk-like objects carved on some of the burial plaques in the Monteverde catacomb at Rome (see illustration at *CIJ* I no. 343) are usually interpreted as the *matzot*, the round pieces of unleavened bread consumed at the former festival. The only certain verbal reference to either known to me occurs in the text cited here – a 2nd (?) century CE epitaph from Hierapolis in Phrygia.

(II.137) (This tomb and the land around it are the property?) of Poplios* Ailios Glykon, (son of?) Damianos, son of Seleukos. In it he himself, his wife (name lost) and their children will be buried. No one else is allowed to be buried in it. He has assigned to the most venerable presidency of the Purple-Dyers two hundred denarii for crowning (his tomb), from the interest on which X (amount lost) is to be given to each (gap in text) on the Feast of Unleavened Bread. Likewise he has left to the Guild of Carpet-Weavers[72] for crowning his tomb one hundred and fifty denarii from (the interest on which there is to be given) ... on the Feast of Pentecost (rest of text missing). (*CIJ* II no. 777)

(e) *Purim*

Celebrated on Adar 14th (February-March), in commemoration of the Jews' deliverance from destruction by the evil Persian vizier Haman, this minor festival was not only the occasion of much jollification but sometimes inter-communal violence as well. Hence the imperial edict cited here. For an attempt by the Jerusalem authorities to persuade the Jews of Alexandria to celebrate it, see **III.66**.

(II.138) The Emperors Honorius Augustus and Theodosius (II) Augustus to Anthemius, Praetorian Prefect. The governors of the provinces are to ban the Jews from burning Aman in a certain ritual of their festival[73] in commemoration of his erstwhile punishment and from setting fire with sacrilegious intent to a form designed, in contempt of the Christian faith, to resemble the Holy Cross, so that they do not associate the sign of our faith with their tomfoolery.[74] They must keep their rites from ridiculing the Christian law. Assuredly they will forfeit what has been permitted until now, if they do not restrain themselves from what has been forbidden. Given on the 4th day before the Kalends of June at Constantinople, during the consulship of Bassus and Philippus. (*Codex Theodosianus* 16.8.18 = Linder no. 36 – 29 May, 408 CE)

(**II.139**) As they came (Pionius and his fellow-Christians) into the agora (of Smyrna), by the eastern stoa and the double gate, the whole agora and the upper storeys of the porches were packed full with Greeks and Jews and women. For they were on holiday because it was a Great Sabbath[75] ... (*Martyrdom of Pionius*, 3.6 = Musurillo, Acts of the Christian Martyrs, no. 10)

(f) Annual local festivals at Alexandria

In celebration of the translation of the Septuagint

(**II.140**) Wherefore (i.e. because of the translation of the Hebrew Scriptures into Greek), even to this day a feast and a public festival is held every year on the island of Pharos.[76] Not only Jews but vast numbers of others make the crossing, both out of reverence for the place in which the light of the translation first shone out and in gratitude to God for an old blessing which is ever being renewed. After the prayers and thanksgiving, they feast with their relations and friends, some having erected tents on the seashore, others just lying in the open on the sandy beach ... (Philo, *Life of Moses* 2.41-2)

In celebration of deliverance from the elephants of a hostile Ptolemy

(**II.141**) Moreover, God himself clearly testified to the justice of Onias' action.[77] For when Ptolemy Physkon was preparing to fight against the army of Onias (text slightly uncertain here) and had arrested all the Jews settled in the city (of Alexandria) together with their children and wives and placed them, bound and naked in front of his elephants, so that they might be trampled on and destroyed, and for that purpose had even made the creatures drunk, his preparations completely backfired. For the elephants, abandoning the Jews who had been placed in front of them, proceeded to attack Ptolemy's friends and killed a great number of them. After this Ptolemy saw a fearful apparition which forbade him to hurt those people (i.e. the Jews). And when his dearest concubine, whom some call Ithaka and others Irene, implored him not to proceed with such an impious act, he gave in to her and repented of both what he had just done and what he was about to do. Whence it is well known that the Jews settled at Alexandria rightly celebrate this day, because manifestly it was through God that they gained their deliverance.[78] (Josephus, *Contra Apionem* 2.53-5)

7. DIVISIONS WITHIN THE JEWISH COMMUNITY

For all the importance Diasporan Jews attached to the *idea* of community, *actual* communities were often riven by deep divisions. While some of these arose out of different responses to Christian missionising, others clearly had an economic basis. In both Egypt and Cyrene around 73 CE a sharp cleavage is attested between the rich few and the many poor. Given the generally aristocratic nature of synagogal communities (seen, for instance, in the life-tenure of offices and the honorary positions accorded the sons of the rich and prominent), it seems safe to surmise that such divisions were widespread.

(a) Divisions between rich and poor

At Alexandria

(II.142) Not content with safety, they (the Sicarii who had taken refuge in Egypt at the end of the First Jewish War) again became involved in revolutionary activities. They persuaded many of their hosts to make a bid for freedom, to think of the Romans as no better than themselves and to consider God alone their master. When some of the Jews of rank tried to oppose them, they liquidated them. The rest they continued to pressurise, pleading with them to revolt. Observing their madness, the leaders of the *gerousia* (council of elders) thought it no longer safe to turn a blind eye to them. On gathering all the Jews together for an assembly, they attempted to prove the madness of the Sicarii by demonstrating that they were responsible for all the troubles ... They begged the community to take precautions against being ruined on account of these men and to justify itself to the Romans by handing them over. Appreciating the magnitude of the danger, the people were persuaded by their arguments. Rushing furiously upon the Sicarii, they made to seize them. Six hundred of them were captured at once. Those who escaped into Egypt and Egyptian Thebes, were soon arrested and brought back (to be handed over to the Romans for torture and execution). (Josephus, *Jewish War* 7.410-16)

In Cyrene

(II.143) Like a disease, the madness of the Sicarii attacked the cities of Cyrene too. For Jonathan, an outright villain and a weaver by trade, who had taken refuge there, persuaded many of the poor to attach themselves to him and he led them into the desert promising to reveal to them signs and portents. Many people failed to notice his fraudulent activities. The men of rank among the Jews of Cyrene, however, reported both his exodus and plans to Catullus, the governor of the Libyan Pentapolis. Despatching cavalry and infantry, he easily overwhelmed the unarmed band. (Josephus, *Jewish War* 7.437-40)

(b) Divisions arising out of Christian missionising

(II.144) Since the Jews were constantly making disturbances at the instigation of Chrestus,[79] Claudius expelled them (from Rome).[80] (Suetonius, *Claudius* 25.4 = Stern II no. 307)

(II.145) Each Sabbath, Paul held discussions in the synagogue (at Corinth) and he tried to win over both Jews and Greeks. After Silas and Timothy came down from Macedonia, he continued with his preaching and kept on affirming to the Jews that Jesus was the Messiah. When they opposed him and verbally abused him, he shook out his garments and said to them, 'Your blood be upon your own heads! I am guiltless. Henceforth I shall go to the Gentiles.' Departing thence, he went to the house of a man called Titius Iustus. He was a Godfearing man[81] and his house was next door to the synagogue. Crispus, the *archisynagogos*,[82] became a believer in the Lord together with his entire household and many of the Corinthians, on hearing (Paul), believed and were baptized. One night the Lord spoke in a vision to Paul (as follows): 'Do not be afraid but go on preaching and do not be silent. For I am with you and no one shall lay a hand upon you to hurt you. The number of my people in this city is great.' (And so) he settled down for eighteen months and taught the word of God among them.

But when Gallio became proconsul of Achaea (*c.* 52 CE), the Jews set upon Paul en masse and brought him before the (Roman) tribunal and declared: 'This man is persuading people to worship God contrary to the Law.' Paul was about to open his mouth when Gallio said to the Jews, 'If some crime or foul misdeed were at issue here, then, of course, I would bear with you. But if it is a matter of words and names and that law of yours, see to it yourselves. I do not wish to be a judge of these things.' And he dismissed them from his tribunal. (*Acts of the Apostles* 18.4-16)

(II.146) I beg you, brothers, in the name of our Lord, Jesus Christ: please all say the same thing and let there not be divisions among you. Be firmly of the same mind and of the same judgement. For, my brothers, it has been revealed to me about you by Chloe's people that there are quarrels amongst you.[83] By which I mean that each one of you is saying: I'm for Paul, I'm for Apollos, I'm for Kephas,[84] I'm for Christ ... (1 *Corinthians* 1.10-12)

(II.147) The Emperor Constantine to Felix, the Praetorian Prefect ... This we order in this same sanction, that if any Jew, in opening for himself the door to eternal life, binds himself to the sacred rites and chooses to be a Christian, he shall not suffer any loss of peace or any molestation at the hands of the Jews. If any Jew thinks a Jewish convert to Christianity should be beaten and injured, we wish the contriver of such contumely to be subjected to avenging penalties that are commensurate with the nature of the crime committed ... Given on the 12th day before the Kalends of November; published on the 7th day before the Ides of March at Carthage during the consulship of Nepotianus and Facundus. (*Constitutio Sirmondiana* 4 = Linder no. 10 – 21 October, 335 and 9 March, 336 CE)

III

Diasporan Jews and the Jewish homeland

1. PILGRIMAGE TO JERUSALEM

The most visible sign of interaction between Diaspora and homeland were the thousands of pilgrims who annually made their way from every corner of the Jewish world to Jerusalem. Their purpose was to try to fulfil the Law's prescription (*Deuteronomy* 16.16) that each year every Jewish male should visit the Temple at Passover, Pentecost and the Feast of Tabernacles to offer prayer and sacrifice. Although distance made it impossible for most Diasporan Jews to meet the full demands of the Law, there is extensive evidence that many thousands of them, women as well as men, proselytes as well as born Jews, did make the often long and hazardous journey to Jerusalem at least once in their lives. Some may have died there. Once in the city, many will have stayed with friends (cf. *Acts of the Apostles* 21.16). Others will have found lodging in guest-houses, some specially built for them by rich members of the local community. Even after the destruction of the Temple in 70 CE and Hadrian's ban on Jewish access to Jerusalem after the Bar Kochba revolt **(IV.69)**, the process did not stop. In the 390s CE Jews were still making their way there: Jerome (*In Sophoniam* 1.16) records them paying a fee to the Christian authorities at that time in order to visit the Temple remains and lament.

(III.1) Countless multitudes from countless cities flock to the Temple at every feast, some by land, some by sea, from east and west and north and south. (Philo, *The Special Laws* 1.69)

(III.2) Theodotos, son of Vettenos, priest and *archisynagogos*, son of an *archisynagogos*, grandson of an *archisynagogos*, has built the synagogue for the reading of the Law and the teaching of the commandments and the guest-house[1] and the rooms and water facilities[2] for a lodging for those from foreign countries who need it. His fathers and the Elders and Simonides laid the foundations. (*CIJ* II no. 1404 = *DF* no. 79 -- Jerusalem; probably before 70 CE)

(III.3) This man (Zamaris)[3] was a bulwark against the Trachonites for both the native Jews and those coming from Babylonia to sacrifice in Jerusalem ... (Josephus, *Jewish Antiquities* 17.26)

(III.4) There is in Syria, on the coast, a city called Ascalon. Being there at a time when I was on my way to the ancestral temple to pray and make sacrifice, I saw countless numbers of doves at the crossroads and every house. When I asked the reason, they said it was not lawful to catch them. (Philo, *De providentia* 2.64)

(III.5) On the other sides (of the Temple) there was one gate to the south and one to the north, through which there was access to the women's court. For it was not permitted to women to enter by the others or to go by way of their own gate beyond the partition wall. This court, however, was accessible for cult purposes equally to Jewesses of the country (of Judaea) and their counterparts from abroad. (Josephus, *Jewish War* 5.199)

(III.6) Helena, the mother of the king (Izates of Adiabene in northern Mesopotamia), seeing that the kingdom was at peace and her son prospering and admired by all, even foreigners, on account of his divinely inspired wisdom, conceived a desire to go to the city of Jerusalem and worship at the universally acclaimed temple of God and make thank-offerings there.[4] She asked her son for permission. Acceding readily to his mother's request, he made lavish provision for the journey and gave her a considerable amount of money. She arrived in Jerusalem, having been escorted a large part of the way by her son. (Josephus, *Jewish Antiquities* 20.49-50)

2. PAYMENT OF ANCESTRAL DUES AND TAXES

Another visible sign of the strong link between Diasporan Jews and the mother country was the annual payment made by the former of various ancestral dues and taxes to the Jerusalem authorities. The most conspicuous was the half-shekel Temple tax, sometimes also referred to in our sources as the didrachm (*Gospel according to Matthew* 17.24) or the two-denarii tax **(IV.53-8)**. Paid by male Jews between the ages of twenty and fifty and escorted to Jerusalem by pilgrims and specially appointed envoys, it was used mainly to finance the daily sacrifices which the Temple cult required. Greeks, resentful of the outflow from their communities of this 'Jewish gold', frequently hampered its export and in consequence sometimes suffered reprimand by Rome **(IV.28)**. But even the Romans were not always above impounding the tax **(III.9)** and after destroying the Temple in 70 CE, they diverted it permanently into the coffers of their own chief protecting deity, Jupiter Capitolinus **(IV.50-1)**. Besides the Temple tax, first fruits and tithes (or their redemption money) also made their way from the Diaspora to Jerusalem. Though not as contentious as the Temple tax or perhaps as widely paid, they too, on occasion, were the source of friction between Jew and Greek and thus the subject of official Roman pronouncements. After 73 CE, the first-fruits were diverted, as the Temple tax had been a few years earlier, to the coffers of Rome.

(III.7) For revenue, the Temple has not only landed estates but also other, far greater resources, which never will be destroyed. For as long as mankind lasts – and it will last for ever – the revenues of the Temple will be preserved. They will co-exist perpetually with the whole universe, for it has been decreed that every male, starting at the age of twenty, shall contribute first-fruits[5] annually ... As one would expect with a people that is exceedingly numerous, the first-fruits too are superabundant. In practically every city there are depositories for the sacred monies, to which it is customary to come and pay in the first-fruits. At stated times, there are appointed as sacred envoys for the monies men who have been selected on merit, namely those in each city of the highest repute. They will escort in safety the hopes of all. For it is on the first-fruits prescribed by the Law that the hopes of the pious are based. (Philo, *The Special Laws* 1.76-8)

(III.8) Nearda in Babylonia is a city which is not only populous but also has a territory which is fertile and extensive. In addition to its other merits, it is densely populated. It is, moreover, not easily liable to enemy attack owing to a bend in the Euphrates which virtually encircles it and to the construction of its walls. The city of Nisibis is also situated on the same bend of the river. For this reason the Jews, trusting in the natural strength of these places, used to deposit there the didrachm which by custom they all pay to their God, as well as such other offerings as they make, and they treated these cities as though they were banks. From there the offerings used to be sent to Jerusalem at the appropriate time. Tens and tens of thousands of Jews participated in the convoy of these monies out of fear of raids by the Parthians to whom Babylonia was subject.[6] (Josephus, *Jewish Antiquities* 18.311-13)

(III.9) There follows the invidious attack connected with the Jewish gold ... Although gold was customarily exported every year from Italy and all our provinces to Jerusalem on the authority of the Jews, Flaccus laid down by edict that it should not be exported from Asia[7] ... At Apamea just under a hundred pounds of gold were openly seized and weighed out at the feet of the praetor in the forum by Sextus Caesius, a Roman knight and a most chaste and upright man; at Laodicea just over twenty pounds by our juryman here, Lucius Peducaeus; at Adramyttium (amount lost) by the legate, Gnaeus Domitius; at Pergamum not much at all. There is agreement on the amount of gold; the gold is in the treasury; no charge of embezzlement has been brought; this is just an attempt to stir up envy[8] (against my client). (Cicero, *Pro Flacco* 28.66-9 = Stern I no. 68 – extracts only)

(III.10) Publius Servilius Galba, son of Publius,[9] proconsul, to the magistrates, council and people of Miletus, greetings. Prytanis, son of Hermas, a citizen of yours, came before me when I was holding an assize at Tralles and revealed to me that contrary to our expressed wish you are attacking the Jews and preventing them from observing the Sabbath and performing their ancestral rites and managing their produce[10] in their customary way ... I wish you to know, therefore, that after listening to the arguments on both sides, I have decided that the Jews are not to be prevented from observing their native customs. (Josephus, *Jewish Antiquities* 14.244-6)

(III.11) Ariston brought his first-fruits from Apamea (in Syria)[11] and they accepted them from him, for they said, 'He that owns (land) in Syria is as one who owns (land) on the outskirts of Jerusalem.' (M. *Hallah* 4.11)

(III.12) On Egypt, because it is near, they have imposed the Poorman's Tithe, so that the poor of Israel may be maintained by it in the Seventh (i.e. Sabbatical) Year. (M. *Yadaim* 4.3)

(III.13) Ptollis, son of Thedetos* has paid in respect of the two-denarii tax on the Jews and the *aparchai* (first fruits)[12] for the 8th year of Domitian 4 drachmas, 4 obols. Year 8, Mesore 6. (*CPJ* II no. 186 – Apollinopolis Magna/Edfu; 89 CE)

3. OFFERINGS TO THE TEMPLE BY DIASPORAN JEWS

Besides paying the dues and taxes noted above, Diasporan Jews and their converts also underlined their attachment to the cult of Yahweh by making free-will offerings to His temple in Jerusalem. Though only the most lavish gifts receive individual mention in our sources, some idea of the vast wealth that accrued from them is to be derived from both the boasts of Josephus **(III.14)** and the pique of Tacitus **(VII.2)**.

(III.14) No one should be amazed at the amount of wealth in our Temple,[13] for all the Jews throughout the inhabited world and those who feared God,[14] even those in Asia and Europe, had been making contributions to it for a very long time. There is no lack of witnesses to the vast quantity of the aforementioned money. It is not boasting on our part nor exaggeration that has made the amount so high. Among the many historians who bear us out is Strabo, the Cappadocian, who writes thus: 'Mithridates, having sent to Cos, took the money which Queen Cleopatra had deposited there and the eight hundred talents of the Jews.' We have no public money except that which belongs to God and it is clear that the Jews in Asia had transferred this money to Cos out of fear of Mithridates.[15] (Josephus, *Jewish Antiquities* 14.110-13)

(III.15) Of the gates (to the Temple), nine were completely covered with gold and silver, as were also the door-posts and lintels. The one outside the Sanctuary, however, was made of Corinthian bronze[16] and it far exceeded in value those overlaid with silver and gold. There were two doors to each gateway, each one thirty cubits high and fifteen wide (i.e. about 45 by $22\frac{1}{2}$ feet) ... The size of the rest were all alike but the one beyond the Corinthian gate, opening out from the Women's Court on the east and facing the gate of the Sanctuary, was far larger. It was fifty cubits high and its doors forty cubits. Its decoration was richer, being overlaid with thick plates of silver and gold. It was Alexander,[17] the father of Tiberius, who had embellished the nine gates in this manner. (Josephus, *Jewish War* 5.201-5)

(III.16) The bones of the family of Nikanor, of Alexandria, who made the gates.[18] Nikanor (and?)[19] Alexas. (*CIJ* II no. 1256 = *MPAT* no. 108 = HN no. 153)

(III.17) During the 20th year [of King Herod (the Great), when Simon son of Boethus was] High Priest, Paris (or Sparis), son of Akeson [a Jew (?)[20] resident] in Rhodes [contributed] towards the paving[21] [...] drachmas. (*SEG* 33 (1983) no. 1277 – Jerusalem; probably 18/17 BCE)

(III.18) King Monobaz (II) made of gold all the handles for the vessels used (in the Temple) on the day of Atonement. His mother, Helena, erected a golden candlestick above the door of the Sanctuary.[22] (M. *Yoma* 3.10)

4. DIASPORAN CHARITABLE AND MILITARY AID
TO PALESTINIAN JEWS

It was not just the Temple and the priesthood that profited from the solidarity Diasporan Jews felt with the 'mother-city'. A clear beneficiary was the general populace. At times of crisis, it received considerable material support from 'world Jewry'.

(a) Charitable aid during the famine of 46-7 CE

(III.19) At this time, certain prophets came down from Jerusalem to Antioch. One of them, a man called Agabos, stood up and, through the Spirit, predicted that an enormous famine was about to come upon the whole world. This actually took place under Claudius. The disciples decided that each of them should send, in accordance with his means, something to help the brothers[23] who lived in Judaea. This they did and they despatched it to the Elders by the hand of Barnabas and Saul. (*Acts of the Apostles* 11.27-30)

(III.20) Helena's arrival[24] was altogether advantageous to the Jerusalemites. For at that time famine was oppressing their city and many were dying from lack of money (to buy food). Queen Helena sent some of her servants to Alexandria to purchase corn for large sums and others to Cyprus to bring back a cargo of dried figs. After their speedy return with these provisions, she distributed food among the needy ... When her son Izates[25] heard about the famine, he sent large sums of money to the leaders of the Jerusalemites. This was distributed among the needy and it gave many of them release from the dire pressures of the famine. (Josephus, *Jewish Antiquities* 20.51-3)

(b) Military aid during the First Jewish War

Although Josephus fails to mention any Diasporan participation in the First

Jewish War, apart from that of a small number of Adiabenians, it is clear from the Roman historian, Cassius Dio, that the Jews of Judaea received widespread support from their Diasporan counterparts.

(**III.21**) Two days later Simon's men attacked the other (Roman) earth-works too ... A certain Gephthaios from the town of Garis in Galilee, and Magassaros, a royal trooper and attendant of Mariamme (sister of Agrippa II), along with Nabataeus' son, an Adiabenian called from his misfortune Keagiras – i.e. Lame Man, snatched up firebrands and rushed at the siege-engines. Throughout the war no braver men than these, nor more frightening, were produced by the city.[26] (Josephus, *Jewish War* 5.473-4)

(**III.22**) The first battles Titus fought (against the Jews) were indecisive. Then, after defeating them, he laid siege to Jerusalem. It had three walls, including the one around the Temple. The Romans, therefore, heaped up mounds against the (outermost) wall and brought up their siege engines. Those who sallied forth against them, they fought and repulsed. Those who positioned themselves on the wall, they kept back with slings and arrows, for they had many (slingers and archers) who had been sent by barbarian kings. The Jews themselves also hurled weapons and stones, some by hand and some by means of mechanical devices. Aiding them were many Jews from Judaea itself and many of their co-religionists, not just from the Roman empire but also from the lands beyond the Euphrates. (Dio, *Roman History* 66.4.1-4 = Stern II no. 430)

5. DIASPORAN JEWS AND THE TRANSMISSION OF INFORMATION TO JERUSALEM

Down to Josephus' day, it seems that the public archives at Jerusalem functioned as a kind of marriage bureau at least for the Jewish priestly class. The contribution which Diasporan Jews made to this service is described briefly here. On the importance of priestly ancestry among Diasporan Jews, see discussion accompanying **II.95-8**.

(**III.23**) For from the beginning not only did they put in charge of this (the keeping of records) men of the highest character who were devoted to the service of God but they took precautions that the priestly stock should remain for ever pure and undefiled. For a man who belongs to the priest-hood must, for the begetting of children, marry a wife of priestly descent. He must not pay attention to wealth or other distinctions but examine carefully the (matter of) pedigree by obtaining from the public archives a genealogy and providing many witnesses. We do this not only in Judaea itself. Wherever there is a community of our people, there an accurate record is kept of priestly marriages. I refer to the Jews in Egypt and Babylon and wherever else in the inhabited world men of priestly stock live in dispersion, for they record and send to Jerusalem the name of the bride, her father and more distant ancestors, together with the names of the witnesses. (Josephus, *Contra Apionem* 1.32-3)

6. IMMIGRATION TO JUDAEA OF DIASPORAN JEWS

Not all Diasporan Jews were content with the intermittent forms of contact with Judaea described so far in this section. Many decided to live in Judaea on a more or less permanent basis. Among such people, particularly conspicuous are those from Alexandria, Babylonia, Cilicia and Cappadocia. A variety of reasons for such immigration can be surmised. Some immigrants probably were returnees from captivity. Others doubtless went to Jerusalem to study the Torah or be near the Temple. Yet others were lured by enhanced career or trading prospects. Two of the High Priests appointed by Herod were of Diasporan extraction and among the traders who ended their days in the prosperous harbour-city of Jaffa a number of Diasporan Jews are to be found. (Besides **III.24**, note also **III.46-53**.)

Diasporan synagogues in the homeland

(III.24) Here lies Isakis*, Elder of the (Community) of the Cappadocians (at Jaffa), a Tarsian (and) a linen merchant. (*CIJ* II no. 931 – Jaffa; 2nd-4th century CE)

(III.25) Rabbi Judah said, '... Rabbi Eleazar, son of Rabbi Tsadok, bought the Alexandrian synagogue in Jerusalem, and did exactly what he wanted with it.' (Tosefta, *Megillah* 2.17)

(III.26) Our master (the Patriarch, Judah I ha-Nasi) was sitting and studying the Torah in front of Babylonian synagogue in Sepphoris ... (Genesis *Rabba* 33)

Persons returned from slavery?

(III.27) Stephen, full of grace and power, was working great miracles and signs among the people (at Jerusalem). There came forward, arguing with Stephen, men from the so-called Synagogue of the Freedmen, comprising Cyrenians and Alexandrians, and Jews from Cilicia and Asia.[27] (*Acts of the Apostles* 6.8-10)

(III.28) (Ossuary of) Theodotos, freedman of Queen Agrippina.[28] (*BASOR* 235 (1979) 33 = Rahmani no. 789 – Jericho; 1st century CE)

Scholarly immigrants

Among the most famous of these was the Babylonian Hillel, from whom the later Patriarchs were descended, and Saul (later Paul) of Tarsus. The Gamaliel at whose feet the latter sat was either the son or grandson of the former.

(III.29) *And Moses was one hundred and twenty years old* (when he died) (*Deuteronomy* 34.7). He was one of four who died at the age of one hundred and twenty, and these were: Moses, Hillel the Elder, Rabban Johanan ben Zakkai and Rabbi Akiba. Moses was in Egypt for forty years and in Midian for forty years and led Israel for forty years. Hillel the Elder came up from Babylonia when he was forty, served the Sages for forty years and led Israel for forty years ...[29] (*Sifre Deuteronomy* 357)

(III.30) When complete silence had fallen, Paul addressed them in the Hebrew language in these words: 'Brothers and fathers, listen to the defence I now make before you.' Hearing that he was addressing them in the Hebrew language, they became quieter and he said: 'I am a Jew, a native of Tarsus in Cilicia but brought up in this city. Trained at the feet of Gamaliel in the fine points of the ancestral law, I am zealot for God, as are you all today.' (*Acts of the Apostles* 21.40-22.3)

(III.31) The bones of those who have immigrated ... the house of Izates.[30] (*CIJ* II no. 1230 – Jerusalem; 1st century CE)

Two Herodian High Priests of Diasporan extraction

(III.32) King Herod immediately deprived Ananel of the High Priesthood. He was, as I said before, not a native (of Judaea) but descended from the Jews who had been transported across the Euphrates. Many tens of thousands of this people had been transported to Babylonia, whence Ananel hailed. He was of High Priestly family and had long enjoyed a close relationship with Herod. Just as Herod had honoured him, when he took over the kingship, so now, in contravention of the Law, he dismissed him[31] in order to put a stop to his domestic troubles. (Josephus, *Jewish Antiquities* 15.39-40)

(III.33) There was a certain Simon, a Jerusalemite, who was the son of one Boethos, an Alexandrian. He was a well-known priest and had a daughter who was considered to be the most beautiful woman of the day. (Josephus goes on to relate how Herod became smitten with her and set about making her one of his wives.) Since Simon did not have enough prestige for a family connection (with royalty) but was too important to be despised, Herod attained his heart's desire in the most reasonable way possible, namely by enhancing the family's status and increasing its honour. He immediately removed Jesus, son of Phabes from the High Priesthood, appointed Simon to the office (*c.* 24 BCE) and established a family relationship with him. (Josephus, *Jewish Antiquities* 15.320 and 322)

7. DIASPORAN BURIALS IN JUDAEA

Among the hundreds of epitaphs from the first four centuries CE that have been discovered at Jerusalem, Jaffa and Beth She'arim, quite a number belong to Jews or proselytes of Diasporan extraction. Were those people visitors to the country, immigrants or life-long Diasporan residents whose remains had been brought to Judaea specifically for burial? As far as those mentioned in the epitaphs from Beth She'arim are concerned, there can be little doubt. By the time those texts were composed (the 3rd-4th centuries), burial in the 'Holy Land' had, largely for eschatological reasons, become common practice among rich and pious Diasporan Jews and the necropolis of Beth She'arim, the Patriarchs' own cemetery, their favourite resting place. Until the town itself was destroyed in the mid-4th century, coffins were regularly conveyed there from all over the eastern Diaspora to be laid in pre-purchased spaces or halls in the nearby catacombs. But what of the people mentioned in the other texts – i.e the ossuary inscriptions from pre-70 CE Jerusalem and those carved on the (mainly 2nd-4th century?) tombstones from the Jaffa necropolis? With regard to the first group, some modification is required of the common view (for which see Safrai and Stern I, p. 194) that they must have been either festal pilgrims or recent immigrants. As the first three entries in this section show, long before the 3rd century, the deliberate transportation of bones to Jerusalem for burial did take place, even if only occasionally. As for the Diasporan Jews mentioned in the Jaffa epitaphs, the probability is that most were immigrants. Some form family groups, which suggests immigration rather than sudden death during travel. With others, their occupations (for the most part, rather humble) suggest that they were part of the city's work-force, rather than international travellers.

(a) At Jerusalem

All the texts in this section, apart from **III.34** and **III.45**, are usually dated to the 1st century CE.

Transportation of bones to Jerusalem

(**III.34**) I, Abba, son of the priest Eleaz(ar), son of Aaron the elder, I, Abba, the oppressed and the persecuted, who was born in Jerusalem and went into exile in Babylonia and brought (back [to Jerusalem]) Mattathi(ah) son of Jud(ah), and I buried him in the cave, which I acquired by the writ.[32] (*MPAT* no. 68 – 1st century BCE or CE)

(**III.35**) Joseph, son of Elasah, (son of?) Artakes, has brought the bones of his mother (name uncertain), to Jerusalem.[33] (Puech no. 26)

(**III.36a**) Izates' mother, Helena, took the news of his death badly, as was to be expected of a mother who had been deprived of a most pious son. She derived some consolation, however, from hearing that the succession had passed to her elder son and hastened to him. When she got to Adiabene, she did not long survive her son Izates. Oppressed by old age and the pain of her grief, she quickly passed away. Monobazus sent both her bones and those of his brother to Jerusalem with orders that they be buried in the three pyramids which his mother had built three furlongs from the city of Jerusalem.[34] (Josephus, *Jewish Antiquities* 20.94-5)

(**III.36b**) Tsaran, the Queen; Tsarah, the Queen.[35] (*CIJ* II no. 1388 = *MPAT* no. 132 – *c.* 50 CE)

Select Diasporan burials at Jerusalem

The three texts listed under **III.37** were all inscribed on the same ossuary. Assuming that it contained only one body, as was the general practice in the burial complex where it was found, then Ariston of Apamea and Judah the proselyte must have been one and the same person, for whom perhaps see also **III.11**. For the assumption of a new name on conversion to Judaism, see note to previous entry.

(**III.37a**) Ariston. (*SCI* 11 (1991-2), p. 150 = *SEG* 41 (1991), no. 1558)
(**III.37b**) Ariston of Apamea. (*SCI* 11 (1991-2), p. 150)
(**III.37c**) Judah, the proselyte. (*SCI* 11 (1991-2), p. 150)

Two epitaphs from the same burial complex in Jerusalem; the bones suggest they were father and daughter:

(**III.38a**) Furius from Africa. (*CIJ* II no. 1227a)
(**III.38b**) Furia from Africa. (*CIJ* II no. 1227b)

(**III.39**) (Ossuary of) Gaios, son of Artemon, of Berenike (in Cyrenaica). (Rahmani no. 404)

(**III.40**) (Bones of) Ioudan*, proselyte of Tyre. (Bagatti-Milik, no. 13a; re-interpreted Puech, no. 27)

(**III.41**) Ioustos from Chalkis.[36] (*CIJ* II no. 1233)

(**III.42**) Maria, wife of Alexander, from Capua. (*CIJ* II no. 1284)

(**III.43**) Maria, the proselyte from Doliche (in Commagene). (*CIJ* II no. 1390, as re-interpreted in Bagatti-Milik, p. 95)

Two epitaphs from the tomb of a Cyrenaican immigrant family. In all, it contained nine inscribed ossuaries:

(**III.44a**) Philon, the Cyrenian. (Bagatti-Milik, no. 9 = *CJZC* no. 29b)
(**III.44b**) Sara, (daughter of) Simon of Ptolemais. (*CJZC* no. 35 = Rahmani no. 99)

(**III.45**) Rabbi Samou[el], *archisynagogos*, a Phrygian from Do[rylaeum?].

The world (?) will glorify him. [Peace on] his resting place (in Hebrew). (*CIJ* II no. 1414 – undated)

(b) At Jaffa

(**III.46**) (Tomb) of Abbomaris, son of Aha, a Levite from Babylon,[37] baker. (*CIJ* II no. 902 = HN no. 145)

(**III.47**) (Burial) place of Eiako*, (the) Cappadocian and Acholia, his wife and Asterios. (*CIJ* II no. 910)

(**III.48**) Here lies Ioudas, son of Ioses*, of Tarsus. (*CIJ* II no. 925)

(**III.49**) (Tomb of) Ioustos, son of Robes*, Alexandrian, rag-dealer. (*CIJ* II no. 928 = HN no. 148)

(**III.50**) (Tomb of) Isas*, son of Lazaros, a priest from Egypt. Peace. Lazar. (*CIJ* II no. 930 = HN no. 149)

(**III.51**) Monument of Kyrillos and Alexander, Alexandrians. Peace (*Shalom*)! (*CIJ* II no. 934 = HN no. 150)

(**III.52**) Memorial of Roubes*, son of Iakob, from the Pentapolis.[38] (*CIJ* II no. 950)

(**III.53**) (Tomb of) Symmachos, of Chios. (*CIJ* II no. 954)

(c) At Beth She'arim

The three texts listed under **III.54** all come from same burial hall and relate to the same man.

(**III.54a**) The tomb of Aristeas from Sidon. (*BS* II no. 172)
(**III.54b**) The entire burial chamber belongs to Aristeas. May your lot be good, Aristeas! (*BS* II no. 171)
(**III.54c**) May your lot be good, Aristeas! May the sleep of the pious Aristeas be in peace. (*BS* II no. 173)

(**III.55**) Here lies Asther*, daughter of Anthos, from Tyre. (*BS* II no. 147)

(**III.56**) Here lies the most distinguished[39] Eusebis*, *archisynagogos* of the people of Beirut. (*BS* II no. 164)

(**III.57**) Germanos, son of Isakios*, from Palmyra. (*CIJ* II no. 1011 = *BS* II no. 100)

(III.58) Iakos* of Caesarea, *archisynagogos*; (originally) from Pamphylia. Peace (*Shalom*)! (*BS* II no. 203)

(III.59) (Tomb of) Iose(s)*, *archisynagogos* from Sidon. (*BS* II no. 221)

(III.60) The tomb of Kaliope of Byblos, the lady. (*BS* II no. 137)

(III.61) The burial hall of Thyme of the family of Amase.[40] (*BS* II no. 11 (text in Greek) and *CIJ* II no. 1024 (text in Palmyrene))

(III.62) A priest from Beirut. (*BS* II no. 148)

(III.63) (Burial place of) the men from Himyar (in southern Arabia). (*CIJ* II no. 1138 = *BS* II no. 111)

8. THE JUDAEAN AUTHORITIES AND THE DIASPORAN SYNAGOGUE FROM THE 2ND CENTURY BCE TO THE MID-2ND CENTURY CE

How much control the Jewish authorities in Judaea exercised over the Diasporan synagogue during this period is difficult to assess and much disputed. As will be seen below, the evidence is not only scanty but, in the main, rather suspect.

(a) Control over the conduct of festivals?

Although the evidence cited in this section reveals the Jerusalem authorities attempting to influence Egyptian Jews in the conduct of festivals, considerable doubt attaches to its authenticity. But even if it is largely fabricated, it is not valueless, for it shows that there were Jews who wanted the bonds between Jerusalem and Egyptian Jewry to be tighter than presumably they were in practice. Who the fabricators were is disputed, some arguing that it was the Jews of Alexandria and others the Jerusalem authorities themselves. For discussion, see *HJPAJC* III, pp. 505 and 533-4.

Instructions from Jerusalem over the celebration of Hanukkah

(III.64) In the year one hundred and eighty eight,[41] the people in Jerusalem and in Judaea, and the council and Judas (Maccabaeus) to Aristoboulos, King Ptolemy's teacher, a man of anointed priestly stock, and to the Jews in Egypt, greetings and health. Having been rescued from great perils by God, inasmuch as we have been in battle against a king, we give thanks to Him. For He has driven out those who were drawn up in battle order in the Holy City. (Account of the death of Antiochus IV Epiphanes follows.) Now that we intend, therefore, to celebrate on the 25th of Chislev the cleansing of the Temple, we have deemed it necessary to send clear instructions to you, so that you too may celebrate (it in the manner of) the Feast of the Tabernacles[42] ... Since we are about to celebrate the purification, we have written to you. Please see to it that you (too) keep the days ... (Extracts from 2 *Maccabees* 1.10-2.17)

(**III.65**) To our brothers, the Jews in Egypt, greetings. Your brothers, the Jews in Jerusalem and those in the country of Judaea, (wish you) good peace. May God do good to you and be mindful of His covenant with Abraham and Isaac and Jacob, His faithful servants. And may He give you all a heart to worship Him and carry out His wishes with a great heart and a willing spirit. May He open your heart in His law and His command-ments and send peace and listen to your supplications and be at one with you and not desert you in time of trouble. And now we here are praying for you.

Reign of Demetrios (II Nikator), year one hundred and sixty nine (of the Seleucid era).[43] We the Jews wrote to you at the height of the troubles that came upon us in the years after Jason and his associates revolted from the holy land and kingdom and burned the porch and poured out innocent blood.[44] And we supplicated God and we were heard and we offered sacrifice and a wheaten offering and we lit the lamps and set out the shewbread. And now (see to it) that you keep the Feast of Tabernacles of the month of Chislev.[45] (2 *Maccabees* 1.1-9)

The promotion of the Festival of Purim

It is thought that the purpose of the justificatory passage cited below, which is found only in the Septuagintal version of Esther, was to promote among the Jews of Egypt the use of the Book of Esther as a festal scroll.

(**III.66**) In the fourth year of the reign of Ptolemy and Kleopatra,[46] Dositheos, who said he was a priest and a Levite, and Ptolemy his son, brought in (to Alexandria) the published Letter of the Phrourai.[47] They declared that it *did* exist and that Ptolemy's son, Lysimachos, who was in Jerusalem, had translated it. (*Esther*, LXX supplement)

(b) Determination of the calendar

Proper celebration of such festivals as those mentioned in the previous section required accurate calendrical knowledge. According to Talmudic sources, this was supplied by the Judaean authorities, first, by means of beacons, and later, through envoys. Not only did the latter pass on the dates, as determined in Jerusalem, for each New Moon, but they also kept (all?) Diasporan communities informed about the decision to intercalate a month, whenever the lunar and solar calendars became too far out of alignment.

(**III.67**) Previously they (the Judaean authorities) used to light beacons, but after the wicked actions of the Samaritans (who lit misleading fires), they enacted that envoys should be sent out. (M. *Rosh ha-Shanah* 2.1)

(III.68) Because of six New moons envoys are sent out: because of Nisan, to determine the time of Passover (= 15th Nisan), because of Ab, to determine the time of the Fast (= 9th Ab),[48] because of Elul, to determine the New Year (= 1st Tishri), because of Tishri, to determine correctly the set feasts (i.e. Yom Kippur and Sukkot), because of Chislev, to determine the time of (the festival of) the Dedication (i.e. Hanukkah) and because of Adar, to determine the time of Purim (= 14th Adar). (M. *Rosh ha-Shanah* 1.3)

(III.69) Rabbi Akiba said: When I went down to Nehardea (in Mesopotamia) to ordain a leap-year, Nehemiah of Bet Deli met me and said ... (M. *Yebamoth* 16.7)

(c) Attempted control of the spread of Christianity?

Christian sources routinely allege that the Jerusalem authorities deliberately set about checking the spread of Christianity within the Diasporan synagogue, by, in the main, the systematic spread of disinformation about the new sect. How much credence to give these reports is difficult to decide. A large measure of anti-Jewish propaganda is to be suspected.

(III.70) Saul, still breathing threats and murder against the disciples of the Lord, approached the High Priest and asked him for letters for the synagogues in Damascus, so that if he found any people, male or female, who were of the Way (i.e. Christians), he might arrest them and bring them to Jerusalem. (*Acts of the Apostles* 9.1-2)

(III.71) When we got to Rome, Paul was allowed to lodge by himself with the soldier who was guarding him. It came about that after three days he called together the leading men of the Jewish community. When they were gathered, he addressed them as follows: 'My brothers, I, who have committed no offence against either the (Jewish) people or our ancestral customs, was bound and handed over to the Romans at Jerusalem. After examining me, they wanted to release me because there was no capital charge against me. But because the Jews raised objections, I was compelled to appeal to Caesar – not that I had any accusations to make against my own people. That is the reason why I have summoned you to see you and talk with you. It is for the hope of Israel that I am in chains like this.' They said to him: 'We have neither received any communication about you from Judaea nor has any of our brothers arrived and reported or said anything bad about you. We would like to hear from you what your own views are. For concerning this sect we know that everywhere it is spoken against.' (*Acts of the Apostles* 28.17-22)

(III.72) When you knew that he (Jesus Christ) had risen from the dead and had ascended into Heaven, as the prophets had predicted would happen, not only did you not repent of your evil deeds but you then chose men and sent them from Jerusalem all over the world, saying that a godless, heretical sect of Christians had arisen. You disseminated the charges that all those who do not know us make against us.[49] (Justin Martyr, *Dialogus cum Tryphone* 17.108)

(d) Control in halakhic matters?

Talmudic sources abound in anecdotes about Judaean rabbis (e.g. Rabban Gamaliel, Rabbi Akiba) debating with their Diasporan counterparts the finer points of halakhah. To infer from such material, however, that the Judaean religious authorities exerted great influence over the Diasporan synagogue in this area would be dangerous. These stories are essentially ahistorical, products of the need to create a vehicle for the exposition of the law rather than straight recordings of events. And the later they are (those in the Babylonian Talmud, for instance, date to around 500 CE), the less likely they are to contain accurate information about the period under review in this section. That Judaean rabbis travelled overseas, visited Diasporan synagogues and preached in them is inherently likely. Witness the activities of Saul/Paul. But how systematically they did this and how much influence the Judaean religious authorities exerted over the interpretation of the law in the Diaspora is both uncertain and unascertainable.

(III.73) It is said of Rabban Gamaliel, Rabbi Joshua, Rabbi Eliezer ben Azariah and Rabbi Akiba that they went to Rome and taught there[50] ... (discussion of what they taught follows) (Exodus *Rabba* 30)

(III.74) Rabbi Mattiah ben Heresh inquired of Rabbi Eleazer ben Azariah at Rome, 'Have you heard about the four types of sin that Rabbi Ishmael use to lecture about?' ... (discussion follows)[51] (bT, *Yoma* 86a)

(III.75) But are there no more (cases of excommunication)? Is there not the case learned by Rabbi Joseph (which goes as follows)? Thaddeus, a man of Rome, habituated the Jews of Rome to eat helmeted goats (i.e. kids roasted whole) on the Passover eve. Simeon ben Shetah sent to him and said: 'Were you not Thaddeus, I would excommunicate you, since you cause Israel to eat holy things outside the precincts (of the Temple)?'[52] (bT, *Berakoth* 19a)

9. THE PATRIARCHS AND THE DIASPORA

With the establishment of the Jewish Patriarchate – i.e. the recognition by Rome, probably in the late 2nd century CE, of the descendants of Hillel the Elder as the leaders of the Empire's Jews, a degree of formal control by the Palestine authorities over the Diaspora comes into existence. A new institution is now attested, the chief functions of which seemingly were (a) the transmission to Diasporan communities of vital information from the Patriarch and (b) the collection from them of contributions for the maintenance of, inter alia, the Patriarch's court in Galilee. The officials who performed these tasks were termed *apostoloi* and the chief impost they collected the *apostole* or *aurum coronarium*. There is evidence also that they had disciplinary duties. Although little is known about the *apostoloi* before the 4th century, it is generally believed that the institution itself goes back at least to the time of Judah I ha-Nasi, the greatest of the Patriarchs, whose rule spanned the late 2nd and early 3rd centuries CE. How tight a control the Patriarchs exercised over the Diaspora through the apostolate is disputed. What is not in doubt is that the prestige of the Patriarchs themselves among Diasporan Jews was considerable, as the appeal to their authority in a number of inscriptions, only one of which is cited here, shows. (For another, see **II.7**.)

(**III.76**) It came about that after Judah the Patriarch had reached maturity[53] ..., he gave to Joseph, in recompense, the revenues of the apostolate. He sent him with despatches into the territory of the Cilicians. On arrival there, he exacted in each town of Cilicia from the Jews who lived in the province the tithes and the first fruits. While lodging quite near to the church in some town or other at that time, he became friendly with the bishop there and secretly asked him for the Gospels, which he read. Since in his capacity as *apostolos* – that, as I have said, is what the office is called by the Jews – he was conducting himself with the utmost gravity and acting with great rigour in restoring discipline – it was for the maintenance of that that he had been chosen and he had reduced in rank and deprived of their dignity on the grounds of unworthiness quite a number of *archisynagogoi*, priests, Elders and Azanitae,[54] as their deacons and assistants are called – he was hated by many. In order to avenge themselves upon him, they were extremely keen to investigate and make enquiries about his activities. Having, for those reasons, carried out the most detailed investigations, they launched a mass attack on Joseph's house and caught him in the very act of reading the Gospels. Snatching the book from his hands, they laid hold of him and threw him to the ground. Then shouting and hurling the most violent abuse at him, they led him to the synagogue and gave him a flogging. (Epiphanius, *On the Heresies* 30.11 = *PG* 41, col. 424)

(**III.77**) And it is the custom of the Jews even now (i.e. the 3rd-4th century CE) to give the name apostles (*apostoloi*) to the bearers of encyclical letters from their rulers. (Eusebius, *In Isaiam* 18 = *PG* 24, col. 213)

(**III.78**) The same two Augusti (Arcadius and Honorius) to Messala, the Praetorian Prefect. It is a matter of shameful superstition that the *archisynagogi*, the Elders of the Jews and those who are sent by the Patriarch at a certain time to demand gold and silver and are called *apostoli*, exact and receive and carry back to him a sum from each synagogue.[55] For this reason, everything that we believe has been collected, when the period of time is considered, is to be sent faithfully to our Treasury. We decree that henceforth nothing is to be sent to the aforesaid (i.e. the Patriarch). Let the peoples of the Jews know, therefore, that we have done away with the operation of this form of spoliation. If any men are sent by that despoiler of the Jews to perform this task of exaction, let them be handed over to the judges, so that sentence may be passed against them as violators of our laws. Given on the 3rd day before the Ides of April at Milan, during the the consulship of the most renowned Theodoros. (*Codex Theodosianus* 16.8.14 = Linder no. 30 – 11 April, 399 CE)

(III.79) The same two Augusti (Arcadius and Honorius) to Hadrianus, the Praetorian Prefect. We ordered some time ago that what by custom was offered to the Patriarchs by the Jews of these regions, should not be offered at all.[56] But now that the first order has been revoked, we want all to know that, in accordance with the privileges established by former emperors, the right of sending (contributions) has, through our clemency, been conceded to the Jews. Given on the 8th day before the Kalends of August at Rome, during the 6th consulship of Honorius Augustus and the (1st) of Aristaenetus. (*Codex Theodosianus* 16.8.17 = Linder no. 34 – 25 July, 404 CE)

(III.80) Peace upon Israel. Amen. Amen. Peace, Shmuel.[57] I, Aurelius Samohil*, have purchased (this) tomb for myself and my wife, Lasi(e?) Erine (= ? Lassia Irene), who completed her allotted span on the 12th day before the Kalends of November, on Venus' day (i.e. Friday), in the eighth month, when Merobaudes was consul for the second time and Satorninus for the first. She lived peacefully for 23 years. I adjure you by the Victories (of those) who rule, and I adjure you by the Honours of the Patriarchs[58] and I adjure you by the Law which the Lord gave the Jews that no one open this tomb and put a foreign body on top of our remains. If anyone opens it, let him give to the Treasury ten pounds of silver. (*CIJ* I² no. 650 = Noy I no. 145 – Catania in Sicily; 21 October, 383 CE)

10. PALESTINIAN INFLUENCE ON THE LANGUAGE OF DIASPORAN INSCRIPTIONS

Given the evidence cited in the last section for Patriarchal relations with the Diaspora from the time of Judah I ha-Nasi onwards, it should cause no surprise that in Diasporan inscriptions of the 3rd-4th centuries Palestinian influence becomes increasingly apparent. (Another contributory factor here may have been current Jewish emigration from Galilee, for which see **I.48-50**.) Phrases which are common in the synagogal inscriptions of 3rd-4th century Palestine (e.g. holy place, hallowed community, May he be remembered for good) start to crop up in contemporaneous synagogal inscriptions in the Diaspora. And the title, rabbi, unknown in earlier Diasporan epigraphy, begins to make an appearance. While its meaning remains disputed (conceivably it is no more than a polite form of address), the very occurrence of this semitic term is indicative of growing Palestinian influence over Diasporan Jewry.

(a) Holy congregation and holy place

With the destruction of the Temple in 70 CE, not only did the synagogue come to replace the Temple as the central institution of Judaism but it also started to acquire something of the Temple's aura. Hence both the synagogal building and the congregation which gathered in it began to be conceived of as hallowed entities. Both Palestinian and Diasporan inscriptions reflect these new ideas.

(III.81) To the most holy community/synagogue (*synagoge*) of the Hebrews in memory of my brother Hermophilos, I, Eustathios, a Godfearer,[59] along with my bride Athanasia, have dedicated the ablution-basin (*maskaules* = Heb. *maskel*). (*CIJ* II no. 754 = *DF* no. 28 – Philadelphia in Lydia; 3rd century CE)

(III.82) Aur(elios) Eusanbatios, Elder (*presbyteros*), and Aur(elia) Epitynch(an)ousa for their own safety and that of their children and ... (have dedicated) to the most holy synagogue/community (*synagoge*) ... out of their own resources. (*DF* no. 32 – Hyllarima in Caria – no earlier than the 3rd century CE)

(III.83) Sacred synagogue/community (*sinagoga*) of Naro. For her own salvation, your servant Julia (of Ptolemais?) has laid the mosaic floor at her own expense. (Le Bohec, no. 13 – Hammam Lif (Naro in north Africa); late 4th century CE)

(III.84) Ilasios, son of Eisakios*, *archisynagogos* of Antioch, has paved with mosaics the entrance (to the synagogue) for the safe-keeping of Photion, his wife, and their children, and for the preservation of Eustathia, his mother-in-law and in memory of Eisakios and Edesios and Hesychion, his ancestors. Peace and mercy upon your hallowed community (*plethos*) in its entirety. (*CIJ* II no. 804 = *IGLS* IV no. 1320 = *DF* no. 39 – Apamea in Syria; 391 CE)

(b) May he be remembered for good

A common phrase in Palestinian donor inscriptions with clear eschatological overtones. It reflects the hope that God will remember the donor kindly in the hereafter because of his benefaction in this world to the holy place.

(III.85) That Ahiah, son of [...]h, of the sons of Levi, may be remembered for good before the God of the heavens. Amen. This (is) a memorial for (his) good. (*CIJ* II no. 845 – Doura-Europos; 3rd century CE)

(III.86) Samouel, son of Sapharas – may he be remembered – has founded this (i.e. the synagogue) in this manner. (*CIJ* II no. 831 = *DF* no. 59 – Doura-Europos; 3rd century CE)

(c) The title, rabbi

For a catalogue of the epigraphic occurrences of this title and a full discussion of their likely meaning, see S.J.D. Cohen, 'Epigraphical Rabbis', *JQR* 72 (1981), pp. 1-17.

(III.87) Vow of Rabbi Attikos. (*CIJ* II no. 736 = *DF* no. 83 – Lapethos, Cyprus; 3rd century CE)

(III.88) Matrona, daughter of Rabbi Yehudah. Peace [on her soul?]. (Le Bohec, no. 80 – Volubilis, Mauretania; 4th century CE(?))

(III.89) Peace (*Shalom*)! Here lies the Rabbi Abba Maris, the honoured one. (Noy I no. 22 – Nola, Italy; 4th-5th century CE)

IV

Jewish interaction with Greek and Roman authorities

1. JEWISH HONOURS FOR PTOLEMAIC RULERS

The two entries in this section, as well as their parallels (e.g. **I.102-3** and **IV.11**) illustrate the way in which the Jews of Ptolemaic Egypt set about demonstrating their loyalty to their rulers without seriously compromising their beliefs. Although these dedicatory inscriptions open with the standard Ptolemaic loyalty formula (on this, see introductory note at **V.38**), the customary references to the rulers' divine status are omitted. This practice is followed in all the synagogue dedications from Egypt known to us.

(IV.1) On behalf of King Ptolemy (III) and Queen Berenike, his sister and wife, and their children, the Jews (of Schedia near Alexandria[1] have dedicated) the prayer-house. (*CIJ* II no. 1440 = HN no. 22 and Plate IX – 246-222 BCE)

(IV.2) On behalf of the Queen and the King,[2] for the great God who listens (to prayers), Alypos* has made the prayer-house. Year 15, Me[cheir ?]. (*CIJ* II 1432 = HN no. 13 – Alexandria; probably 1st century BCE)

2. PTOLEMAIC AND SELEUCID PRIVILEGES FOR THE JEWS

Although Josephus frequently implies (as, for instance, at *Jewish Antiquities* 14.186) that the privileges awarded by Hellenistic kings to the Jews were extensive, those actually attested are rather modest.

Inviolability for a Jewish prayer-house in Egypt

(IV.3) (In Greek) On the orders of the Queen and King,[3] let what is written below be inscribed in the place of the previous plaque about the dedication of the prayer-house: King Ptolemy Euergetes[4] (has proclaimed) the prayer-house inviolate (*asylon*).[5]

(Added in Latin) The Queen and the King have ordered. (*CIJ* II no. 1449 = HN no. 125 and Plate XXIX)

Olive oil concession at Antioch

(IV.4) He (Seleukos I Nikator) ordered that the Jews (of Antioch) who did not wish to use foreign (and therefore ritually impure) olive oil should receive from the gymnasiarchs a fixed sum of money for the purchase of (their own kind of) olive oil. When the people of Antioch in the recent war[6] proposed to revoke the privilege, Mucianus, the then governor of Syria, upheld it. (Josephus, *Jewish Antiquities* 12.120)

3. JEWS IN THE SERVICE OF THE SELEUCIDS AND PTOLEMIES

Although the Seleucids made considerable use of Jews in buttressing their regime (**I.18**), individual cases of Diasporan Jews who were in their service are not attested. The focus in this section, therefore, is exclusively on Jews who served the Ptolemies. The examples cited all come from Egypt. They represent just a small sample of the abundant papyrological material available.

(a) Jews in the army

Throughout the Ptolemaic period, Jews are attested at every level of the military: we know of river guards, reservists (the so-called Jews of the Epigone), high-ranking officers (*taktomisthoi*) and commanders-in-chief. That they were at their most prominent under Ptolemy VI Philometor is not surprising: he was by far the most philosemitic member of the dynasty.

(**IV.5**) Notification from Herakon, superindentent of the lands of Peitholaos, to Amosis, scribe of the village of Apollonias. On the ... of Epeiph, Theophilos, son of Dositheos, Philistion, [son of ...] and Timaios, son of Telouphis, all three Jews of the Epigone, coming upon the orchard of the aforesaid Peitholaos, which lies in the vicinity of the aforesaid village, stripped the fruit from 10 vines. When Horos the guard ran out against them, they set upon him and beat him on any part of his body they could get hold of and went off with a vine-dresser's pruning-hook. The aforesaid robbers are inhabitants of Kerkeosiris. I estimate that the fruit stripped off (will make) 6 measures[7] of wine. (*CPJ* I no. 21 – Apollonias, Fayum; 210 BCE)

(**IV.6**) In the seventh year of Ptolemy (VI), the son of Ptolemy and of Kleopatra, gods Epiphaneis ... on the thirteenth of the month Gorpiaios, (being) Phamenoth the thirteenth, in Trikomia in the division of Themistes in the Arsinoite nome. Ioudas, son of Iosephos, Jew of the Epigone, has lent to Agathokles, son of Ptolemy, a Jew of the infantry detachment of Molossos, stationed in the Herakleopolite nome, (and) a *taktomisthos*,[8] two talents and five hundred drachmas of copper coinage for twelve months from the date written above, with interest at the rate of two drachmas per mina per month.[9] This loan is the amount which Agathokles (still) owed Ioudas out of the five talents which he had received from Ioudas as as advance towards a joint retail business[10] according to a written agreement of which Ananias, the son of Ionathas*, a Jew of the

Epigone, is the guardian. Agathokles shall repay to Ioudas the aforesaid loan and the interest in the month Mecheir of the eighth year. If
he does not repay it in accordance with what has been written, he shall
pay it increased by half. This agreement is valid. The witnesses (are):
Deinias, the son of Aineas, Thraseas, the son of Sosibios, Thebon, the
son of Phanokles, Samaelos*, the son of Ioanes, (all) four Jews of the
Epigone, Theodoros, the son of Theodoros, who is also called Samaelos*,
Nikanor, the son of Iason, both Jews of the First Hipparchy of
Dositheos, (and) eighty-arourai holders.[11] (*CPJ* I no. 24 – Trikomia,
Fayum; 174 BCE)

(IV.7) In the twenty-ninth year of the reign of Ptolemy (VI) and Kleopatra,
children of Ptolemy and Kleopatra, gods Epiphaneis ... on the seventh of
the month Panemos, being Tybi the seventh, in Alexandrou-Nesos in the
division of Themistes in the Arsinoite nome. Simon, son of Theodoros and
his partners, Jews of the ... (being) *taktomisthoi*[12] ... agree with Euarchos,
son of Heliodoros, of the deme Aiakide (and) one of the court *Diadochi*[13]
that they have contracted from him all the viticultural works (text uncertain here) in the vineyard belonging to Melankomas, the *archisomato-
phylax* (chief of the bodyguard) and *strategos*, formerly called Lampros'
(vineyard) at a fee of one thousand seven hundred copper drachmas per
aroura, the aroura being estimated, minimally, at four hundred vines. And
Simon and his partners[14] ... (rest of text barely intelligible). (P. Köln III
no. 144 = *New Docs*. VI no. 24 – 152 BCE)

(IV.8) At this time (*c*. 107 BCE), not only were the Jews in Jerusalem and
the land (of Judaea) flourishing but also those who dwelled at Alexandria
and in Egypt and Cyprus. For Queen Kleopatra (III), who was fighting a
civil war against her son Ptolemy (IX), nicknamed Lathyros (i.e. chick-
pea), appointed as her generals Chelkias and Ananias, the sons of the
Onias who had built the temple at Heliopolis after the manner of the one
at Jerusalem[15] ... (Josephus, *Jewish Antiquities* 13.284-5)

(IV.9) Eleazaros, son of Nikolaos, the officer,[16] (has dedicated) the sundial
and well on behalf of himself and his wife, Eirene. (*CIJ* II no. 1531 = HN
no. 115 – provenance unknown; late (?) Ptolemaic)

(IV.10) Turning back from the Euphrates, Gabinius set about restoring
him (Ptolemy Auletes) to Egypt (55 BCE). For the campaign, Hyrcanus and
Antipater put themselves entirely at his disposal. Besides producing
money, arms, corn and soldiers, Antipater also persuaded the local Jews
who guarded the river mouths at Pelusium to let Gabinius through.
(Josephus, *Jewish War* 1.175)

(b) Jews in the police force

(IV.11) On behalf of King Ptolemy and Queen Kleopatra, Ptolemy, son of Epikydes, the chief of police,[17] and the Jews in Athribis, (have dedicated) the prayer-house to the Most High God. (*CIJ* II no. 1443 = HN no. 27 – Athribis; 2nd-1st century BCE)

List of witnesses to a loan document from Hephaisteas in the Fayum (173 BCE):

(IV.12)
Ptolemy ...
... of Kineas of the Second Hipparchy
... a Jew, policeman
Spartakos, son of Alexander. (*CPJ* I no. 25)

(c) Jewish civil servants

Although only a few Jewish civil servants are attested, they include two high-flyers – a head of one of the two royal secretariats and possibly a *strategos* of the Heliopolite nome.

(IV.13) Philon to Zenon, greetings. If you, as well as those whom you wish to be so, are in good health, that would be good. I myself am well. Please make every effort to handle expeditiously the matters concerning which my brother Ptolemy sailed up (the Nile) to you, so that he may return quickly to me and I may not be prevented from sailing up the river should the need arise. For I must be off from here (i.e. Alexandria) shortly. I wrote to you earlier about Hermokrates too, because I realised that you were exerting yourself on his behalf and had myself made this clear to him and I really do think that he will be out (i.e. set free) within a few days. Many other people too have troubled themselves on his behalf but Kaphisophon, the son of Philip the doctor has been the most effective. The written report of the enquiry, which acquits him of all the charges, is already in the hands of Dositheos[18] the *hypomnematographos*[19] (memorandum-writer), so that the king may, in accordance with established procedure, read it before his release ... (*CPJ* I no. 127a – Philadelpheia in the Fayum; 240 BCE)

(IV.14) Heroides to Onias,[20] greetings. King Ptolemy (VI) is well and King Ptolemy his brother and Queen Kleopatra his sister and their children and their affairs are as usual. If you are in good health and the rest of your affairs in order, that would be as we wish. We ourselves are going along well enough. The copy of the letter to Dorion, the *hypodioiketes* (lit. under-manager) is appended for you. Understanding, therefore, that it is incumbent upon all alike who are concerned with administration to show consideration for those engaged in sowing, please make every effort and take every precaution that neither those who are incapable of farming are impressed nor those who are capable are sheltered on any pretext whatsoever. Let everything be done in the manner set out in the document that has been sent to you by us. Look after yourself, so that you remain in good health. Farewell. Year 6. Mesore 24. (*CPJ* I no. 132 – vicinity of Memphis; 164 BCE)

(IV.15) I, Horos, district scribe, acting through Onias,[21] (my) secretary, have posted up (this edict) opposite the one that was published before. Year 3, Hathyr (.)5. (*CPJ* I no. 137 – exact provenance unknown; 50 BCE)

(d) Jewish financial officials/tax collectors

(IV.16) Year 27. Psenamounis, son of Horos, has handed over in respect of the chaff-levy due for the same (i.e. above) year 40 jars. Total: 40 jars. (Signed by) Iosepos.[22] (*CPJ* I no. 100 – Upper Egypt; 155/4 BCE)

(IV.17) Year 28. Simon, son of Abietos, has handed over for the above year 100 jars of chaff. Total: 100. (Signed by) Iosepos; Iason; Simon, son of Abietos. (*CPJ* I no. 101 – Upper Egypt; 154/3 BCE)

(IV.18) Year 30. Mecheir 17. Paid to the bank at Koptos, of which Dositheos[23] is head, as payment of a fine for the twenty-ninth year (by) Panechares, son of ...eteaios, one thousand five hundred drachmas. Total: 1,500. Also the taxes due, (paid) double. Dositheos, banker. 2,030. (*CPJ* I no. 69 – Koptos; 140 BCE)

(IV.19) (1st hand) Simon, son of Iazaros,[24] tax farmer controlling the fourth (part) of the fisher's tax for the 28th year, to Mesoeris, greetings. I have received from you for the tax on you and your sons, in the month Tybi, four thousand drachmas of copper. Total: 4,000. Dellous has written (this) at Simon's request, because he is illiterate. (*CPJ* I no. 107 – probably Thebes; 154/3 BCE)

4. JEWISH HONOURS FOR ROMAN EMPERORS

Since participation in the imperial cult was incompatible with the worship of God, Jews had to find other ways of assuring the Roman authorities of their loyalty. Thus, in Judaea itself, they offered each day in the Temple at Jerusalem sacrifices to God on the emperor's behalf (Philo, *Legatio ad Gaium* 280) and in the synagogues of the Diaspora passed intermittent resolutions honouring the emperor, his family and officials (for an example of the last, see **V.35**). Benefactions to the synagogue too were often made either on the emperor's behalf or expressly for his well-being.

(IV.20) Gathering together great hordes of men, they (the Greeks of Alexandria) attacked the prayer-houses, of which there are many in every section of the city. Some they vandalised, others they totally destroyed by torching and burning them to the ground, in their fury and mindless frenzy paying no heed at all to the nearby houses, for nothing is faster than fire once it fastens on timber. I say nothing about the simultaneous destruction and burning of objects set up to honour the Emperors – shields and gilded crowns and stelai and dedicatory inscriptions, consideration for which should have made them spare the rest.[25] (Philo, *Legatio ad Gaium* 132-3)

(IV.21) For the safety of the Emperor(s?). Mindis Phaustos (i.e. Mindius Faustus) with [his family?][26] has, from his own donations, built and made (this)[27] and set up the ark for the Holy Law. (Noy I no. 13 and Plate VI – synagogue at Ostia; 2nd-3rd century CE)

(IV.22) For the safety of the Emperors L(ucius) Sept(imius) Severus Pertinax and M(arcus) Aur(elius) Antoninus, the Augusti,[28] and Iulia Augusta, Mother of the Camps,[29] [Secu]ndus has restored from the foundations the prayer-house fallen from age.[30] (*CIJ* I² no. 678a = Scheiber no. 8 – Mursa in Pannonia; between 195 and 209 CE)

5. PRIVILEGES FOR JEWS WHO WERE ROMAN CITIZENS

These were modest: the exemption from military service **(IV.23)** was simply an ad hoc ruling of the Roman civil war era (i.e. the 40s-30s BCE). That it had no permanent or universal validity, is shown by Tiberius' conscription of the Jews of Rome for military service in Sardinia (**I.53-4** and **IV.45**). The special arrangements for collecting the corn dole at Rome **(IV.24-5)** applied only to those Jews domiciled there who possessed full citizen rights.

Exemption from military service

(IV.23) Lucius Lentulus (Crus), the consul (in 49 BCE), declared: Those Jews who are Roman citizens and observe Jewish rites and practise them in Ephesus, I released from military service[31] on religious grounds before the tribunal on the twelfth day before the Kalends of October,[32] in the consulship of Lucius Lentulus and Gaius Marcellus ... (Josephus, *Jewish Antiquities* 14.228)

Special collection arrangements for the corn dole at Rome

(IV.24) Moreover, in the monthly distributions in his own city (i.e. Rome), when all the people receive in turn either cash[33] or corn, Augustus never put the Jews at a disadvantage in sharing the bounty. If it came about that the distribution occurred on the Sabbath when it is forbidden either to receive or give anything or perform any workaday task, and especially those connected with commerce, he gave orders that those who carried out the distribution should keep back for the Jews until the next day their share of the common largesse. (Philo, *Legatio ad Gaium* 158)

Two entries from fragments of an Urban Prefect's edict[34] in which eligibility for free corn is denied to certain offenders, among whom are the following:

(IV.25a) Felix Tineosus, a Jew.
(IV.25b) Cretic[u]s, a Jew.
(*CIJ* I no. 530 = Noy II no. 601 – Rome; 4th century CE)

6. ROMAN PROTECTION OF THE JEWISH WAY OF LIFE

In order to practise their traditional way of life in what, for a variety of reasons, was often a hostile environment, Diasporan Jews frequently needed official protection. Presented in the first part of this section is a small number of the many (allegedly) original documents that Josephus cites in his *Jewish Antiquities* to illustrate how the pagan Roman authorities honoured the Jews and protected their interests. They have been chosen specifically to illustrate Roman handling of the commonest problems encountered by the Jews of the Diaspora in both war and peace. No attempt has been made to assess the authenticity of this material. For help with that difficult question, the reader is referred to, in the first instance, the specialist works listed in Appendix J of vol. VII of the Loeb edition of Josephus and, in the second, the following articles: H. Moehring, 'The *Acta pro Judaeis* in the *Antiquities* of Flavius Josephus: a study in Hellenistic and modern apologetic historiography' in J. Neusner (ed.) *Christianity, Judaism and Other Greco-Roman Cults, Studies for Morton Smith at Sixty* III (Leiden, 1975), pp. 124-58; E. Bickermann, 'Une question d'authenticité: les privilèges juifs' in *Studies in Jewish and Christian History* II (Leiden, 1980), pp. 24-43; T. Rajak, 'Was there a Roman charter for the Jews?', *JRS* 74 (1984), pp. 107-23; M. Pucci Ben Zeev, 'Greek and Roman documents from Republican times in the *Antiquities*: what was Josephus' source?', *SCI* 13 (1994), pp. 46-59. We conclude this section by setting out an imperial enactment from near the end of our period, the purpose of which was to protect the Jews against a new and increasingly serious threat – Christian fanaticism. Analogous documents are to be found at **V.93-4**.

(IV.26) In the presidency of Artemon, on the first day of the month of Lenaeon (i.e. 24 January 43 BCE), Dolabella, Imperator, to the magistrates, council and people of Ephesos, greetings. Alexander, son of Theodoros, ambassador of Hyrkanos, son of Alexander, High Priest and Ethnarch of the Jews, has pointed out to me the inability of his fellow-Jews to undertake military service since they cannot bear arms or march on the days of the Sabbath. Nor can they obtain the traditional foodstuffs to which they are accustomed. I, therefore, like the governors before me, grant them exemption from military service and permit them to observe their native customs – namely, assembling for the sake of sacred rites in accordance with their law and for (making) contributions towards their sacrifices.[35] I wish you to inform the various cities of these things in writing. (Josephus, *Jewish Antiquities* 14.225-7)

(IV.27) Decree of the people of Halikarnassos. 'In the priesthood of Memnon, son of Aristeides ... the people passed the following decree on the motion of Markos Alexander. Since we at all times have the deepest regard for piety towards the divine and holiness, following the example of the people of Rome, who are the benefactors of all mankind, and in conformity with what they have written to our city about their friendship and alliance with the Jews, namely that their religious rites and their customary festivals and their meetings are to be carried on, we have deemed it right that those Jewish men and women who so wish may keep the Sabbath and carry out their sacred rites in accordance with Jewish Laws, and build prayer-houses by the sea, as is their native custom.[36] If anyone, whether community official or private person prevents them, he shall be liable to this fine[37] and owe it to the city.' (Josephus, *Jewish Antiquities* 14.256-8)

(IV.28) Caesar Augustus, Pontifex Maximus, with tribunician power,[38] decrees: since the Jewish nation has been found well disposed towards the Roman people not only at the present time but also in the past, and especially in the time of my father the Imperator Caesar, as has their High Priest Hyrkanos, it has been decided by me and my council under oath, with the consent of the Roman people, that the Jews are to follow their own customs in accordance with their ancestral law, just as they did in the time of Hyrkanus, High Priest of the Most High God, and their sacred monies are to be inviolable and despatched to Jerusalem and handed over to the treasurers in Jerusalem, and they need not give bond (to appear in court) on the Sabbath or on the day of preparation for it after the ninth hour. If anyone is caught stealing their sacred books or their sacred monies from a synagogue or a community hall,[39] he shall be regarded as sacrilegious and his property made over to the public treasury of the Romans. The decree they have given to me in honour of the dutifulness (*pietas*) I show towards all men and in honour of Gaius Marcius Censorinus,[40] and this edict here I order to be set up in the most conspicuous part of the temple assigned to me by the federation (*koinon*) of Asia at Ancyra. If anyone contravenes any of the above ordinances, he shall pay a heavy penalty. (Josephus, *Jewish Antiquities* 16.162-5)

(IV.29) The same two Augusti (Honorius and Theodosius II) to Johannes, Praetorian Prefect (of the East). Let no one dare to violate or seize and occupy what are known to be frequented by associations of Jews and go by the name of synagogues, since all ought to retain what is their own, without their religion and cult being subjected to stress or their rights disturbed.[41] Furthermore, since ancient custom and habit have preserved for the above-mentioned Jewish people the sanctity of the Sabbath day, we also decree the following: let no judicial summons, under the pretext of public or private business, constrain a man of the above-mentioned religion, since the rest of the time seems perfectly adequate for the public laws and it is most in keeping with the moderation of the age that long-held privileges should not be violated ... Given on the 7th day before the Kalends of August at Ravenna, during the 9th consulship of Honorius Augustus and the 5th of Theodosius Augustus. (*Codex Theodosianus* 16.8.20 = Linder no. 40 – 26 July, 412 CE)

7. JEWS IN THE SERVICE OF THE ROMAN GOVERNMENT

Although the banning of Jews from the army and civil service in 418 CE (**IV.73**) indicates that at that time, at least, Jewish bureaucrats and military men did exist, very few can be clearly identified, either then or in the preceding centuries. Diasporan Jews in general did not use Hebrew names and those who were totally assimilated, as members of the public services by definition will have been, tended not to advertise their Jewishness. The few who can be detected show that Jews operated at all levels of the army and the civil service. Only in one instance, however, that of the high-flying Tiberius Julius Alexander, can a public career be reconstructed in any detail.

(a) Tiberius Julius Alexander

Son of Alexander the alabarch and nephew of Philo the philosopher, this rich and totally assimilated Alexandrian Jew governed two Roman provinces, Judaea and Egypt, under Claudius and Nero respectively, played a prominent advisory role in 63 CE in Rome's war against King Tiridates of Armenia and was a major player in the in-fighting that followed the end of Julio-Claudian rule in 68 CE. So successful was his political manoeuvring at that time, that he was early admitted to the friendship of the Flavians and given major responsibilities in the war that they were conducting in Judaea. It is possible that they may even have appointed him Prefect of the Praetorian Guard at Rome as a reward for his services.

(**IV.30**) Fadus' successor (as governor of Judaea)[42] was Tiberius Alexander, the son of Alexander, the *alabarch* in Alexandria, a man who surpassed all his fellow citizens in both birth and wealth.[43] In piety towards God he far excelled his son Alexander. For the latter did not abide by the native traditions (of the Jews). (Josephus, *Jewish Antiquities* 20.100)

(**IV.31**) On the appointed day (sometime in 63 CE), Tiberius Alexander, an illustrious Roman knight[44] who had been appointed campaign-advisor,[45] and Annius Vinicianus, Corbulo's son-in-law, who, though below senatorial age, was acting-legate of the fifth legion, entered Tiridates' camp. Their visit was both an honour and a guarantee against treachery. (Tacitus, *Annals* 15.28.3 = Stern II no. 292)

(**IV.32**) Ioulios Demetrios, *strategos* of Oasis in the Thebaid. I have inscribed for you below a copy of the edict that was sent to me by the Lord Prefect, Tiberios Ioulios Alexander,[46] so that you may know and enjoy his benevolence. Year 2 of Imperator Lucius Livius Augustus Sulpicius Galba[47] ... (*SEG* 15 (1958) no. 873)

(**IV.33**) The gaps in the four legions caused by the drafts which Vespasian had sent with Mucianus to Italy (in 69 CE) were filled with the troops who had arrived with Titus. For two thousand picked men from the armies of Alexandria followed him, as well as three thousand from the garrisons on the Euphrates. With these was the most outstanding in loyalty and intelligence of all his friends, Tiberius Alexander. Formerly he had controlled Egypt in their (i.e. the Flavians') interest but now he was judged worthy of commanding armies,[48] for he had been the first to welcome the dynasty as it was rising and with splendid faith had attached himself to its fortunes while they were still unclear. As an advisor in a war-situation, he was pre-eminent, by virtue of both his age and experience. (Josephus, *Jewish War* 5.43-6)

(**IV.34**) ... of Tiberios Ioulios Alexander, the former Prefect (of Egypt), who became also Praetorian Prefect.[49] (*CPJ* II no. 418b)

(b) Jewish officials in Roman Egypt

An alabarch

(**IV.35**) At the same time (i.e. sometime between 48 and 54 CE) Mariamme (the sister of Agrippa II) repudiated (her husband) Archelaos and began to live in wedlock with Demetrios, an Alexandrian Jew, prominent by virtue of both birth and wealth. At that time he held the office of *alabarch*.[50] (Josephus, *Jewish Antiquities* 20.147)

A tax-collector

(**IV.36**) Ischylos, son of Iosephos to Tryphas, son of Nikon. I agree that I have had from you for the bath-tax for the 3rd year, 6 drachmas, with regard to you and Nikon, son of Antonios Rouphos, and Theodotos, his brother.[51] (*CPJ* II no. 240 – Apollinopolis Magna/Edfu; 70/71 CE)

Jewish sitologoi

(**IV.37**) List of *sitologoi*[52] for the 5th year of our Lord, Trajan Caesar. Kephalion, son of Dorion; Ioses*, called Teuphilos*, descendant (?) of Dosthon; Achorimphis, son of Panther; Pakysis, son of Pnepheros; Straton, called Isakis*; Eleazaros, son of Ptolemaios ...[53] (*CPJ* II no. 428 – Fayum; 101/2 CE)

An official of the state alum monopoly

(IV.38) Aurel(ios) Makrobios, lessee of the alum industry, through me, Kaisarios, scribe, to Aurelios Isak*, manager, greetings. I have sent to you one Italian pound of alum through Isidoros (and) 2 ounces, 8 carats (?) of cardamum. Year 16 and 15 and 8. Tybi 28. (*CPJ* III no. 477 – Oxyrhynchos; 300 CE)

(c) Jewish officials in areas other than in Egypt

A Jewish palatinos of Palmyrene extraction

(IV.39) Tomb of Leontios, father of the Rabbi Paregorios and the *palatinos*,[54] Ioulianos. Former goldsmith.[55] (*CIJ* II no. 1006 = *BS* II no. 61 – 4th century CE)

A one-time procurator at Sardis

(IV.40) Aur(elios) Basileides – former procurator.[56] (Hanfmann, *Sardis*, fig. 272 – 3rd or 4th century CE)

(d) Jews in the military

A centurion

(IV.41) Thanoum, son of Simon, grandson of Beniamin, the *centenarius*[57] from Parembole.[58] Peace (*Shalom*)! (*CIJ* II no. 920 = HN no. 147 – Jaffa; 2nd-4th century CE)

A guard-post superintendent

(IV.42) To the everlasting God, for the safety of our lord Severus Alexander, Pius, Felix, Augustus, and of the mother of Augustus, Julia Mamaea Augusta, Cosmius, superintendent of the guard-post at Spondill, a member of the Jewish community, willingly repaid his vow. (*CIJ* I[2] no. 677, re-edited in Scheiber no. 3; for further re-editing, see *AE* 1990 no. 823 – Intercisa, Pannonia; 233-235 CE)

A trooper

(IV.43) Flavia Optata (wife/daughter?) of a soldier from the troop of the Royal Emesene Jews.[59] If anyone after my death wishes to open the tomb, he shall pay to the resources of the treasury one pound of gold. (*CIJ* I no. 640 = Noy I no. 6 – Concordia, a military camp near Aquileia; 4th century CE)

8. MEASURES TAKEN OR THREATENED AGAINST THE JEWS BY THE ROMAN AUTHORITIES

Although the Romans of the late Republic and early Empire were willing to support the Jews in their desire to live in accordance with their ancestral customs and usually upheld their petitions over the infringements of their rights, there were limits to their toleration. They disapproved of the deliberate spreading among non-Jews of Jewish (and, therefore, in their eyes, anti-social and atheistic) ways and tended to react ruthlessly to riotous or criminal behaviour. Action, usually in the form of a general expulsion, was several times taken against Jews at Rome on one or other of those grounds. Rebellion, of course, was deemed intolerable and when this happened, as, for instance, in Judaea in 66 and 132 CE, the whole of Jewry was subsequently made to suffer. Hence, inter alia, the empire-wide imposition of the Jewish tax in 70 CE and the banning of all Jews from Jerusalem in 135 CE. From Constantine onwards, the grounds for threatening to proceed against the Jews were rather different. Christian emperors viewed with intense dislike the possibility of Jews, whether as slave-owners, spouses or public officials, exerting influence over Christians. Hence their repeated (because they were largely ineffectual?) rulings to counteract it in both the private and the public spheres. Of the many examples available, only three are presented here. For a comprehensive collection, see A. Linder, *The Jews in Roman Imperial Legislation* (Michigan, 1987).

(a) Action against Jews at Rome

(i) An expulsion in 139 BCE

Mentioned briefly in two late and rather confused epitomes or summaries of a work written in the early Julio-Claudian period, this expulsion was probably a small-scale affair involving Jewish visitors to Rome. There probably was no permanent Jewish community there at that time.

(**IV.44a**) In the consulship of M(arcus) Popilius Laenas and L(ucius) Calpurnius, Cnaeus Cornelius Hispalus, the *praetor peregrinus*[60] ordered the Chaldaeans (i.e. Babylonian astrologers) by edict to leave the city and Italy within ten days, since they were causing confusion in the minds of the frivolous and stupid by their fallacious interpretation of the stars and mercenary lying. The same magistrate ordered the Jews [and those] who were trying to contaminate the Roman way of life with the rituals of Jupiter Sabazius[61] to return to their homes. (Valerius Maximus, *Facta et Dicta Memorabilia* 1.3.3, from the Epitome of Iulius Paris – 4th century CE(?) = Stern I no. 147b)

(**IV.44b**) Cornelius Hispalus, therefore, expelled the Chaldaeans from the city and ordered them to leave Italy within ten days, to prevent them selling their foreign knowledge. The same Hispalus also banished from the city Jews, who were trying to transmit their sacred rites to the Romans, and he removed from public places their private altars.[62] (Valerius Maximus, *Facta et Dicta Memorabilia* 1.3.3, from the Epitome of Ianuarius Nepotianus – 4th/5th century CE(?) = Stern I no. 147a)

(ii) Coercive measures under Tiberius, 14-37 CE

On these, see now M.H. Williams, 'The expulsion of the Jews from Rome in AD 19', *Latomus* 48 (1989), 765-84 and L.V. Rutgers, 'Roman policy towards the Jews: expulsions from the city of Rome during the first century CE', *Classical Antiquity* 13 (1994), pp. 56-74. Both stress that the need to preserve law and order in the capital was of paramount importance to the Roman authorities.

(IV.45) Tiberius suppressed foreign cults, especially the Egyptian and Jewish rites, compelling those who were in the grip of that superstition to burn their religious vestments along with all the instruments of their cult.[63] Under the pretext of military service he assigned the Jewish youth to provinces of less healthy climate;[64] the rest of that ethnic group and those who held similar beliefs he expelled from the city, on pain of perpetual servitude if they did not obey. (Suetonius, *Tiberius* 36 = Stern II no. 306)

(IV.46) As the Jews were flocking to Rome in great numbers and bringing over to their ways many of the local people, Tiberius drove most of them out.[65] (Dio, *Roman History* 57.18.5a, as cited by the Christian writer, John of Antioch = Stern II no. 419)

(iii) Coercive measures under Claudius, 41-54 CE

Besides closing down the synagogues of Rome in 41 CE, as described here, Claudius also expelled the Jews from the city *c.* 49 CE. See **I.21** and **II.144**.

(IV.47) As for the Jews who had multiplied again to such an extent that only with difficulty could they have been banned from the city without immense disorder on account of their numbers, Claudius did not drive them out but ordered them, while adhering to their traditional way of life, not to assemble. (Dio, *Roman History* 60.6.6 = Stern II no. 422)

(iv) An undated expulsion of the Jews from Rome

(IV.48) A man well fitted to beg at the Arician Gate or Slope among the Jews, who had gone to Aricia[66] after they had been expelled from the city.[67] (*Scholium* on Juvenal, *Satires* 4.11 = Stern II no. 538)

(b) The closure of the Temple at Leontopolis, *c.* 73 CE

This was ordered by the emperor Vespasian in the aftermath of the First Jewish War for the reasons set out in following passage.

(IV.49) At that time Lupus was in charge of Alexandria and he speedily notified Caesar (Vespasian) about this disturbance.[68] Viewing with suspicion the unquenchable appetite of the Jews for revolution, and fearing that they might gather together in force and attract others to their cause, he ordered Lupus to pull down the Jewish temple in the so-called Land of Onias[69] ... Lupus, the governor of Alexandria, on receipt of Caesar's communication, went to the temple, removed some of the offerings and shut up the building. Lupus died shortly afterwards and Paulinus, his successor in office, stripped the temple of its offerings, issuing dire threats against the priests if they did not hand over everything. He forbade would-be worshippers to approach the precinct and shut the gates, making the place completely inaccessible. The result was that not a trace of God-worship was left at the site. (Josephus, *Jewish War* 7.420-1 and 433-5)

(c) The tax on the Jews and the *fiscus Iudaicus*

(i) Imposition of the tax in 70 CE

(**IV.50**) Thus was Jerusalem destroyed on the very day of Kronos (= Saturn = the Sabbath), a day which even now Jews reverence more than any other. From that time it was ordered that those who continued to adhere to their ancestral customs should pay annually to Capitoline Jupiter two drachmas. (Dio, *Roman History* 66.7.2 = Stern II no. 430 (final section))

(**IV.51**) On all Jews, wherever they lived,[70] he (the emperor Vespasian) imposed a tax. He ordered that every Jew should pay two drachmas every year to the Capitol (i.e. the temple of Jupiter on the Capitol), just as formerly they had paid them to the Temple at Jerusalem. (Josephus, *Jewish War* 7.218)

(ii) Payment and collection of the tax in Egypt

Part of a tax register from Arsinoe, 73 CE

(**IV.52**) From Herakleides, *amphodarch*[71] of the Camp of Apollonios.[72] Liability for the Jewish tax for the fifth year of the Emperor Caesar Vespasian Augustus, being an abstract according to the statement of the fourth year.

The number of Jews taken up by previous accounts is as follows: adult males – 5; adult females – 6, of whom one is over age and was adjudged as such, being 59 years of age in the fourth year; minors – one, being four years of age in the fourth year. Total of names – 12.

And those being taken up through a transcript of the preceding *epikrisis* (examination), having been shown to be three years of age in the fourth year, having been one year old in the second year, (are as follows:) males – Philiskos, son of Ptollas, the son of Philiskos, mother, Erotion; females – Protous, daughter of Simon, the son of Ptolemy, mother, Dosarion. Total – 2. Grand Total – 14, comprised of 5 adult males; 1 male minor, who is four years old in the fifth year; 6 adult females; 1 female minor, who is five years old in the fifth year; 1 female minor, who is four years old in the fifth year. Total of names – 14.

In addition there is enrolled for the Jewish tax in the fifth year of the Emperor Caesar Vespasian Augustus, from minors who in the third year were one year old and so in the fifth year three years old, of males taken up, Seuthes, son of Theodoros, the son Ptolemy, mother, Philous. Found to be two years old in the fourth year, in the examination of the fourth year. Total of names – 15, comprised of 5 adult males; 1 male minor, who is four years old in the fifth year; 1 male minor, who is three years old in the fifth year; 6 adult females; 1 female minor, who is five years old in the fifth year; 1 female minor, who is four years old in the fifth year. Grand Total – 15, of whom the adult males listed as liable to the maximum rate of the *laographia* (poll tax) are 5. The remaining names (are 10), who individually are as follows:

Adult females: Tryphaina, daughter of [...]spas, the son of Kales, mother, Dosarion. (She is) from those who are over age (and is) 61 years old, having been adjudged 59 years in the fourth year. Dosarion, daughter of Iacob, the son of Iacob, mother, Sambous, husband, Simon, aged 22 years. Philous, daughter of [...]os, mother, Ptollous, husband, Theodoros, aged 20 years. Sambathion, daughter of Sabinos, mother, Herais, husband, The(a)genes, 18 years old. S[...], daughter of [...]os, mother, Theodous, husband, Sambath(ion?), aged [...]. Erotion, daughter of [...]on, mother Euterpe, husband, Ptollas, aged 22 years. Total – 6.

Male minors, who were four years old in the fifth year: Philiskos, son of Ptollas, the son of Philiskos, mother Erotion – 1 name.

(Male minors), who were three years old in the fifth year: Seuthes, son of Theodoros, the son of Ptolemy, mother Philous – 1 (name).

Female (minors), who were five years old in the fifth year: Protous, daughter of Theodoros, mother, Philous – 1 (name).

(Female minors), who were [four years old in the fifth year]: Protous, daughter of Simon, the son of Ptolemy, mother, Dosarion – 1 (name).

Total of names – 10. Together with the 5 names of those liable to the maximum rate of the poll tax, total, as above, 15 names, at 8 drachmas, 2 obols each, 125 drachmas. For the *aparchai* (first fruits), 15 drachmas. (Grand) total 140 drachmas. A copy has been deposited with the royal scribe through Amoutio... the scribe. Fifth year of Vespasian, Germanikios[73] 20. (*CPJ* II no. 421)

A collector of the Jewish tax

(**IV.53**) ...naios, son of Kallistratos, collector of the Jewish tax, to Tryphas, son of Nikon, greetings. I have received through ..., son of Apollonios, the two-denarii tax on the Jews from you and from ... for the 2nd year of our Lord, Titus Caesar, 16 drachmas and 4 obols and for the *aparchai* (first fruits) 2 drachmas. Year 3, Hathyr 18. (*CPJ* II no. 181 – Apollinopolis Magna/Edfu; 80 CE)

Individual tax receipts

The texts listed here, a small selection of the large number of the tax receipts found in the Jewish quarter of Apollinopolis Magna/Edfu in Upper Egypt, have been chosen to illustrate (a) the rigorous collection of the two-denarii tax on the Jews by Vespasian and his imposition on them in 73 CE of an additional levy, the *aparchai* (first fruits), (b) the alleviation of the tax burden by Titus, (c) the merging of the two taxes under Domitian and (d) the decreasing regularity in the payment of the Jewish tax under Trajan.

Payment of the tax under Vespasian

(IV.54) Niger, son of Antonios Rouphos, (has paid) in respect of the two-denarii tax on the Jews for the 4th year of Vespasian 8 drachmas, 2 obols. Mecheir 3. (*CPJ* II no. 162 – 72 CE)

(IV.55) Teuphilos*, son of Simon, in respect of the two-denarii tax on the Jews for the 5th year of Vespasian, 8 drachmas, 2 obols (and) for the *aparchai* (first fruits) 1 (drachma). Eunous, son of Dolchous, similarly, 8 drachmas, 2 obols (and) in respect of the *aparchai* (first fruits), 1 (drachma). Year 5, Pharmouthi 2. (*CPJ* II no. 167 – 73 CE)

(IV.56) Theodotos, also called Niger, son of Antonios Rouphos, has paid in respect of the two-denarii tax on the Jews for the 11th year of Vespasian 8 drachmas, 2 obols (and) for the *aparchai* (first fruits) 1 (drachma). Year 11, Pachon 3. (*CPJ* II no. 178 – 79 CE)

Alleviation of the tax burden by Titus

Note in **IV.58** the payment of the tax in half-yearly instalments. This was seen by Tcherikover (*CPJ* II, p. 115) as an attempt by the tax officials to lighten the Jews' burden.

(IV.57) Kaekillias, freedman[74] of Sarra, daughter of Sakax (?), for the 2nd year of Titus in respect of the two denarii tax on the Jews, 8 drachmas, 2 obols and for the *aparchai* (first fruits) 1 (drachma). Year 2, Pachon, 28. (*CPJ* II no. 179 – 80 CE)

(IV.58) Tryphas, son of Nikon, in respect of the two-denarii tax on the Jews for the 3rd year of Titus, 4 drachmas, 1 obol and for the *aparchai* (first fruits), 3 obols. Year 3, Payni 25. For the 4th year, similarly, 4 drachmas, 1 obol (and) for the *aparchai*, 3 obols. (*CPJ* II no. 182 – 81 CE)

The tax under Domitian

Note the treatment in **IV.59** of the *aparchai* and the two-denarii tax as a single levy. This merging of the two dues has been seen as an example of Domitian's well-known drive for administrative efficiency. The payment of odd amounts, to be seen in **IV.60**, becomes increasingly frequent in the years leading up to the great revolt under Trajan (illustrated here by **IV.61-2**). Whether this reflects Jewish inability or unwillingness to pay the full tax at once cannot be determined.

(IV.59) Iosepos*, son of Aischylos, in respect of the dyke-tax for the 4th year of our Lord, Domitian, 6 drachmas, 4 obols; in respect of the bath-tax, 2 obols; in respect of the Jewish tax (*telesma*), 9 drachmas, 2 obols. Year 4, Payni 24. (*CPJ* II no. 183 – 85 CE)

(IV.60) Paid by Thedetos*, son of Alexion, in respect of the Jewish tax for the 14th year of Domitian, 4 drachmas; by his son Philippos, 4 drachmas. Total 8. Year 14, Mesore 25. (*CPJ* II no. 192 – 95 CE)

The tax under Trajan

(IV.61) Mariamos, son of Simon, in respect of the Jewish tax for the 3rd year of our Lord, Trajan, 4 drachmas, 4 obols. Year 4, Thoth 30. (*CPJ* II no. 195 – 100 CE)

(IV.62) Damas, son of Harbinos, in respect of the dyke-tax for the 9th year of our Lord, Trajan, 6 drachmas, 4 obols; in respect of the bath-tax, 2 obols; in respect of the Jewish tax, 1 (drachma), 2 obols ... (*CPJ* II no. 203 – 106 CE)

(IV.63) Meious, son of Thedetos*, in respect of the Jewish tax for the 19th year of our Lord, Trajan Optimus Caesar, 4 drachmas. Year 19,[75] Pharmouthi 25. (*CPJ* II no. 228 – 116 CE)

Later history of the tax in Egypt

The next entry, part of a list of taxes collected at Karanis either in 145/6 or 167/8 CE, shows that (a) the Jewish tax continued to be collected in Egypt after the Trajanic revolt and at the same rate as before and (b) the formerly large Jewish community of Karanis had probably been wiped out in the revolt. There is now only one payer of the Jewish tax.

(IV.64) For Karanis, year 9.
Poll tax – 6 talents, 2,312 (drachmas).
Pig-tax – 1,275 (drachmas), 2 ob(ols).
Ferry-tax – 2 (drachmas), 2 chalkoi.
Tax on craftsmen – 90 (drachmas), 2 ob(ols).
Tax on perquisites (of priestly office) – 3 (drachmas).
Jewish tax – 9 (drachmas), 2 ob(ols).
(*CPJ* III no. 460)

(iii) Operation of the fiscus Iudaicus

An official of the fiscus Iudaicus at Rome

(IV.65) To T(itus) Flavius Euschemon, freedman of Augustus, who was *ab epistulis* (imperial secretary) and *procurator* for the capitation tax on the Jews. Flavia Aphrodisia has set up (this memorial) to her patron and well-deserving husband. (*CIJ* I no. 532 = Noy II no. 603 – Rome; probably 1st century CE)

Abusive administration of the fiscus Iudaicus under Domitian

Precisely who the victims of this abuse were is unclear and much disputed. While L.A. Thompson, 'Domitian and the Jewish tax', *Historia* 31 (1982), pp. 329-42, followed by M. Goodman, 'Nerva, the *Fiscus Judaicus* and Jewish identity', *JRS* 79 (1989), pp. 40-4, argues for the specific targetting of Jewish apostates, M.H. Williams, 'Domitian, the Jews and the "Judaizers" – a simple matter of *cupiditas* and *maiestas*?', *Historia* 39 (1990), pp. 196-211, has suggested that in the general persecutory atmosphere of Domitianic Rome 'many people whose physical appearance, dietary habits or religious practices and institutions made them appear to be Jewish' may well have fallen foul of the authorities. Besides non-religious Jews, other likely victims are circumcised peregrini (suggested also by Thompson), Jewish Christians and pagan Judaizers.

(IV.66) Besides other taxes, that on the Jews was levied with particular harshness: accusations were laid against those who were living as Jews, without admitting (their attachment to Judaism), as well as those who had concealed their Jewish origin and not paid the tax that had been imposed upon their nation. I remember as a young man being present when an old man of ninety was inspected by the procurator in a very crowded court to see if he was circumcised. (Suetonius, *Domitian* 12.2 = Stern II no. 320)

Removal of the above-mentioned abuses by Nerva

The appearance of the following legend on the emperor Nerva's first three coin issues (early 96 CE) indicates very clearly how scandalous the abuses connected with the Jewish tax must have become by the end of Domitian's reign. See Williams, art. cit. (previous entry), p. 200.

(IV.67) FISCI IVDAICI CALVMNIA SVBLATA = Removal of the Calumnies associated with the *Fiscus Iudaicus*. (*RIC* II, 227-8, nos. 58; 72 and 82)

(iv) The last reference to the tax

In the following extract from Origen, written probably in the first half of the 3rd century CE, we have the last reference in antiquity to the payment of the tax. What happened to it after that is not known. It may either have lapsed during the great inflation of the 3rd century (A.H.M. Jones, *The Later Roman Empire* II (Oxford, 1964), p. 947) or been abolished by the Emperor Julian.

(IV.68) It must be said that there is nothing surprising in great nations after their conquest winning permission from their ruler to use their own laws and lawcourts. At the present time the Romans are the rulers and the Jews pay the didrachm tax to them. Yet those of us with experience know that the ethnarch,[76] with Caesar's permission, has such authority over them (i.e. the Jews) that his rule is indistinguishable from that of a king. (Origen, *Epistola ad Africanum* 14 = *PG* 11, cols. 81-2)

(d) The total ban on Jewish access to Jerusalem in 135 CE

(IV.69) From that time on,[77] the whole race has been completely banned from setting foot on the territory around Jerusalem by a legal decree and ordinances of Hadrian, which ensured that not even from afar could they see their ancestral land. (Eusebius, *The History of the Church* 4.6.3)

(IV.70) You yourselves are aware[78] that care is taken by you to prevent any Jew from coming there, and that death is pronounced against any Jew who attempts to enter. (Justin Martyr, *Apologia* 77)

(e) Anti-Jewish rulings of the early Christian emperors

(IV.71) The Emperor Constantine (II) Augustus to Evagrius (Praetorian Prefect of Italy). If any Jew believes that he must buy a slave of another sect or nation, the slave shall immediately be made over to the state treasury. If he circumcises the slave he has bought, he shall not only be penalised by the loss of the slave but even be punished with a capital sentence.[79] If a Jew does not hesitate to buy slaves who are associated with the venerable faith (i.e. Christianity), all those who are found with him shall immediately be removed and there shall be no delay in depriving him of possession of those men who are Christians ... Given on the Ides of August during the 2nd consulship of Constantius Augustus and the 1st of Constans Augustus. (*Codex Theodosianus* 16.9.2 – Linder no. 11 = 13 August, 339 CE)

(IV.72) The Emperors and Augusti, Valentinian (II), Theodosius (I) and Arcadius, to Cynegius, Praetorian Prefect. Let no Jew take in marriage a

Christian woman, nor a Christian engage in matrimony with a Jewess. If anyone performs an act of this kind, he shall be charged for this crime as for adultery, with the freedom to lay an accusation being allowed to the general public. Given on the day before the Ides of March at Thessalonica, during the consulship of Theodosius Augustus for the second time and Cynegius, the Most Renowned. (*Codex Theodosianus* 3.7.2 = Linder no. 18 – 14 March, 388 CE)

(**IV.73**) The same two Augusti (Honorius and Theodosius II) to Palladius, the Praetorian Prefect. Those living in the Jewish superstition are henceforth to be obstructed in their attempt to enter the public service. To those among either the Executive Agents (civil administrators) or the Palatini (financial officials) who have taken the oath of service, we give the opportunity of completing it and terminating it at its statutory term, ignoring the situation rather than favouring it. The concession we are prepared to make to a few at the present time is not to be allowed in future. We decree, however, that those in thrall to this nation's perversity who are proven to have entered the Military Service, are to be discharged forthwith, without deriving any credit or protection from former meritorious conduct. Of course we are not preventing Jews who have been instructed in the liberal arts from practising as advocates and we permit them to enjoy the honour of curial liturgies,[80] which they possess by virtue of the prerogative of birth and the splendour of their family. Since they ought to be satisfied with these things, they should not consider the ban on State Service as a mark of infamy. Issued on the 6th day before the Ides of March at Ravenna, during the 12th consulship of Honorius and the 8th of Theodosius, both Augusti. (*Codex Theodosianus* 16.8.24 = Linder no. 45 – 10 March, 418 CE)

V

The Jews among the Greeks

1. JEWS AS CITIZENS OF GREEK CITIES

The consensus nowadays is that Jews resident in the Greek cities of the eastern half of the Mediterranean were not *in general* citizens of those *poleis*. It seems that they were categorised as resident aliens (in Greek, *metoikoi*) – a classification which caused deep resentment, particularly at Alexandria, in long-established and well-integrated Jewish communities (see discussion at **V.80**). There are, however, a number of cases of *individual* Jews who apparently did enjoy full citizenship. Those who appear in lists of ephebes (i.e. gymnasium graduates) from Cyrene and elsewhere may reasonably be assumed to have done so: a gymnasium education (*paideia*), a *sine qua non* for the young citizen male in the Hellenistic and Roman periods, is usually taken as virtual proof of the possession of citizen status. And absolutely unambiguous is the evidence from Cilicia and Sardis: in a number of texts relating to those places, Jews explicitly state that they are in possession of local Greek citizenship. How they had come to acquire that coveted status is not known. There is, however, no doubt about its importance to them, in terms of both the financial benefits and the social clout it brought (**V.3-4**).

(a) Jewish gymnasium graduates at Cyrene

The following texts, extracts from ephebic lists found at Cyrene, each reveal one gymnasium graduate who almost certainly was Jewish: the names Iesous (**V.1**, line 2) and Ioudas (**V.2**) seem never to have been used by Greeks. For further Jewish graduates of the gymnasium, see **V.21-4**. For discussion of the onomastic criteria for establishing the likelihood of Jewish extraction, see introductory note at **V.21**.

(**V.1**) Iason, son of Karnis
Iesous*, son of Antiphilos
Ithannyras, son of Apollodoros
Orion, son of Orion
(*CJZC* no. 6, col. II – 1st century BCE)

(**V.2**) Chaireas, son of Ioudas. (*CJZC* no. 7c, line 13 – 1st century CE)

(b) A case of disputed citizenship at Alexandria

Despite the very fragmentary state of the following text, it is clear that the point at issue is the Alexandrian citizenship of the Jew, Helenos. While his father had been a citizen and he himself had been brought up as if he were a citizen too (i.e.

he had been given the appropriate gymnasium education), for reasons that are now unclear his status had been downgraded and he had thus become liable to the poll-tax. The confusion over his status is neatly illustrated by the scribal correction at the beginning of the document. It is generally assumed that the substitution there of Jew of Alexandria for Alexandrian came about because Helenos had initially given, perhaps unintentionally, misleading information about his civic status.

(V.3) To Gaios Tyrannios (Roman governor of Egypt), from Helenos, son of Tryphon, an Alexandrian (this word has been crossed out and corrected as), a Jew of Alexandria. Most mighty governor, although my father was an Alexandrian citizen and I myself have always lived here and received, as far as my father's means allowed, the appropriate education (*paideia*), I am in danger of not only being deprived of my native country (i.e. my Alexandrian citizenship) but also ... (text defective here). For it has come about that Horos, the public administrator ... of the month Tybi(?) ... for the reason of ... my father to his ancestral gymnasium (?) ... forcibly ... from the ephebate ... Kaisar ... written ... poll-tax ... the month Mecheir ... the remaining time for the poll-tax because of the age-limit of sixty. I beseech you, saviour of all, not to reject my plea, since I have not been troubled by either the first governors or you ... (*CPJ* II no. 151 – Alexandria; 7-4 BCE)

(c) Jewish citizens in Cilicia and at Sardis

For further examples, see **I.91** and Trebilco, *Jewish Communities*, p. 209, n. 34 (at Sardis); **V.10** (in Cilicia).

(V.4) Paul said, 'I am a Jew, from Tarsos in Cilicia, a citizen of no mean city. I beg you to allow me to speak to the people.' (*Acts of the Apostles* 21.39 – 1st century CE)

(V.5) Here lies Alexander, citizen of Anemurion,[1] a Jew, together with his wife. If anyone disturbs us, he shall pay to the most sacred treasury 2,500 denarii. (*CIJ* II no. 786 = *MAMA* III 222 – Korykos; 3rd century (?) CE)

(V.6) Pegasios, son of Pegasios, citizen of Sardis, with ... (*DF* no. 26 – 3rd or 4th century CE)

(V.7) Aur(elios) Alexander, also called Anatolios, citizen of Sardis, councillor, has adorned the third bay (of the synagogue) with mosaics. (Trebilco, *Jewish Communities* 2.4.5 = Kroll (forthcoming) no. 3 – 3rd or 4th century CE)

2. JEWS AS COUNCILLORS, MAGISTRATES AND OFFICIAL ENVOYS

The advantages to Jews of possessing full Greek citizenship were not just social and financial. Participation in the political life of the *polis* also became possible. Those with means (and an accommodating attitude towards the religious rituals of the Greek city-state) might even hope to sit on the city council (*boule*) and eventually hold public office. From the period before the third century CE, we have very few examples of either Jewish city councillors (*bouleutai*) or magistrates. But after that date, there are quite a number. There are two likely reasons for the increase: (1) epigraphic evidence of all kinds becomes more abundant from the third century onwards; (2) around 200 CE measures were taken by the emperors Severus and Caracalla to boost the number of Jews serving on city councils and holding local magistracies. The pride with which Jews after that date record their civic honours demonstrates how welcome this imperial initiative was to them, even though it had been inspired largely for fiscal reasons.

(a) As city councillors

General enablement for Jews to serve on city councils

(V.8) The divine Severus and Antoninus[2] permitted adherents of the Jewish religion (lit. *superstitio*) to hold public office but imposed upon them (only) such duties as did not offend against their religion. (*Digest* 50.2.3.3 = Linder no. 2)

Some individual councillors

Besides those listed here, see **I.91-2** and Trebilco, *Jewish Communities*, pp. 46-7 and 209, n. 34 (councillors from Sardis); **V.14-15**; **VI.6** and **21** (councillors from other cities of the Roman East).

(V.9) He (Didius Julianus, emperor briefly in 193 CE) built in Antioch the Great the so-called Plethrion because they had held the wrestling at the Olympic festival in the theatre. And because of a petition from the land-owners of the city of Antioch, who made the request, he granted them money for the construction of the Plethrion. They built it near the Kais-arion, having purchased the house that belonged to Asabinos, a councillor of the city who was a Jew by religion. It was situated near the Xystos and the Bath of Commodus.[3] (John Malalas, *Chronographia* 290 = *PG* 97, col. 440)

(V.10) Sarcophagus of Aur(elios) Eusanbatios, son of Menander, citizen of Korykos, councillor, and of his wife, the peerless and unforgettable Matrona, also called Photion. Here she lies and Photion, (the) grandson of Matrona and (Photi?)os, *doukenarios*[4] from Seleukeia[5] and their sweetest children. If anyone else wishes to place (another body) here, he shall pay to the heirs of the same Eusanbatios ... ounces (?) of gold. Do not lose heart, for no one is immortal, save the One who has ordered that this (i.e. the punishment for disturbing the grave) take place, (He) who has transposed us to the sphere of the stars.[6] (*CIJ* II no. 788 = *MAMA* III no. 262 – Korykos; 3rd century CE)

(V.11) I, Euphrosynos, councillor, have fulfilled my vow, together with my (text lost), Euphrosynos. (*DF* no. 24 – Sardis; 3rd or 4th century CE)

(V.12) I, Pegasios,[7] a councillor, have fulfilled my vow. (*DF* no. 25 – Sardis; 3rd or 4th century CE)

(b) Jews as local magistrates

A Jewish nomophylax at 1st century CE Cyrene

The *nomophylakes* (lit. guardians of the law) at Cyrene were annually elected magistrates, whose functions included the control of the public archives.

(V.13) (Year) 90 and (Year) 91.[8] During the priesthoods of Istros and Asklapos, the sons of Philiskos, the *nomophylakes* who held office together (were as follows): Lysis, son of P(oublios) Kointilios Apollos; Elazar[9] son of Iason; Gemellos, son of Alopex; Damis, son of Arimmas; Thrasymachos, son of Lysimachos ... (*CJZC* no. 8)

Two Jewish high-flyers at 3rd century CE Akmonia in Phrygia

An epitaph in four segments (here, (a)-(d)) from an altar-shaped tomb. While (a) is on the main face, (b), (c) and (d) each occupy one of the other three sides.

(V.14)
(a) Made in the year 328 (= 243-4 CE).
T(itos) Fl(abios) Alexander has built the tomb during his lifetime for himself and his wife Gaiana, as a memorial, having been councillor, held public office, lived an honourable life (and) harmed no one. After the interment of me, Alexander, and my wife, Gaiana, should anyone open the tomb, there will fall upon him the curses that have been written against his sight and the whole of his body and his children and his life.[10] If anyone tries to open (this tomb), he shall pay to the treasury a fine of 500 denarii.

(b) Office for maintaining peace (*eirenarchia*). Office of the corn supply (*seitonia*).

(c) Presidency of the council (*boularchia*). Office of market-regulator (*agoranomia*).

(d) Office of strategos (*strategia*). Office of corn supply (*seitonia*).[11]
(*CIJ* II no. 770)

A bi-partite epitaph (here, (a) and (b)) inscribed on the principal face and left hand side of the tomb.

(V.15)
(a) Year 333 (= 248-9 CE) Aur(elios) Phrougianos, son of Menokritos, and Aur(elia) Iouliane, his wife, have constructed (this tomb), during their lifetime, for Makaria his (or her) mother and Alexandria, their sweetest daughter, as a memorial. If anyone after their deposition places another corpse in it or transgresses by purchasing it, there shall be upon him the curses written in Deuteronomy.[12]

(b) Office of market-regulator (*agoranomia*). Office of corn supply (*seitoneia*). Office of police commander (*paraphylakeia*). Having undertaken all offices and liturgies and been *strategos*.[13]
(*CIJ* II no. 760.)

(c) A Jewish envoy?

(V.16) The people of Ptolemais in Cyrene to A(ulus) Terentius Varr(o) Murena, son of Aulus, their patron, through their envoys Itthallammon, son of Apellas and Simon, son of Simon.[14] (*CJZC* no. 36 – Lanuvium; 2nd half of the 1st century BCE)

3. JEWISH INFLUENCE UPON GREEK CIVIC LIFE

The only clear evidence for Jewish influence upon Greek civic life comes from second and third century CE Apamea in Phrygia, a city with a thriving Jewish community which probably went back to early Seleucid times (**I.18**). The evidence consists of numerous examples of the coin-type shown overleaf, on which is depicted, in the manner of a film-strip, the legend of Noah (in Greek, *Noe*) and the Ark. Two episodes from the story can be clearly identified: on the right of the coin, on top of Noah's now open but still floating Ark (neatly labelled with his name), we see the dove that had been sent out to discover if the flood-waters were subsiding but had returned 'not having found rest for her feet ... because the waters were on the whole face of the earth' (LXX *Genesis* 8.9), and, on the left, Noah and his wife leaving the Ark after it had finally 'beached' on Mt Ararat (LXX *Genesis* 8.18). The bird and the branch over-arching the space between the floating Ark and Noah's departing figure probably should be taken as an (inexact) allusion to a third, intervening, episode in the story – the dove's second return with the olive twig (here a rather substantial branch!), which had indicated to Noah that the flood-waters were indeed subsiding and land was near (LXX *Genesis* 9.11). Although this particular coin dates from the reign of Philip the Arab, Roman emperor from 243-9 CE, the type had been issued regularly since the 190s CE. For a full discussion of its design and social significance, see now Trebilco, *Jewish Communities*, pp. 86-95.

(V.17)
Legend around edge of coin: (Issued) under M(arkos) Aur(elios) Alexander, son of Alexander, High Priest of Apamea.
On the Ark itself: *Noe* (LXX form of Noah).
(Sketch based on Goodenough, *Jewish Symbols* III, fig. 700.)

4. JEWISH INVOLVEMENT IN GREEK CULTURAL LIFE

Besides participating in the political life of the *polis*, some Diasporan Jews also became involved in its cultural activities. Although Gentile writers of the Hellenistic and early Roman imperial periods are silent on this subject, from the Jewish writer Philo, a few inscriptions from Asia Minor and the writings of the Byzantine historian John Malalas (6th century), a tiny amount of information can be gleaned about Jewish donations to civic projects, Jewish attendance at the gymnasium and Jewish participation in Graeco-Roman leisure activities.

(a) Contributions to civic projects in Asia Minor

Presented here are two brief extracts from donor lists from western Asia Minor. While the contribution in the first was towards a festival in honour of Dionysos, the precise purpose of the donation in the second is unknown. From the rest of the document (not quoted here) it may safely be inferred, however, that it was for some kind of civic project.

(V.18) Niketas, son of Iason, a Jerusalemite[15] – 100 denarii. (*CIJ* II no. 749 – Iasos; mid-2nd century BCE)

(V.19) The former Jews[16] – ten thousand drachmas. (*CIJ* II no. 742 – Smyrna; reign of Hadrian – i.e. 117-138 CE)

(b) Jews and the gymnasium

A gymnasium at Jerusalem in the Hellenistic period

Although the following passage relates to Judaea and not the Diaspora, it has been included as it gives a much clearer picture than the inscriptions in **V.21-4** of what attendance at the gymnasium actually involved for Jews.

(V.20) When Seleukos (IV) died and Antiochos called Epiphanes took over the kingdom (175 BCE), Iason corruptly secured the High Priesthood (of the Jews) by offering the king at an audience three hundred and sixty talents of silver and eighty talents from some other source. In addition to these, he promised to pay another one hundred and fifty talents as well, provided he was allowed, with the king's authority, to set up for him a gymnasium and an ephebate (i.e. a body of youths to be trained in the gymnasium) and enrol the Jerusalemites as Antiochenes.[17] Once the king had given his approval and Iason had gained control of the office (of High Priest), he immediately made his compatriots switch to a Greek lifestyle. Setting aside the royal privileges secured for the Jews by John, the father of Eupolemos ..., he destroyed the traditional way of life and brought in new practices that were contrary to the Law. For he eagerly established a gymnasium under the very citadel and he induced the noblest of the youths to wear the *petasos*.[18] There was such a flowering of Greek fashion and such an advance of foreign practices through the extreme impurity of the impious Iason – no High Priest he! – that the priests were no longer keen to carry out their sacrificial duties. Despising the Temple and neglecting the sacrifices, they hurried to take part in the unlawful activities (i.e. nude wrestling and athletics) that were being laid on in the palaestra ... (2 *Maccabees* 4.7-14)

Extracts from ephebic lists

In the following extracts from ephebic lists of the early Roman imperial period, only for those ephebes whose names are italicised can a Jewish origin be either assumed or argued. For those with the Hebrew names and/or patronymics Elazar, Ioudas and Ioses (a shortened form of Joseph) such an origin is virtually certain – Greeks did not use Hebrew names. Strongly suggestive of a Jewish origin are the names Theodotos, Theudas (its shortened form) and Dosas (an abbreviated form of Dositheos). Not only are they (in their full form) precise literal translations of the common Hebrew 'gift of God' names, Yehonatan and Mattathiah/Nathanel, but they are known to have been popular with Greek-speaking Diasporan Jews. Simon, son of Pothon (**V.21**, line 1) may also have been of Jewish extraction. The name Simon, while greatly favoured by Jews because of its similarity to Simeon, was not much used by Greeks. For these (and other) names used by Diasporan Jews, see Tcherikover, *CPJ* I, *Prolegomena*, pp. 27-30; N. Cohen, 'The names of the translators in the Letter of Aristeas: a study in the dynamics of cultural transition', *JSJ* 15 (1984), pp. 32-64; M.H. Williams, 'Palestinian Jewish personal names in Acts', in R. Bauckham (ed.), *The Book of Acts in its Palestinian Setting = The Book of Acts in its First Century Setting* 4 (Grand Rapids, Michigan 1995), pp. 79-113.

(**V.21**) *Simon, son of Pothon*
Timarchos, son of Akesandros
Alexis, son of Alexis
Apollodoros, son of Thaliarchos
Aristis, son of Dionysios
Theukrisios, son of Patron
Theudotos*, son of Theudotos*
Dionysios, son of Olympos
Bartybas, son of Bartybas

Elaszar (sic), son of Elazar
Agathokles, son of Elazar
Onomarchos, son of Leonidas
Alexander, son of Poseidonios
Aiglanor and Ptolemy, the sons of Ptolemy
(*CJZC* no. 7a, right hand column, lines 39ff. – Cyrene; 3/4 CE)

(**V.22**) Dionysios, son of Dionysios
Hieronymos, son of Eirenaios
Dosas*, son of Dosas*
Ioudas, son of Euodos
Tryphon, son of Tryphon
Dionysios, son of Dionysios
Theophilos, son of Theophilos
Artemeisios, son of Theudas*.
(*REJ* 101 (1937), 85-6 – Iasos; early imperial period)

(**V.23**) *Aur(elios) Ioses**
Aur(elios) Ioses*
(*CIJ* I² no. 721c – Coronea (Greece); 246 CE)

A young men's association at Hypaepa (near Sardis)

A late 2nd century CE inscription that possibly functioned as a seat marker in the palaestra at Hypaepa, a town to the south of Sardis. The younger Jews mentioned in it (in Greek: *neoteroi*) probably belonged to a young men's association. Such associations were comprised of recently graduated ephebes. Though primarily devoted to gymnastic exercise, they also played a role in political and public life. See Trebilco, *Jewish Communities*, p. 177.

(**V.24**) Of the younger Jews. (*CIJ* II no. 755)

(c) Participation in Greek entertainments

(i) Jews at the theatre

Those who have difficulty with the idea of Jews attending the theatre in antiquity claim that Philo in the passage immediately below is producing nothing more than a few conventional remarks on a well-worn theme and he himself never witnessed the pagan entertainment he describes. Given the existence of unambiguous epigraphic evidence for Jewish attendance at the theatre (**V.26**), such fastidiousness on his part seems unlikely.

(**V.25**) I have often noticed when I happened to be in the theatre the different effects (on the audience) of a single tune produced by the tragic actors on the stage or the players of the lyre. Some are so carried away that in their excitement they join together and involuntarily shout out their approval. Others are so unaffected that you might think them no different than the lifeless seats on which they are sitting. Others, again, are so put off that they actually leave the performance, blocking their ears with their hands as they go ...[19] (Philo, *On Drunkenness* 177)

A Jewish seat-marker in the theatre at Miletos

The second half of this probably late 2nd/early 3rd century CE inscription has been much debated. For a summary of views, see Trebilco, *Jewish Communities*, pp. 159-62. The translation here is in accordance with E. Schürer's widely accepted emendation of the text, for which see *Geschichte des jüdischen Volkes im Zeitalter Jesu Christi*[4] III (Leipzig, 1909), p. 174, n. 70. What is not in doubt is *Jewish* occupancy of seats in the theatre.

(V.26) Place of the Jews and of the Godfearers. (*CIJ* II no. 748)

(ii) Jews at the hippodrome

Philo at the hippodrome

(V.27) If people through heedlessness go unarmed, unprepared and without fear into the lairs of wild beasts, let them blame themselves for the consequences and not Nature, because they neglected to take precautions when they could have done. I have seen people yielding to folly at the hippodrome. By standing in the middle, when they should have been sitting down and watching in an orderly fashion, they were knocked over by the rush of the four-horse chariots and crushed under the hooves and wheels. (Philo, *De providentia* 2.58)

Jews as supporters of the Blue circus faction

Since in the sources for our chosen period Jewish support for the Blues is only implied (see **V.28**), I have decided to include here two slightly later texts which make the link explicit.

(V.28) From the first year of Gaius Caesar (37 CE) and for the three years until the end of his reign, the Green faction[20] ruled the roost both at Rome and in the cities generally. It assumed from him its licence to act as it pleased, for he was its supporter.[21] In the third year of his reign in Antioch in Syria, the members of the Blue faction of that city chanted in the theatre against the local Greens, 'Time raises up and Time casts down. The Greens are lechers.' Pronoios,[22] the consular governor, was watching at the time. A great public riot broke out and disaster befell the city, for the Greeks of Antioch, doing battle with the Jews of the city, killed many of them and burned down their synagogues. (John Malalas, *Chrono-graphia* 244 = *PG* 97, col. 373)

(V.29) Those in the Green faction of the city of Antioch started a stone-fight against the Blues during a spectacle at the hippodrome, while Thalassios, the consular governor (*c.* 490 CE) was watching ... Six months later the Antiochenes of the Green faction gathered again and, during a riot at the hippodrome, killed many people. They burned down the synagogue called after Asabinos[23] because the Jews were supporters of the Blue faction. And they plundered all that was in the synagogue and those who lived there. (John Malalas, *Excerpta de insidiis* 166-7)

A 5th-6th century CE *seat-marker from the Odeon at Aphrodisias*

(**V.30**) Place of Blues, of the elder Jews (*Hebreon ton paleion*). (*SEG* 37 (1987) no. 846 = Roueché, no. 180.iii.)

5. GREEK CULTURAL INFLUENCES ON THE JEWS

Apart from the widespread adoption by Diasporan Jews of Greek personal names, most notably illustrated in **I.107** above, the clearest indication of Greek cultural influence on them is their heavy use from the 3rd century BCE onwards of Greek itself. Nearly all the texts in this book, whether emanating from the Greek-speaking East or the predominantly Latin-speaking West, were originally written in it. Indeed, until the re-Hebraization of the Diaspora in the Byzantine period, it was the principal language not only of everyday converse but of literature and the synagogal liturgy. To document this fully is beyond the scope of this volume. (For a brief overview of some of the more important works of Jewish Diasporan literature, see now J.M.G. Barclay, *Jews in the Mediterranean Diaspora* (Edinburgh, 1996) chs 6, 7 and 12.) In this section a selection of texts is presented which illustrate Greek influence on Jewish civic, religious, legal and funerary practices. The fact that most of this evidence is epigraphic is not fortuitous: the epigraphic habit itself was a Jewish borrowing from the Greeks.

(a) Greek cultural influence in the civic sphere

Although Diasporan Jews in general were not citizens of the *poleis* in which they had made their homes, they were nonetheless profoundly affected by Greek civic practices. This can be seen in (i) their adoption of Greek civic terms for their own community institutions and officials, (ii) the official-sounding Greek titles borne by Jewish women of high social status, (iii) the Greek-style public honours formally granted to synagogal benefactors (e.g. gold crowns, gilded shields, privileged seating) and (iv) the Greek phraseology employed by the richer members of the Jewish community when making public benefactions.

(i) Greek influence on Jewish community terminology

This is most clearly seen in the widespread adoption by the Jews of the common Greek constitutional terms *gerousia* (council of elders) and *archon* (ruler) for (respectively) the synagogal council and its chief executive officer. Besides the passage quoted here, see also Synagogal officers and dignitaries (**II.19-75**). Nearly all the titles listed there were either borrowed directly from the Greeks or patterned on Greek usage.

(V.31) Of the members of the *gerousia*,[24] three men, Euodos and Tryphon and Andron, had become dispossessed of their property, having been despoiled in one fell swoop of everything they had in their houses. Flaccus knew perfectly well what they had suffered, for he had been told all about it when he had summoned our *archons*[25] earlier, ostensibly to bring about a reconciliation between the Jews and the rest of the city. (Philo, *In Flaccum* 76)

(ii) Community titles borne by women

In a small number of inscriptions mainly of the fourth century and later we meet Jewish women with titles of a type more commonly borne by male officers of the synagogal community (e.g. *archisynagogos*). Were these women also serving officers of the community, as has been argued by Brooten, or were their titles largely honorific, as has traditionally be assumed? The Jewish evidence on its own permits no conclusion to be drawn, for the only activity in which these women are shown engaged is making benefactions (**V.32** and **VI.37**). Evidence from Greek society, however, whence the practice of bestowing official-sounding titles upon Jewish women clearly was derived (there is no evidence for it among the Jews of Judaea/Palestine), suggests that they were largely honorific. For although women were often active and influential in the communal life of the cities of the Greek East, in the process of government itself they generally were not involved. On this controversial subject, see, for example, B. Brooten, *Women Leaders in the Ancient Synagogues* (Chico California, 1982); A. Cameron and A. Kuhrt (eds), *Images of Women in Antiquity*[2] (London, 1993), chs 4 and 14; W. Horbury, 'Women in the synagogue' in *CHJ* III (forthcoming). For other female title-bearers in this collection, see **II.53-5** (*presbyterai*); **II.71-3** and **VII.30** (Mothers of the Community); **VI.37** (*archisynagogos*).

(V.32) From Theopempte, *archisyn(agogos)* and her son Eusebios [as a result of a vow?]. (*CIJ* II no. 756 = *DF* no. 29 – Myndos, Caria; 4th-5th century CE(?))

(V.33) Sophia from Gortyn, *presbytera* and *archisynagogissa* of Kisamos, lies here. The memory of the just is for ever. Amen. (*CIJ* I^2 no. 731c – Crete; 4th-5th century CE)

(V.34) Tomb of Peristeria, *archegissa*.[26] (*CIJ* I^2 no. 696b – Phthiotic Thebes; undated)

(iii) Greek-style honours awarded by Jewish communities

Two honorific decrees of the Jewish politeuma at Berenice

Greek influence is revealed in these decrees by, inter alia, their original language (Greek), the nature of the honours awarded, the decision to leave a public record of them on a costly and prominently displayed marble stele and the final voting formula.

(V.35) Year 55,[27] Phaophi 25, at the assembly of the Feast of Tabernacles (*skenopegia*),[28] in the archonship of Kleandros, the son of Stratonikos; Euphranor, son of Ariston; Sosigenes, son of Sosippos; Andromachos, son of Andromachos; Markos Lailios Onasion, the son of Apollonios; Philonides, son of Hagemon; Autokles, the son of Zenon; Sonikos, son of Theodotos; Iosepos*, son of Straton: because Markos Tittios, son of Sextos, of the Aemilian tribe, a worthy and excellent man, since coming to the province to administer public affairs[29] has directed their governance with benevolence and skill and in his behaviour consistently shown himself to be of an eirenic disposition, and has behaved unoppressively both in these (public matters) and with regard to those of the citizens who have approached him privately, and because for the Jews of our *politeuma*[30] both publicly and privately his administration has been useful and he has not ceased to perform deeds in keeping with his own essential nobility of character, therefore the *archons* and the *politeuma* of the Jews in Berenice have decided to laud him and crown him 'by name' at each gathering and each New Moon with a wreath of olive leaves and (a fillet of) wool. The *archons* are to inscribe the decree on a stele of Parian stone (i.e. marble) and to place it in the the the most conspicuous part of the amphitheatre.[31] All (pebbles) white (i.e. decided unanimously).[32] (*CJZC* no. 71)

(V.36) (Year)[33] ... Phamenoth 5, in the archonship of Arimmas, son of (name lost); Dorion, son of Ptolemy; Zelaios, son of Gnaios; Ariston, son of Araxa[...]; Sarapion, son of Andromachos; Nikias, son of (name lost); (name lost), son of Simon. Since Dekmos* Oualerios Dionysios, son of Gaios ... remains a fine and good man [in word and deed and inclination] and does good, whenever he can, both publicly and privately, to each of the citizens, and has plastered the floor of the amphitheatre and decorated the walls with paintings, the *archons* and *politeuma* of the Jews in Berenice have decided to enrol him in the ... of the ... and exempt him from all liturgies (i.e. public duties in the Jewish community). Likewise (they have decided) to crown him 'by name' at each meeting and New Moon with a wreath of olive-leaves and (a fillet of) wool. After inscribing this decree on a stele of Parian stone (i.e. marble), the *archons* are to place it in the most conspicuous part of the amphitheatre. All (the voting pebbles) white (i.e. decided unanimously).[34]

Dekmos Oualerios Dionysios, son of Gaios, has plastered the floor and the amphitheatre and painted it at his own expense as a contribution to the *politeuma*. (*CJZC* no. 70)

Public honours for a female benefactor at 3rd century(?) CE Phokaia in Ionia

(V.37) Tation, daughter of Straton, the son of Enpedon, out of her own resources has built the house (i.e. the synagogue) and the enclosed court-yard and graciously given them to the Jews. The Jewish community (*synagoge*) has honoured Tation, daughter of Straton, son of Enpedon, with a golden crown[35] and (the) privilege of *proedria*.[36] (*CIJ* II no. 738 = *DF* no. 13)

(iv) Use of typical Greek phraseology in making public benefactions

The Ptolemaic 'loyalty formula'

The opening words of the inscription below constitute 'the regular "loyalty for-mula" used in Ptolemaic dedications to deities both Greek and Egyptian' (see P.M. Fraser, *Ptolemaic Alexandria* I (Oxford, 1972), pp. 282-3). It was attractive to Jews because it enabled them, while expressing their wishes for the safety and well-being of the their rulers, to avoid ascribing divinity to them. For other examples, see **I.102-3**, **IV.1-2** and **11**.

(V.38) On behalf of King Ptolemy and Queen Kleopatra and their children, Hermias and his wife Philotera and their children (have given) this *exedra* (annexe?) to the prayer-house. (*CIJ* II no. 1444 = HN no. 28 – Athribis; 2nd or 1st century BCE)

'Out of his / their own resources'

For other Jewish examples of this heavily used evergetist phrase, see **II.7** and **61**; **VII.11** and **17**.

(V.39) Ptolemy, son of Leukios, citizen of Tlos, has built the tomb (*heroon*) from its foundations out of his own resources (for) himself and on behalf of his son Ptolemy, son of Ptolemy, son of Leukios, on account of the archon-ship which he has held amongst us Jews.[37] It is to be the property of all the Jews[38] and no one else is to bury anyone else in it. If anyone is discovered burying someone else (in it), he shall pay to the people of Tlos (amount lost) drachmas (rest of text missing). (*CIJ* II no. 757 = *TAM* II.2, no. 612 – perhaps late 1st century CE)

(b) In religious matters

(i) Greek influence on the language of the synagogue

The enormous impact of Greek culture on Diasporan Jewry can be seen very clearly in the need felt by the Alexandrian Jews, probably as early as the first part of the 3rd century BCE, to start making a Greek translation of the Hebrew

Scriptures. The validation legend of this ambitious project, which took decades, if not centuries, to complete, and culminated in the production of the Septuagint, first surfaces in, and forms a large part of, the so-called *Letter of Aristeas*, a pseudonymous Jewish work produced in Ptolemaic Egypt, probably in the 3rd or 2nd century BCE. Only a few extracts of this long text, a paraphrase of which is to be found in Josephus, *Jewish Antiquities* 12.11-118, are quoted here. The Septuagint itself remained the 'Bible' of the Greek-speaking Diaspora until the 2nd century CE, when its hijacking by the Christians resulted in the use in the synagogue of newer and more literal translations of the Hebrew Scriptures, such as those of Aquila and Theodotion (**VII.25**).

The validation legend of the translation of the Septuagint

(**V.40**) King Ptolemy (II Philadelphos) to Eleazar, the High Priest, greetings and good health. Since it has come about that many Jews have settled in our country, some dragged away from Jerusalem by the Persians during the time when they were in power and others coming into Egypt with our father (Ptolemy I) as prisoners of war ... Now since we wish to favour both these and all the Jews in the inhabited world and those yet to be born, we have decided that your Law is to be translated into Greek from the so-called Hebraic characters in use among you, so that we may have it in our library along with the other royal books. You will be acting nobly and worthily of our zeal if you select elderly men of good character, who are skilled in the Law and able to translate. (There are to be) six from each tribe, so that from many (contributions) agreement may be reached. For it is an investigation into weighty matters and we are of the opinion that when it has been completed we shall win great renown ... Farewell.

To this letter Eleazar replied to the best of his ability (as follows): Eleazar, the High Priest, to King Ptolemy, his true friend, greetings. Good health to you yourself, your sister, Queen Arsinoe, and your children ... We, too, are in good health. When we received your letter, we were overjoyed on account of your decision and fine plan. We assembled the whole people and read it out to them, so that they might know of your piety towards our God ... And the whole people prayed that everything might turn out for you as you wish, and that God, who is the Lord of All, might preserve your kingdom in peace with honour, and that the transcription of the Holy Law might be to your advantage and security. Then, in the presence of all, we selected elderly men of noble character, six from each tribe, and sent them off bearing (the books of) the Law. We beseech you, O righteous king, when the transcription of the books has taken place, to give orders that the men may be returned safely to us. Farewell. (*Letter of Aristeas*, extracts from 35-45)

(**V.41**) After three days (of banqueting with King Ptolemy), Demetrius (the royal librarian) took them (the translators from Jerusalem) and traversed the breakwater, seven stades long, to the island (of Pharos). He crossed the bridge and proceeded to the northerly parts (of the island). On calling a meeting in a house built by the seashore, which was magnificently appointed and very secluded, he urged the men to carry through the work of translation. For everything of which they had need had been amply supplied. And they did carry it out, arriving at unanimity on each point through mutual comparison. An exact fair copy was made under Demetrius' direction of the agreed version. The sessions went on until the ninth hour. After that, they would break off to take care of their bodily requirements. Everything of which they had need was lavishly provided. Further, each day Dorotheus[39] made available to them everything that he had prepared for the king, for he had been ordered to do so by the king. Every day, early in the morning, they would present themselves at court. Having greeted the king, they would go off to their own place. They would wash their hands in the sea, as is the custom with all the Jews. Once they had prayed to God, they would turn to reading and the clarification of each passage ... And so it came about that in seventy-two days the work of transcription was completed. It was as if through some design that a coincidence such as this[40] had taken place. (*Letter of Aristeas*, extracts from 301-7)

Use of the LXX and the Aquila translation of the Scriptures by Diasporan Jews

This is best exemplified by setting out three epitaphs of approximately the same date and origin (i.e. 3rd-4th century Rome), in each of which there appears a Greek version of *Proverbs* 10.7 (the memory of the righteous one (be) for a blessing). While in the first, we see an attempt to replicate the rather loose Septuagintal translation of this passage (the memory of the righteous ones (be) with praises), in the second the more exact Aquilan rendering of the passage is reproduced. In the third a mixture of both versions has been discerned (e.g. by van der Horst, *Ancient Jewish Epitaphs*, pp. 37-8). After the re-Hebraization of Diasporan Jewry in the 5th to 6th centuries, the passage, when used in epitaphs, appears consistently in Hebrew (see, for instance, *CIJ* I nos. 625 and 635).

(**V.42**) To ...tos, a teacher of the Law (*nomod[idaskalos]*). The memory of the righteous one (be) with praise. In peace your sleep. (*CIJ* I no. 201 = Noy II no. 307)

(**V.43**) Here lies Makedonis*, the Hebrew, from Caesarea in Palestine, son of Alexander. The memory of the righteous one (be) for a blessing. In peace your sleep. (*CIJ* I no. 370 = Noy II no. 112)

(**V.44**) Here lies Amachis*, also called Primos. The memory of the righteous one, whose praises are true, (be) for a blessing. In peace your sleep. (*CIJ* I no. 86 = Noy II no. 276)

(ii) Ex voto benefactions to the synagogue

For other *ex voto* synagogue inscriptions, **II.7**; **66** and **75**; **V.11-12**.

(V.45) To God,[41] the invincible, and to the sovereign synagogue, I, Aurelios Protoktetos, having prayed and seen my prayer answered, have dedicated (this) as a thank-offering. (*DF* no. 35 – Amastris in Paphlagonia; 3rd century CE)

(V.46) Eupithis, having prayed for herself, and her husband, and her children, and her whole household, has made the place (i.e. covered part of the synagogue floor with mosaics).[42] (*IGLS* IV no. 1336 = *DF* no. 55 – Apamea in Syria; 391-2 CE)

(iii) Visitation of Jews to pagan temples

The following, much discussed, graffiti come from rocks near the Temple of Pan near Apollinopolis Magna/Edfu in Upper Egypt. They are generally thought to date from the 2nd-1st century BCE.

(V.47) Praise to God! Theudotos*, son of Dorion, a Jew, safe from the sea.[43] (*CIJ* II no. 1537 = HN no. 121)

(V.48) Praise God! Ptolemy, son of Dionysios, a Jew. (*CIJ* II no. 1538 = HN no. 122)

(V.49) I, Lazaros,[44] have come for the third time. (HN no. 123)

(iv) Participation in Greek religious rituals

Incubation at the Amphiareion at Oropos

The following inscription comes from a stele, erected by the Jew, Moschos, at the shrine of Amphiaraos at Oropos on the border between northern Attica and Boeotia probably in the first half of 3rd century BCE following his incubation there – i.e. sleeping within the precincts of the shrine, in order to receive a dream vision from the resident deity.

(V.50) ... Phrynidas (will release) Moschos to be free, dependent on no one. If anything happens to Phrynidas before the time (of the *paramone*)[45] elapses, let Moschos go free, wherever he wishes. With good fortune. Witnesses: Athenodoros, son of Mnasikon, of Oropos; Biottos, son of Eudikos, of Athens; Charinos, son of Anticharmos, of Athens; Athenades, son of Epigonos, of Oropos; Hippon, son of Aischylos, of Oropos.

Moschos, son of Moschion, a Jew, as a result of a dream (has set up this stele) at the command of the god Amphiaraos and Hygeia, in accordance with the orders of Amphiaraos and Hygeia to write these things on a stele and set (it) up by the altar. (*CIJ* I² no. 711b)

Participation in ruler cult in Egypt

(V.51) In the twenty-fifth year of King Ptolemy,[46] son of Ptolemy and of Arsinoe, gods Adelphoi, when Dositheos, the son of Drimylos[47] was the priest of (the deified) Alexander and of the gods Adelphoi and the gods Euergetai ... (*CPJ* I no. 127d)

Sacrifice Greek-style at Antioch, 66 CE

(V.52) Antiochos (the apostate son of a Jewish *archon* at Antioch) further inflamed the fury (of the Greeks of Antioch against the Jews). Thinking that he would provide proof of his conversion and hatred of Jewish ways by sacrificing in the Greek manner, he recommended that they compel the other Jews to do the same. (Josephus, *Jewish War* 7.50-1)

(c) Greek influence in legal matters

From stray inscriptions and papyri that have turned up in various parts of the Graeco-Roman world it can be seen that some Diasporan Jews at least were prepared to conduct their affairs according to local (Gentile) usage even though that might involve using common pagan oath-formulae, attendance at pagan temples or even contravening the Torah. How widespread such behaviour was, we have no means of knowing. For discussion of the papyrological evidence, some of which is cited in (iii) below, see J. Mélèze-Modrzejewski, 'Jewish law and Hellenistic legal practice in the light of Greek papyri from Egypt' in N.S. Hecht et al (eds), *An Introduction to the History and Sources of Jewish Law* (Oxford, 1996).

(i) Use of the common Greek juridical formula – By Zeus, Earth and Sun

The Jewish identity of the next two inscriptions has been inferred mainly from the divine epithets that appear in them.

(V.53) To God, Most High, All-powerful and Blessed. In the reign of King Mithridates (?), the Friend of (text uncertain) and the Lover of the Fatherland, year 338 (of the Bosporan era), month Deios. Pothos, the son of Strabon, has dedicated to the prayer-house, in accordance with his vow, his home-bred slave, named Chrysa, on the condition that she be unharmed and unmolested by all (his) heirs. By Zeus, Earth and Sun. (*CIJ* I² no. 690 = *CIRB* no. 1123 – Gorgippia in the Crimea; 41 CE)

(V.54) To God, Most High, All-powerful and Blessed. In the reign of King Rheskouporis, the Friend of Caesar and the Friend of Rome, the Pious, year 364 (of the Bosporan era), month Daisios. I, Neokles, son of Athenodoros, set at liberty under Zeus, Earth (and) Sun ... (text defective at this point) with the assent of my father Athenodoros, son of Athenaios, on condition that they be unharmed and unmolested by all my heirs. They are to go wherever they desire because of the valid order made by me. (*CIJ* I² no. 690a = *CIRB* no. 1126 – Gorgippia; 67-8 CE)

(ii) Attendance at pagan shrines to conduct legal transactions

(**V.55**) During the archonship of Herakleidas, in the month of Poitropios, Ioudaios,[48] son of Pindaros, has, with the agreement of his son Pindaros, sold to Apollo for five silver minas a male slave, Amyntas by name, for the purpose of freeing him and he (Apollo) has the money. Guarantor: Kleon, son of Kleudamos. Amyntas is to stay with Ioudaios for as long as Ioudaios lives, doing everything that is required of him to the best of his ability. If he does not, Ioudaios is empowered to punish him as he thinks fit but he may not sell him. If anything happens to Ioudaios (i.e. should he die), Amyntas shall be free. Inasmuch as Amytas has entrusted the sale to the god, so he is to be free and totally immune from seizure for the rest of his life. If anyone does lay hands on Amyntas in order to enslave him, let him who chances to be by rescue him since he is free and let the guarantor guarantee the sale to the god. Witnesses: the archons [Nikatas, Sostratos, Kallia]s; laymen, Timokles, Xenokritos, Sostratos, Tarantinos, [Phil]okrates. (*CIJ* I no. 711 – Delphi; 119 BCE)

(iii) Adoption of Ptolemaic loan procedures in Egypt

In several papyri from Ptolemaic Egypt we see Jews lending money to each other at interest, a practice which was in flagrant contravention of *Deuteronomy* 23.19. In these transactions the standard Ptolemaic rate of two drachmas per mina per month was routinely used. Besides the two documents presented here, note also **IV.6**.

(**V.56**) Mousaios, son of Simon, a Jew of the Epigone (i.e. army reservist), has lent to Lasaites, son of Izi..is, Jew of the Epigone, 108 drachmas of copper at par, the interest (being) 2 drachmas per month ... Keeper of the contract, Dositheos.[49] Charge: 4 obols (?). (*CPJ* I no. 20 – Tebtynis; 228-221 BCE)

(**V.57**) In the twenty-fourth year of the reign of Ptolemy son of Ptolemy (V) and Arsinoe, gods Philopatores, the priest of Alexander and the gods Adelphoi and the gods Euergetai and the gods Philopatores and the gods Epiphaneis, and the *athlophoros* of Berenike Euergetis, and the *kanephoros* of Arsinoe Philadelphos and the priestess of Arsinoe Philopator being those officiating at Alexandria, on the twenty-eighth of the month of Dystros, being Thoth twenty-eighth, in Krokodilopolis in the Arsinoite nome. Apollonios, son of Protogenes, Jew of the Epigone (army reservist), has lent to Sostratos, son of Neoptolemos, Jew of the Epigone, two talents three thousand drachmas of copper money without interest for one year from the date above written on the security of the house belonging to him and courtyard and all the appurtenances situated at Apias in the division of Themistes, of which the measurements are, from south to north twenty cubits, from west to east twenty cubits (approx. 100 square yards), the adjacent features being, at the date written above, to the south, the house of Sopatra, to the north and east, streets, to the west, the house of Harpalos and Sostratos. Sostratos shall repay this loan to Apollonios within the year. If he does not repay it in accordance with what has been written, Apollonios shall have the right to lay claim to the security in accordance with the (royal) edict. Sostratos shall guarantee to Apollonios this security and shall produce it unencumbered, unpledged, unliable for another debt and free from royalties. If he does not guarantee it or produce it in accordance with what has been written or if any risk occurs with regard to this security whether in whole or in part in any way, Sostratos shall repay this debt to Apollonios immediately within the year. If he does not repay it in accordance with what has been written, Sostratos shall forthwith forfeit to Apollonios the loan increased by one half and for the overtime interest at the rate of two drachmas per mina per month. This contract shall be valid everywhere.

(2nd hand) Through Boubakes also called Stheneus.[50]

(3rd hand) Apollonios, about 35 years old, tall, fair-skinned, with bright eyes and ears that stick out. Sostratos, about 35 years old, of medium build, fair-skinned ... with a scar over his right eyebrow.[51] (*CPJ* I no. 23)

(d) Greek influence on funerary practice

Jewish tombs in Judaea, at least in the first centuries BCE and CE, tend to be anonymous. When they do bear an epitaph, it seldom contains anything more than the name of the deceased and his/her patronymic. Funerary epithets, elaborate metrical epitaphs and instructions relating to the maintenance and protection of the tomb – all common features of the Greek funerary scene – are very rare. Among many Diasporan Jews, this low-key attitude to burial long continued. In the catacombs used by Roman Jewry, the greater part of which was Greek-speaking, most of the burials are anonymous. Epitaphs tend to be simple and formulaic. Although epithets do occur, they are distinctly a minority usage. In some Diasporan communities, however, most notably those of Asia Minor, Jews were considerably influenced by what their Gentile neighbours did. They erected tombs similar to theirs, and on those tombs, many of them situated in the common city cemetery, they had epitaphs inscribed in the prevailing local idiom. These often included instructions for the maintenance of the grave and threats against those who tried to re-use it. Usually the only reason we can tell that these graves are Jewish is the rare presence of a Hebrew name, the epithet *Ioudaios* (Jew) or a Jewish symbol such as the menorah.

(i) Funerary epithets

Adjectives and phrases emphasising the estimable qualities of the deceased are a common feature of Greek epitaphs and, through Greek influence, Latin ones as well. (The best treatment of the whole subject is still R. Lattimore's *Themes in Greek and Latin Epitaphs* (Urbana, Illinois, 1942).) Given the widespread nature of the practice in the Graeco-Roman world, it is not surprising that some Jews in some places adopted the habit too and the epithets they tended to favour were those popular with the local gentiles. To illustrate the appearance in a Jewish context of *Greek* funerary epithets and the considerable variation in usage between one area and another, a small but representative selection is presented here of epitaphs from our two richest sources of Jewish funerary material – Leontopolis in Lower Egypt and Rome.

Leontopolis

(V.58) O Eleazar, untimely dead, excellent fellow, everyone's friend. About 20 years old. Me[cheir?] ... (*CIJ* II no. 1453 = HN no. 42 – 2nd century BCE – 1st century CE)

(V.59) Ioan(n)es, son of Ioan(n)es, bridegroom, untimely dead, everyone's friend and harmer of none, excellent fellow, farewell. Aged about 30. (*CIJ* II no. 1468 = HN no. 57 and Plate XVI – 2nd century BCE)

(V.60) Year 30. Pharmouthi 27. Iesous, son of Sambaios, untimely dead, childless, excellent fellow, farewell. (*CIJ* II no. 1476 = HN no. 65 and Plate XXIII – 1st century CE(?))

(V.61) Mari(o)n, priestess,[52] an excellent woman, everyone's friend, who did no harm and loved her neighbours, farewell. About 50 years. In the 3rd year of Caesar, Payni 13. (*CIJ* II no. 1514 = HN no. 84 – Leontopolis; 27 BCE)

Rome (Greek epitaphs only)

Although all the common Greek 'family-loving' funerary epithets (e.g. *philopator, philometor, philadelphos*) are attested in Jewish epitaphs at Rome, their numbers are tiny. By far the most frequently occurring Greek epithets are *glukus/glukeia* (sweet), which is applied not just to children but adult men and women too, and *kalos biosas(a)* (he/she, who has lived a good life). For *philogoneus* (parent-loving) and other uniquely Jewish epithets that have been patterned on Greek usage, see Community Values at Chapter II § 4 (a), (c), (d) and (e).

(V.62) (a) Theodotos, foster-father, to his sweetest child. Would that I who reared you, Ioustos, my child, could place you in a coffin of gold. Now, O Lord, in your righteousness, (grant that) the sleep of Ioustos, an incomparable child, (be) in peace.

(b) Here I lie, Ioustos, aged 4 years (and) 8 months, sweet to my foster-father.[53] (*CIJ* I² no. 358 = Noy II no. 25 – 3rd-4th century CE(?))

(V.63) Here lies Thaiophilos (*sic*), *gerousiarch*, who lived a good life and was well regarded. Theophilos and Eusebi(o)s (have set this up) for their sweetest father. (May) your memory (be for a blessing?). (*CIJ* I² no. 119 = Noy II no. 354 – 3rd-4th century CE(?))

(V.64) Here lies Probos, a child, who lived for two years, 1 month and three days, a lover of his father (and) a lover of his mother. In peace your sleep. (*CIJ* I no. 152 = Noy II no. 254 – 3rd-4th century CE(?))

(ii) Metrical epitaphs

Since the composition of metrical epitaphs in Greek and (through Greek influence) Latin, was widespread in Graeco-Roman antiquity, it is not surprising that the Jews were aware of the practice and occasionally practised it themselves. Most of the examples known to us come from Leontopolis in Lower Egypt and are Greek. (For a comprehensive listing and discussion of these epitaphs, see now P. van der Horst, 'Jewish poetical tomb inscriptions' in *SEJE*, pp. 129-47.) Three only are presented here (for another, see **II.26**), but without any attempt at metrical translation. Of these, the most accomplished is the first, the sole Jewish instance of that well-known Greek epitaph-form – the dialogue between the deceased and the passer-by. On the congruity of the ideas expressed in these Greek-style epitaphs with those found in Jewish literature, see W. Horbury, 'Jewish inscriptions and Jewish literature in Egypt, with special reference to Ecclesiasticus' in *SEJE*, pp. 9-43.

(V.65) The stele has a tale to tell!

(*Passer-by:*) 'Who are you who lie in the dark tomb? Tell me both your country and parentage.'

(*Arsinoe:*) '(I'm) Arsinoe, daughter of Aline and Thedosios (*sic*). It's called the Land of Onias,[54] the place that nourished us.'

(*Passer-by:*) 'How old were you when you slipped down the dark slope of Lethe?'

(*Arsinoe:*) 'At twenty I went down to the mournful place of the dead.'

(*Passer-by:*) 'Were you yoked in marriage?'

(*Arsinoe:*) 'I was.'

(*Passer-by:*) 'Did you leave him a child?'

(*Arsinoe:*) 'Childless I went to the halls of Hades.'

(*Passer-by:*) 'May earth, the guardian of the dead, lie lightly upon you.'

(*Arsinoe:*) 'And for you, stranger, may she bring forth fruitful crops.'

In the 16th year, Payni 21. (*CIJ* II no. 1530 = HN no. 38 and Plate XII – Leontopolis; 2nd-1st century BCE)

(V.66) I am Iesous*, my father was Phameis, passer-by. Sixty years old, I have come to Hades. Weep together all of you for the one who has suddenly passed to the depths of eternity, to dwell in darkness. You, too, Dositheos, weep for me. You have an obligation to pour forth upon my tomb the bitterest of tears. You are my child,[55] for I have departed childless. Weep all together for the wretched Iesos* (*sic*). (*CIJ* II no. 1511 = HN no. 34 and Plate XI – Leontopolis; 2nd century BCE – 2nd century CE)

(V.67) Citizens and strangers, all of you weep for Rachelis, a chaste woman and the friend of all. (She was) about 30. Do not vainly shed empty (tears?) for me (text uncertain here).[56] Even if my allotted life-span was short, nonetheless I await a good hope of mercy.

Also Agathokles, about 38.[57] (*CIJ* II no. 1513 = HN no. 36 – Leontopolis; 2nd century BCE – 2nd century CE)

(iii) Tomb maintenance

The maintenance of the tomb after the interment of the deceased was very important to the Greeks. Many regarded it, quite literally, as their 'eternal home' (see **VI.24**) and they expected it to be properly looked after and their memory regularly honoured at it. Common commemorative practices in Asia Minor were its annual decoration with wreaths (*stephanoi*) or flowers, often followed by a public banquet or the distribution of money. Instructions and funds left by the deceased would determine the precise form of the rituals and pay for their cost. That the Jews of Asia Minor were not unaffected by these practices emerges from two inscriptions. One, arranging for the decoration of the tomb on the Feast of Unleavened Bread and the Pentecost, is to be found at **II.137**. The other, whose Jewish nature has been inferred from the presence of the Hebrew name Matthew, is presented here.

Tri-partite text (here labelled (a), (b) and (c)) from 3rd century Akmonia referring to the annual decking of a grave with roses. Note that (b) is a later insertion in the main text, which consists of (a) and (c):

(V.68) (a) [Aur(elios) A]risteas, son of [Apol]lonios, has bought from Markos Math(i)os* an empty plot measuring 10 by 10 cubits (approx. 25 square yards), in the year [300 or 380].[58]

(b) Alexander and Kallistratos his children have built (this tomb) for their father and mother in remembrance.

(c) He (i.e. Aurelios Aristeas) has undertaken (to provide) the Neighbourhood of the First Gate[59] with two two-pronged implements, hired by the month, and a (noun lost) for digging.[60] He has given (them the plot) on the condition that they decorate each year with roses (the grave of) my wife Aurelia. [If they are not willing] to decorate (it) each year with roses, they will have to reckon with the justice of God. (Trebilco, *Jewish Communities* 3.6.1.)

(iv) Tomb protection

Threats of fines and other punishments against would-be tomb-violators are a common feature of Greek epitaphs, especially those from Asia Minor. What people primarily feared, and thus tried to protect themselves against, was the re-use of their tomb after their death by those without entitlement to it rather then its defacement or the theft of its contents. In this area of funerary practice the Jews seem to have been considerably influenced by the Greeks. Most of the Jewish instances of this type of epitaph have been found in the area where Greek examples abound – i.e. Asia Minor. Even the few cases which have been discovered in Palestine occur in a location where Greek influence is particularly strong – namely the 3rd-4th century catacombs at Beth She'arim in Galilee. As in other areas of funerary practice (e.g. funerary epithets) where the Jews were influenced by the Greeks, they did not simply copy but innovated too. In dreaming up punishments for would-be tomb violators, much use was made of Jewish cultural traditions.

In dealing with this type of epitaph, attribution is often a serious problem, for it was used by not only Greeks and Jews but Christians also in due course. The boundaries between the three groups were often blurred and that is reflected in the language of the epitaphs. Both Jews and Christians tend to invoke the wrath of God or threaten the tomb-violator with Divine Judgement. Many simple 'fine' epitaphs which are categorised as Greek may well be Jewish, for Jews tended to use Greek names and only rarely referred to themselves as Jews. The five examples presented here have been chosen because they are either definitely Jewish or generally considered to be so.

Threat of a fine

For further examples of this common type of epitaph, see **I.110**, **V.5** and **V.10**.

(V.69) Here lie Ioudas and Alexas, the sons of Nisaios, Jews. If anyone disturbs us, he shall pay to the most sacred treasury 2,500 denarii. (*CIJ* II no. 791 = *MAMA* III no. 440 – Korykos; early imperial)

The curses that are written in Deuteronomy (chs 27-9)

For similar examples of this threat, see **V.14** and **15** (also from Akmonia).

(V.70) ... (beginning of text missing) ... (nor) will anyone else be permitted to open the burial-vault,[61] except for his (i.e. the tomb owner's) little daughters, Domne and Alexandria. If they marry, it will not be permitted to open (the vault at all). Whoever dares to put in another (body), shall pay to the most sacred treasury 1,000 Attic drachmas and still be liable to a charge of grave-robbery. Such a man shall accursed and may such curses as are written in *Deuteronomy* be upon him and his children and his grandchildren and his whole family. (*MAMA* VI no. 335 = Trebilco, *Jewish Communities* 3.3.2 – Akmonia, 2nd-3rd century CE)

The Law of the Jews

(V.71) I, Aur(elios) Rouphos, son of Ioulianos, the son of Ioulianos, have built the tomb for myself and my wife, Aur(elia) Tatiane. No one else is to be placed in it. If anyone does inter (another body), he knows the Law of the Jews. (*CIJ* II no. 774 = Trebilco, *Jewish Communities* 4.5.1 – Apamea in Phrygia; 3rd century CE)

The sickle of the curse

This particular curse is based on the Septuagintal rendering of *Zechariah* 5.1-5: And I turned and I raised my eyes and saw and behold a flying sickle. And he (the Lord) said to me, 'What do you see?' And I said, 'I see a flying sickle, twenty cubits in length and ten cubits in width.' And he said to me, 'This is the curse which is going out over the face of all the earth ... it will enter the house of the thief and into the one who swears falsely by my name and it will come down into the middle of the house and it will destroy it and its timber and its stones.'

Two-part inscription (here labelled (a) and (b)) from 2nd or 3rd century Akmonia, carved on the face and right-hand side of a tomb:

(V.72) (a) ... (beginning of text missing) ... has made this [for himself and] his wife Trophime. Ti(tos) Tedios Amerimnos, having repaired the tomb of his grandfather, has interred in it his wife Aur(elia) Onesime, daughter of Euelpistos. It will be permitted for Amerimnos, who has repaired his ancestral tomb, also to be interred in it. If anyone else attempts after the deposition of Amerimnos to inter another corpse, he shall pay to the [treasury] (amount lost).

(b) If anyone by sleight of hand inserts a body,[62] may he be overtaken by the same kind of sudden fate as their (*sic*) brother Amerimnos. If anyone of them is not deterred by these imprecations, may the sickle of the curse enter their dwellings and leave no one behind. (*CIJ* II no. 768 = *MAMA* VI no. 316)

The judgement of God

For similar imprecations, see **I.25**, **I.108** and **VII.48** (with note).

(V.73) I, Aur(elios) Kyrion, during my lifetime, have built this tomb for myself and my wife, Aur(elia) Ioulias. It is my wish that after my deposition no one else, except my child, is placed in it. If anyone acts in contravention of this, he will undergo judgement before God. Blessing upon all. (*Hellenica* 11-12 (1960), 392-4 – Nikomedeia in Bithynia; 3rd century CE)

6. INTERMARRIAGE BETWEEN JEWS AND GREEKS

Although Philo's disapproving remarks about intermarriage points to the practice of exogamy among Jews at Alexandria, it is very hard to find instances of Jews either there or anywhere else who had married Gentiles. Egyptian papyri provide none, *CPJ* I no. 128 and II no. 144, which are sometimes cited in this context, both being exceedingly doubtful. Outside the Herodian dynasty, quite a few of whose princesses did marry Gentiles (see note to **V.77**), our sole certain case of intermarriage is provided by the parents of the Christian disciple, Timothy. Those cited by R. Kraemer, 'On the meaning of the term "Jew" in Graeco-Roman inscriptions', *HTR* 82 (1989), p. 48, n. 37 are all hypothetical.

(V.74) Do not, Moses says, enter into a marriage-parnership with a foreigner, lest, defeated by warring customs, you one day give in and inadvertently miss the road to piety by turning into a place that has no roads. You yourself perhaps will hold out, having been fortified from your first youth by the very best of instructions. Your parents, by endless repetition of these, taught you the Holy Laws. But there is much to be feared for your sons and daughters. Enticed perhaps to give preference to spurious customs over genuine ones, they will run the risk of unlearning how to honour the one God, which is the beginning and end of the most grievous ill-luck. (Philo, *The Special Laws* 3.29)

(V.75) Paul went on to Derbe and Lystra. There he found a disciple, named Timothy, the son of a Jewish Christian mother and a Greek father. He was well spoken of by the brothers (i.e. Christians) at Lystra and Iconium. Paul wanted him to accompany him on his travels. So he took him and circumcised him on account of the Jews who were in those parts, for all knew that his father was a Greek. (*Acts of the Apostles* 16.1-3)

(V.76) Boukolion, son of Hermias and of Pontiana, the Jewess.[63] (*CIJ* I no. 697 – Larissa in Thessaly – no date)

(V.77) This Tigranes (Jewish ruler of Armenia)[64] had a son called Alexander, who married Iotape, the daughter of King Antiochos of Kommagene. Vespasian made the latter king of Ketis in Kilikia. Alexander's offspring immediately from birth abandoned the observance of the customs native to the Jews[65] and ranged themselves with the Greek tradition. (Josephus, *Jewish Antiquities* 18.140-1)

7. FRICTION BETWEEN JEWS AND GREEKS

Despite the peaceful interaction noted so far in this section, relations between Jews and Greeks were not always harmonious. In the century before the First Jewish War, the many privileges Diasporan Jews enjoyed through the protection of Rome (for which, in particular, see Chapter IV §§ 5-6) often acted as an irritant to their Greek neighbours. On the Jewish side, there was frequently great resentment at the petty restrictions Greek city authorities imposed on them in contravention of official Roman policy. While there is clear evidence of mild friction in several parts of the eastern Mediterranean during this period, only at Alexandria, where special factors served to exacerbate the situation, is serious ethnic violence attested. In the period after the First Jewish War, the unpopularity of the Jews with the Roman authorities (for which see Chapter IV § 8 (b) and (c)) is thought to have led to a general worsening of their position *vis à vis* the Gentile inhabitants of the empire. Although the process itself is difficult to document (the principal surviving evidence, the *Acts of the Pagan Martyrs*, relates only to Alexandrian Jewry and is of dubious historicity), its consequences are clearly to be seen in the cataclysmic communal conflicts that erupted towards the end of Trajan's reign in Egypt, Cyrene and Cyprus. While Egyptian and Cyrenaican Jewry emerged from them decimated, the Cypriot community disappeared altogether.

(a) Tension in Asia Minor and Cyrene during the reign of Augustus

(**V.78**) While they (Agrippa and Herod the Great) were in Ionia (in 15 BCE), a vast number of the Jews who inhabited its cities took advantage of the chance to speak out freely. They approached them and told them of the abuses which they had suffered – not being allowed to observe their own laws, being compelled to go to court on holy days through the high-handedness of the examining judges, being deprived of the monies set aside for Jerusalem and forced to participate in military exercises, undertake civic duties (lit. liturgies) and spend sacred monies on those things, even though they had been granted exemption, since the Romans had always allowed them to live in accordance with their own laws. (Josephus, *Jewish Antiquities* 16.27-8)

(**V.79**) Marcus Agrippa to the magistrates, council and people of Cyrene, greetings. The Jews in Cyrene, on whose behalf Augustus has already communicated with Flavius,[66] the former governor of Libya and the other officials with responsibility for the province, to the effect that their sacred monies may be sent unhindered to Jerusalem, as is their ancestral custom, have now complained to me that they are being harassed by certain informers and prevented (from sending those monies) on the pretext of owing taxes, which are not owed at all. I therefore order restoration (of those monies to the Jews), who are not to be molested in any way, and if sacred monies have been taken from any of the cities, those answerable for these matters are to rectify them for the Jews there. (Josephus, *Jewish Antiquities* 16.169-70)

(b) Tension between Jews and Greeks in Alexandria in the 1st century CE

In Alexandria, an additional source of communal tension in the early Roman period was the *laographia* or poll-tax. Instituted by Augustus sometime in the 20s BCE, it was imposed on all but the Greek citizen élite. Payment hit not only a person's pocket but his pride – tax liability was a clear sign of social inferiority. Hence the desperate efforts of gymnasium-educated Jews like Helenos (**V.3**) to cling on to the citizenship they thought they possessed and of others to have their metic status upgraded. To the local Greeks such aspirations were an anathema and they did all they could to block the entry into the citizen body of 'uncultured and uneducated' elements (*CPJ* II no. 150 – the so-called '*Boule*' papyrus, not included here). Matters came to a head under the emperor Gaius, whose lack of sympathy for the Jews was well known. Full-scale race riots broke out, the Jews were effectively ghettoised and such rights as they did possess curtailed. (Philo's two accounts of these events are too long to be quoted here but short extracts from them are cited at, inter alia, **I.51**; **56**; **77** and **79** and **V.31**.) Although there was a return to calm and the status quo under Claudius, the underlying problem remained. Relations between Jews and Greeks were often tense and there were serious outbreaks of trouble in both 66 and 115 CE. Of the innumerable analyses of Judaeo-Greek relations in Alexandria and the question of the Jews' civic rights there, the following are to be noted: Tcherikover, *CPJ* I, *Proleg.*, pp. 57-74; A. Kasher, *The Jews in Hellenistic and Roman Egypt* (Tübingen, 1985); Zuckermann in *SCI* 8-9 (1985-88), pp. 171-85 (review of Kasher); Lüderitz, 'What is the politeuma?' in *SEJE*, pp. 183-225; Barclay, *Jews in the Mediterranean Diaspora*, pp. 60-71. On the further trouble between the two communities in the Byzantine period, see **V.99**.

Extract from Claudius' letter to the city of Alexandria, 10 November, 41 CE

(**V.80**) With regard to the disturbances and rioting, or rather, if one must speak the truth, the war against the Jews, and who was to blame, although your ambassadors, and especially Dionysios, the son of Theon, put up a long and spirited defence at the public hearing, I have not wished to conduct a minute enquiry, though I do harbour within myself immutable anger against those who renewed the conflict. I simply tell you that unless you put an end to this destructive and stubborn hatred of each other I shall be forced to show you what a benevolent ruler is like when he has turned to righteous anger. Even now, therefore, I earnestly beg the Alexandrians to behave gently and in a kindly manner towards the Jews who have long been living in the same city and not dishonour any of the traditional practices connected with the worship of their god,[67] but to allow them to observe their customs as they did under the deified Augustus, customs, which I, having listened to both sides, have confirmed. The Jews, on the other hand, I order not strive for more than they had before, nor in future to send out two embassies as if they lived in two cities, a thing that has never been done before, and not to insinuate themselves into the games presided over by the *Gymnasiarchs* and *Kosmetai*,[68] since they already have the benefit of what is their own and in a city that is not their own[69] enjoy an abundance of all good things. Nor are they to bring in or invite Jews to come in by sea and river from Syria or Egypt, behaviour which will force me to conceive (even) graver suspicions. If they do, I shall proceed against them in every way as fomenting a common plague for the inhabited world. If both of you change your ways and are willing to live with gentleness and kindliness towards each other, then I too will care for the city as much as I can, as one which has been closely connected with us for generations ... Farewell. (*CPJ* II no. 153, line 73 – end)

Racial violence in Alexandria at the start of the Jewish War

(V.81) Now that there was general confusion,[70] trouble flared up there (in Alexandria) more strongly than ever. When the Alexandrians were holding a meeting to discuss the embassy they were planning to send to Nero, a large number of Jews poured into the amphitheatre with the Greeks. Their opponents, seeing them, immediately cried out, 'Enemies, spies!' Jumping up, they made to lay hands on them. Most took to their heels and scattered but three were captured and dragged off to be burnt alive. The whole Jewish community rose in their defence. First they pelted the Greeks with stones. Then, picking up torches, they rushed to the amphitheatre, threatening to make a bonfire of the people in it, right down to the last man. And they would have got away with this, had not Tiberius Alexander, the governor of the city, curbed their fury.[71] (Josephus, *Jewish War* 2.490-2)

(c) Evidence of tension in Alexandria under Trajan

The following text, despite its lacunose state and novelettish character, shows that the suspicion in which the Alexandrian Greeks and Jews held each other continued unabated in the decades after the First Jewish War. It is one of the large number of propaganda pieces, popular in extreme Greek nationalist circles in Alexandria in the first two centuries CE, that go by the name Acts of the Pagan Martyrs. Although it is impossible to determine precisely where fact ends and fiction begins in any of these concoctions, there is no doubt that each does contain a core of hard fact. The people mentioned in them certainly existed and the basic situations in which they were involved (i.e. going to Rome as envoys or to face trial) are likely to have been historical. As for the consistent hostility displayed by the Alexandrian 'martyrs' towards the Roman authorities and their fellow Jews, that is entirely plausible. Much, though, is clearly fanciful.

(V.82) ... Dionysios, who had held many procuratorships, and Salouios, Ioulios Salouios, Teimagenes, Pastor, a gymnasiarch, Ioulios Phanias, Philoxenos, gymnasiarch-elect, Sotion, a gymnasiarch, Theon, Athenodoros (and) Paulos, a Tyrian by birth, who had volunteered to act as an advocate for the Alexandrians. Learning of this, the Jews also elected envoys from their own community (*ethnos*) and there were chosen Simon, Glaukon, Theudes*, Onias, Kolon, Iakoumbos* and, as advocate for the Jews, Sopatros, an Antiochene by birth. They set sail, therefore, from the city (Alexandria), each group carrying its own gods, the Alexandrians [a bust of Sarapis, the Jews ...]

... and when the winter was over, they dropped anchor at Rome. The emperor (Trajan) heard that envoys of the Jews and Alexandrians had arrived and he fixed the day on which he would give a hearing to both parties. Plotina (Trajan's wife) went (and persuaded)[72] the senators to oppose the Alexandrians and support the Jews. The Jews, entering first, greeted the emperor Trajan. Caesar greeted them most warmly, for he had already been won over by Plotina. After them the Alexandrian envoys entered and greeted the emperor. The latter did not go to meet them but said: 'Do you greet me as though you deserved a greeting, after the dreadful things that you have dared to do to the Jews?' ...

[Caesar (Trajan) said] ... 'You must want to die, since you have such a contempt of death as to answer even me with insolence.'

Hermaiskos[73] said: 'But we are grieved that your council has been packed with impious Jews.'

Caesar (Trajan) said: 'Look, I'm telling you a second time, Hermaiskos, you're giving me an insolent answer, because you're relying on your noble birth.'

Hermaiskos said: 'How is my answer insolent, O greatest of emperors? Enlighten me.'

Caesar said: 'Making out that my council is full of Jews.'

Hermaiskos: 'So the word Jew is offensive to you, is it? You ought, then, to help your own people and not play the advocate for the impious Jews.'

As Hermaiskos was saying this, the bust of Sarapis that the envoys were carrying suddenly broke into a sweat. Trajan, seeing this, was astonished. And shortly after, crowds of people rushed into Rome and numerous shouts rang out and everyone made off for the highest parts of the hills ... (*CPJ* II no. 157, lines 3-15; 22-37; 40-55)

(d) Racial conflict in Egypt, Cyrene and Cyprus, 115-117 CE

Of unprecedented length and severity was the inter-communal violence that erupted in these three areas towards the end of Trajan's reign. The accounts of Eusebius and Dio, brief though they are, are confirmed in their essentials by inscriptions and papyri from Cyrene and Egypt, a small sample of which is included here. They illustrate well both the extent of the physical damage caused by the Jews as well as the fears their activities sometimes aroused.

(V.83) When the emperor (Trajan) was about to enter the eighteenth year of his reign, a rebellion of the Jews again broke out and destroyed a vast number of them, for in Alexandria and the rest of Egypt and also in Cyrene they rushed into a faction fight against their Greek neighbours, as if seized by some terrible spirit of revolt.[74] After increasing greatly the level of communal violence (*stasis*), they embarked in the following year upon a full-scale war (*polemos*). The governor of the whole of Egypt at that time was Lupus. It came about that in the first clash they triumphed over the Greeks. The latter, however, having fled to Alexandria, captured and killed the Jews of the city ...[75] (Eusebius, *The History of the Church* 4.2)

(V.84) Meanwhile the Jews in the region of Cyrene, taking a certain Andreas as their leader, killed both the Romans and the Greeks (stereotypic details of atrocities follow). In Egypt, they committed many similar outrages, and in Cyprus too under the leadership of a certain Artemion. There two hundred and forty thousand people perished. For this reason no Jew is allowed to set foot on the island and if any, driven by the wind, should end up on it, he is put to death. (Dio, *Roman History* 68.32.1-3 = Stern II no. 437)

Greek fears about Jewish excesses, 116 CE(?)

(V.85) ... with the goodwill of the gods, especially Hermes the Unconquerable, may they (the Jews) not roast you. As for the rest, I hope that you and all yours are flourishing. Your daughter, Heraidous, who is free from harm, sends her greetings. Epeiph, 6.

(On the back of the document) To Apollonios. (*CPJ* II no. 437)

Clearing up after the violence, 117 CE

(V.86) Apollonios, *strategos* of Apollinopolis-Heptakomias to Rammios Martialis, the mighty prefect (of Egypt), greetings. I attach the copy, (my) Lord prefect, of the letter I previously wrote to you, so that, by your favour, you may allow me sixty days to set my affairs in order, especially now, when I think ... I pray that you are well, (my) lord prefect. The (first) year of Imperator Caesar Traianus Hadrianus Augustus, Choiak, 2.

To Rammios Martialis, the mighty prefect, Apollonios, *strategos* of Apollinopolis-Heptakomias, sends greetings ... For not only have my affairs become totally neglected through my long absence, but also, because of the attack of the impious Jews, almost everything that I own in the villages of the Hermoupolite nome and in the metropolis requires attention from me. If you assent to my request, once I have sorted out my affairs to the best of my ability, I shall be able to approach my duties as *strategos* in a better frame of mind. (*CPJ* II no. 443)

(V.87) Imperator Caesar Traianus Hadrianus Augustus, son of the deified Traianus Parthicus, grandson of the deified Nerva, Pontifex Maximus, holder of tribunician power for the second time, consul for the second time, has ordered that the Caesareum[76] which was damaged and burned in the Jewish 'tumult' be restored for the community of Cyrene. (*CJZC* no. 17 – Cyrene; 118 CE)

(V.88) Imperator Caesar Traianus Hadrianus Augustus, son of the deified Traianus Parthicus, grandson of the deified Nerva, Pontifex Maximus, holder of tribunician power for the third time, consul for the third time, has ordered that the baths with their colonnades and ball-courts and other adjoining facilities[77] which were damaged and burned in the Jewish 'tumult' be restored for the community of Cyrene. (*CJZC* no. 23 – Cyrene; 119 CE)

8. JEWISH RELATIONS WITH CHRISTIANS IN
THE GREEK EAST

So far in this chapter, we have been concerned only with relations between Jews and pagan Greeks. From the mid-first century CE onwards, however, and especially after the so-called 'Triumph of Christianity' in the fourth century, an increasingly large element in the population of the Greek East (how large we cannot say) became (nominally, at least) Christian. Jewish relations with these Christianised Greeks, particularly in the period before Constantine, are difficult to document, owing to the lack of hard historical data. The purpose of the passages assembled here is to show the different kinds of interaction, peaceful and otherwise, that might take place. How prevalent each of them was is impossible to say. What the evidence does suggest is that after the accession of the hardline orthodox emperor Theodosius I in 378 CE, Judaeo-Christian relations underwent a distinct change for the worse.

(a) Jewish hostility to Christians

At Smyrna c. 156-7 CE

(**V.89**) After the herald had made this announcement (that Polycarp had confessed that he was a Christian), the entire mob which was comprised of both pagans and the Jews who dwelt in Smyrna cried aloud with uncontrollable anger, 'This is the teacher of Asia, the father of the Christians, the destroyer of our gods, the one who teaches many neither to sacrifice nor to pay respect (to the gods).' While they were saying this, they cried out and requested Philip the Asiarch to let loose a lion against Polycarp. He said, however, that it was not possible for him (to do this), since the days of the animal games were past. Thereupon they decided to cry out all together that Polycarp should be burned alive ... These things happened much faster than can be related. In a moment the mob gathered timber and brushwood from the workshops and public baths, the Jews, as usual, eagerly helping them with this ... (*Martyrdom of Polycarp* 12.1-13.1 = Musurillo, *Acts of the Christian Martyrs*, no. 1)

Jewish destruction of churches under Julian the Apostate, 361 CE

(**V.90**) If I were pleading in accordance with the law of nations, I would mention how many of the Church's basilicas the Jews burned down in the reign of Julian – two at Damascus, of which one has scarcely been repaired ... (and) the other is a pile of ugly ruins. Basilicas were burned down at Gaza, Ascalon, Beirut and almost everywhere in those regions, and no one sought revenge. At Alexandria, too, a basilica which was of outstanding beauty was burned down by pagans and Jews, but the Church was not avenged ... (Ambrose, *Epistulae* 40.15 = *PL* 16, col. 1107)

Jewish crucifixion of a Christian boy at Inmestar in Syria, c. 415 CE

(V.91) Shortly after this, the Jews paid the penalty for their disgusting acts against the Christians. At a place called Inmestar, which lies between Chalkis and and Antioch in Syria, the Jews were indulging in their customary amusements and in the course of play perpetrating many mindless acts. Carried away by drink, they started to ridicule both Christians and Christ himself in the course of their play. While mocking the Cross and those who had put their trust in the Crucified One, they thought up the following 'prank': they seized a Christian boy, bound him to a cross and hung him up. First of all they proceeded to mock and jeer but not long afterwards, being by now out of their minds, they tortured the child to death. At this, a sharp conflict broke out between them and the Christians. When this became known to the authorities, orders were issued to the officials of the province to search out those who were responsible and punish them. Thus the Jews there paid the penalty for the wicked deeds that they had committed while at play.[78] (Socrates, *Ecclesiastical History* 7.16 = *PG* 67, cols. 769-72)

(b) Christian aggression towards Jews

Burning of a synagogue at Callinicum on the Euphrates in 388 CE

(V.92) (Ambrose, Bishop of Milan, is addressing the emperor, Theodosius I in December, 388 CE) ... It was reported by the count of military affairs in the East that a synagogue had been burned down, and that the deed had been done at the instigation of a bishop. You have ordered that punishment is to be meted out to the culprits (lit. the rest) and that the synagogue is to be rebuilt by the bishop himself ... Let it be, however, that no one bring an action against the bishop for performing his duty. I plead for your clemency ... Shall there be made out of the spoils of the Church a place for Jewish perfidy and shall this patrimony, which Christians acquired through the favour of Christ, be transferred to the coffers of traitors? We read that in ancient times temples were founded for idols out of Cimbrian plunder and from spoils taken from other enemies. This is the inscription that the Jews will write on the façade of their synagogue: 'The Temple of Impiety, constructed from the spoils of the Christians.'
... There is, therefore, no reasonable cause for such agitation (on your part), for such severe punishment being meted out for the burning of a building, particularly so when it is (only) a synagogue, a place of perfidy, a house of impiety, a refuge for madness, which God Himself has condemned ... God forbids that intercession be made with Him for those who you think must be avenged. (Ambrose, *Epistulae* 40.6-14 (extracts only) = *PL* 16, cols. 1103-7)

Christian attacks upon synagogues in the East

(V.93) The same three Augusti (the emperors, Theodosius I, Arcadius and Honorius) to Addeus, Count and Master of Both Services (i.e. the army and the civil service) in the East. It is sufficiently established that the sect of the Jews is prohibited by no law. For this reason we are gravely disturbed that their assemblies have been banned in some places. Your Sublime Magnitude shall, therefore, upon the receipt of this order, repress with appropriate severity the excesses of those who, in the name of the Christian religion, presume to commit illegal acts and attempt to destroy and plunder synagogues. Given on the 3rd day before the Kalends of October at Constantinople, during the 3rd consulship of Theodosius Augustus and the (1st) of Abundantius. (*Codex Theodosianus* 16.8.9 = Linder no. 21 – 29 September, 393 CE)

(V.94) The same two Augusti (the emperors Honorius and Theodosius II) to Asclepiodotus, Praetorian Prefect (of the East). It is decreed that in future no synagogues of the Jews anywhere are either to be seized or set on fire. If, in some recent undertaking after (the passage of) the law,[79] any synagogues were seized or converted into churches[80] or consecrated to the venerable mysteries, there shall be offered to them (i.e. the Jews), in compensation for them, sites on which they may construct (new synagogues) up to the size of those that have been taken away. If any votive offerings have been removed, they too are to be restored to them, provided that they have not yet been dedicated to the sacred mysteries. If a venerable consecration does not permit restitution, the exact price for them is to be made over (to them). Henceforth no further synagogues are to be constructed and old ones are to remain in their present state. Given on the 15th day before the Kalends of March at Constantinople during the consulship of Asclepiodotus and Marinianus. (*Codex Theodosianus* 16.8.25 = Linder no. 47 – 15 February, 423 CE)

(c) Co-operation between Jews and Christians

The official pronouncements against Christian socialising with Jews that are set out here provide good, if unwitting, testimony to the friendly relations that often existed between the two groups.

(V.95) It is not fitting (for Christians) to accept from Jews or heretics gifts sent at festival-time or to celebrate festivals with them. (Council of Laodicea in Phrygia, Canon 37 (360 CE) = Mansi II, col. 580)

(V.96) It is not fitting (for Christians) to accept unleavened bread from the Jews or to take part in their impieties. (Council of Laodicea in Phrygia, Canon 38 (360 CE) = Mansi II, cols. 580-1)

(V.97) Another very serious illness calls for any cure my words can bring, an illness which has become implanted in the body of the Church ... What is this disease? The festivals of the pitiful and miserable Jews are soon to march upon us one after the other and in quick succession: the Feast of Trumpets,[81] the Feast of Tabernacles, the fasts.[82] There are many in our ranks who say they think as we do but some of them are going to watch the festivals and others will join the Jews in keeping their feasts and participating in their fasts.[83] It is this wicked practice that I wish to drive out now from the Church. (John Chrysostom, *Adversus Iudaeos* 1.1 = *PG* 48, col. 814)

(V.98) When they (i.e. people like Job) have suffered and endured such misfortunes, what kind of excuse will we give, if, because of a touch of fever or some trivial injury, we run to the synagogues and invite poisoners and sorcerers[84] into our homes? (John Chrysostom, *Adversus Iudaeos* 8.6 = *PG* 48, col. 936)

(d) Conflict between Jews and Christians
at Alexandria, *c.* 415 CE

(V.99) It came about that at this same time the Jewish inhabitants were expelled from Alexandria by Cyril the bishop for the following reason. The populace of Alexandria, more than any other people, rejoices in faction-fighting. If ever it finds a pretext, it breaks out in intolerable excesses. Nor will it let up until blood has flown. It happened at that time that the people fell to rioting, not for any deep-seated reason but because of the vice then fashionable in all the cities – I mean the enthusiasm for pantomimic dancers. Since the dancers used to attract considerable crowds of people on the Sabbath, for the reason that the Jews, not being at work, spent their leisure time not in listening to the Law but in theatrical amusements, the factions of the populace would come to blows on that day. Although a measure of control was exerted by the prefect of Alexandria, the Jews nonetheless remained antagonistic towards the men of the other faction. While they were always hostile to the Christians, on account of the dancers they were all the more inclined to come to blows with them. When Orestes, the prefect of Alexandria, was about to issue an edict in the theatre ..., supporters of Cyril the bishop were present, since they wished to find out what regulations were being laid down by the prefect (presumably in connection with the pantomimes). Among them was a man called Hierax, an elementary school teacher, who was a fervent adherent (lit. auditor) of Cyril the bishop and a most enthusiastic applauder of his sermons. The Jews, on seeing Hierax in the theatre, immediately cried out that he was there for no other purpose than to create a riot among the populace. Now Orestes, even before this, had come to hate the power of the bishops, who were gradually depriving of much of their authority those who had been sent out as governors by the emperor. And he particularly disliked Cyril because the latter was wont to spy upon his actions. And so he seized Hierax and proceeded to subject him to public torture in the theatre. When Cyril found this out, he summoned the leaders of the Jews and threatened them with the utmost severities if they did not cease feuding with the Christians. The Jews, on learning of the threat, became even more contentious and devised schemes to injure the Christians, the chief one of which I shall narrate, for it was the cause of their expulsion from Alexandria. Taking as a pre-arranged signal a finger-ring made of the bark of a palm branch, they plotted a night attack upon the Christians. One night they sent men into the (various) parts of the city to cry out that the church named after Alexander was being consumed by fire. On hearing this the Christians came running out, one from here and one from there, in order to save the church. The Jews immediately set upon them and killed them. While they held off from each other by displaying their rings (lit. fingers), they slaughtered those Christians who fell in with them. At daybreak the perpetrators of the atrocity were revealed. Moved by this, Cyril arrived with a large crowd at the synagogues of the Jews – for so they name their houses of prayer. While he confiscated these, he drove them from the city and gave over their properties to be plundered by the crowd. Thus the Jews, who had dwelt in the city from the time of Alexander of Macedon, were expelled from it, bereft (of all their possessions) and scattered, some in one direction and some in another. (Socrates, *Ecclesiastical History* 7.13 = *PG* 67, cols. 761-4)

VI

The Jews among the Romans

1. JEWS AND THE ROMAN CITIZENSHIP

Until 212 CE, when the emperor Caracalla through his enactment, the *Constitutio Antoniniana*, granted all the free inhabitants of the empire Roman citizenship, probably only a minority of Jews enjoyed that privileged, and hence highly coveted, status. Regular ways of coming by it were by descent from someone to whom Roman citizenship had been granted, through manumission by a Roman citizen and through military service. Sometimes, however, it was acquired irregularly – e.g. as a personal gift, for services rendered, from a powerful Roman. The evidence presented here shows Jews obtaining it by each of these means. But no matter how people came by Roman citizenship, their transition from non-citizen to citizen status was marked by a standard change in name-form – henceforth their personal name was preceded by the family name (e.g. Iulius, Claudius, Flavius) of the Roman who had enfranchised them. To illustrate this we have given in (e) below a few examples of the many Jews (or their ancestors) who gained Roman citizenship through the *Constitutio Antoniniana*. Their newly-acquired status is revealed by their first names – Aurelius/os in men, Aurelia in women. These were derived from the (adopted) family name of Caracalla, otherwise known as Marcus Aurelius Antoninus.

(a) As a personal gift for services rendered

Julius Antipater, father of Herod the Great

(VI.1) Later, after he had settled affairs in Egypt and returned to Syria (*c.* 47 BCE), (Julius) Caesar bestowed upon Antipater Roman citizenship and exemption from taxation and by means of other honours and marks of courtesy made him an object of envy.[1] (Josephus, *Jewish War* 1.194)

Flavius Josephus, the historian

(VI.2) Vespasian gave me lodging in the house that had been his before he became Emperor and honoured me with Roman citizenship and gave me a pension.[2] (Josephus, *Vita* 423)

(b) By descent

(VI.3) But when they had tied him up with thongs, Paul said to the centurion who was standing by, 'Is it lawful for you to flog a man who is a Roman citizen and has not been found guilty?' When the centurion heard this, he went and reported it to the commandant and said, 'What do you intend to do? This man is a Roman citizen.' The commandant came to Paul and said, 'Tell me, are you a Roman citizen?' 'Yes,' he said. The commandant replied, 'This citizenship of mine I acquired through (paying) a hefty sum.'[3] Paul said, 'Mine was by birth.'[4] (*Acts of the Apostles* 22.25-8)

(VI.4) Through the foresight of Tiberios Klaudios Theogenes of Paiania, the *epimeletes* of the city, the council of the Areopagos and the council of 600 and the people (of Athens have honoured) the Great Queen Ioulia Bereneike,[5] daughter of King Ioulios Agrippa and descendant of Great Kings who have been benefactors of the city. (*OGIS* I 428 – Athens; 1st century CE)

(VI.5) In the year 28 (88 CE) of the Great King Markos Ioulios Agrippa,[6] Lord (*Kyrios*), Friend of Caesar, Pious, Friend of Rome, son of ... (rest of text missing). (*Syria* 5 (1924), 324 – from the region of Syria called the Hauran)

(c) Through manumission by a Roman citizen

(VI.6) We, [Aurelios ...] of the illustrious and most illustrious city of Oxyrhynchos, and his sister by the same mother, [Aurelia ... daughter of ...] the former *exegetes* and councillor of the same city, with her guardian ... the admirable ... have manumitted [and released] *inter amicos*[7] our house-born slave Paramone,[8] aged 40 years, and [her children ...] with a scar on the neck, aged 10 years, and Iakob, aged 4 years ... from all the rights and powers of the owner, fourteen talents of silver having been paid [to us for the manumission and] release by the community (*synagoge*) of the Jews through Aurelios [Dioskoros ... and Aurelios Ious]tos, councillor of Ono in Syria Palestina (and) Father of the [Community ...] And, the question being put, [we have agreed that we have manumitted and released them], and that for the same manumission and release [we have been paid the aforementioned sum], and that we do not have any rights or powers over them from [the present day, because] we have been paid and [received for them, once and for all, the aforementioned] money, through Aurelios Dioskoros and Aurelios Ioustos. Transacted in the illustrious and [most illustrious] city of Oxyrhynchos ... [in the 2nd consulship of Tiberianos] and the first of Dion, year 7 of Autokrator (i.e. the emperor) Kaisar [Gaios Aurelios Oualerios Diokletianos and year 6] of Autokrator Kaisar Markos Aurelios Oualerios [Maximianos, Germanikoi, Megistoi, Eusebeis, Eutycheis, Sebast]oi. Pharmouthi ... nineteenth day. (*CPJ* III no. 473 – Oxyrhynchos in Egypt; 291 CE)

(d) Through military service

Generally those who acquired the citizenship in this way had completed twenty-six years service in the auxiliary services, recruitment into the legions normally being confined to those who already were Roman citizens. The one-time Jewish marine who is being awarded the citizenship here owed his recruitment as a legionary to the political upheavals of 68 CE. His unit, the Legio I Adiutrix, was the scratch force that Nero, in a desperate attempt to shore up his position, put together from rowers in the fleet.

(**VI.7**) Imperator Ser(gius/vius) Galba, Caesar, Augustus, Pontifex Maximus, holder of tribunician power, consul designate II, has granted to the veterans of the Legio I Adiutrix whose names are listed below an honourable discharge and citizenship for themselves, their children and descendants, and right of marriage with the wives they had when the citizenship was granted them or, if they were single, with those they might marry afterwards, the limit being one wife for each man. (Enacted) on the 11th day before the Kalends of January, during the consulships of C(aius) Bellicus Natalis and P(ublius) Cornelius Scipio (i.e. December 22, 68 CE)

To Matthaius*,[9] son of Polaus, from Syria.

Certified copy taken from the (bronze) tablet posted at Rome on the Capitol at the altar (of the Julian family). (*CIL* XVI, Diploma no. 8)

(e) Through the *Constitutio Antoniniana*

(**VI.8**) Aurel(ius) Ioses* (and) Aurel(ia) Auguria have set up (this plaque) to their well-deserving son Agathopus, who lived for 15 years. (*CIJ* I no. 209 = Noy II no. 325 – Rome; 3rd-4th century CE(?))

(**VI.9**) Aurelia Protogenia has set up (this memorial) to Aure(elia) Quintille, her dearest mother who lived for 60 years (and) 5 months. To a well-deserving (woman). (*CIJ* I no. 217 = Noy II no. 284 and Plate XI – Rome; 3rd-4th century CE(?))

(**VI.10**) Aurelius Alexander has set up (this memorial) to Aurelia Helenes, his well-deserving wife. (*CIJ* I no. 219 = Noy II no. 279 – Rome; 3rd-4th century CE(?))

(**VI.11**) Year 342. Aur(elios) Alexander, a Jew, has built this tomb during his lifetime. (*CIJ* II no. 764 – Akmonia; 257/8 CE)

(f) Privileges attached to the citizenship

Protection against the violent exercise of power by Roman provincial governors

(**VI.12**) Then (i.e. after Paul's revelations about his Roman citizenship) those who were about to examine him by torture hastily withdrew and the commandant was filled with fear, when he realised that Paul was a Roman citizen and he had fettered him.[10] (*Acts of the Apostles* 22.29)

Ius trium liberorum (lit., the right of three children)

Introduced by Augustus as part of his programme to increase the birth-rate of the Roman upper classes, this right conferred a number of privileges upon citizens who had produced at least three legitimate children. Women were allowed, for instance, to dispense with a legal guardian (*tutor*). Among the perquisites it brought to men was priority in standing for public offices, municipal, as well as urban. Not all who held the right had actually produced three children. Augustus began the practice, still current in Pliny's day, of conferring it as a favour on those who technically did not qualify for it.

(VI.13) Aurelious Dionysious (*sic*), a Jew from Tiberias, aged 50, father of three children. (*CIJ* I² no. 680 – Senia in Dalmatia; 3rd century CE(?))

(VI.14) Nebia* Kyria, also called Maplika, mother of three children <three children>, lies here. (*CIJ* I² no. 47 = Noy II no. 486 – Rome; 3rd-4th century CE)

2. JEWISH INVOLVEMENT IN LOCAL GOVERNMENT IN THE WEST

Although it may be safely deduced from the attempts of the emperors, Constantine and Honorius, to regulate the conditions under which Jews served on the town councils (*curiae*) of the West that Jewish town councillors (*decuriones*) did exist, specific cases are hard to come by.

Imperial attempts to regulate Jewish conditions of service

(VI.15) The same Augustus (Constantine, later 'the Great') to the decurions of Colonia Agrippinensis (Cologne in Lower Germany). We permit all town councils as a general rule to nominate Jews to the *curia*. But, so that something from the former system[11] shall be left to them by way of consolation, we allow as a perpetual privilege that two or three (Jews in each *curia*) shall be exempt from all nominations (to offices).[12] Given on the 3rd day before the Ides of December in the consulship of the Caesars Crispus and Constantine, both for the second time. (*Codex Theodosianus* 16.8.3. = Linder, no. 7 – 11 December, 321 CE)

(VI.16) The same two Augusti (Arcadius and Honorius) to Theodorus, Praetorian Prefect (of Illyricum, Italy and Africa). We have discovered that large numbers of town councils throughout Apulia and Calabria (in southern Italy) are enfeebled because they belong to the Jewish superstition[13] and consider that under a certain law that has been passed in the East they should be protected from the obligation of undergoing liturgies. In this decree, therefore, we order that this law, if it is observed anywhere, is to cease, since it is agreed that it is harmful my (*sic*) territories. All who are in any way obliged to serve legally on the council, no matter what their superstition, are required to perform the liturgies of their towns. Given on the Ides of September at Milan in the 4th consulship of Honorius Augustus and the 1st of Eutychianus. (*Codex Theodosianus* 12.1.158 = Linder no. 29 – 13 September, 398 CE)

Some individual councillors

At Volubilis in Mauretania

(VI.17) Here lies Caecilianus the *protopolites*[14] (lit. the first citizen), Father of the Community of the Jews. Aged 45 years, 8 months (and) 3 days. (Le Bohec, no. 79 – 3rd century CE)

At Oescus on the Danube

(VI.18) Ioses*, *archisynagogus* and *principalis* (leading decurion?),[15] son of Maximinus of Pannonia, dedicated (this) during his lifetime as a memorial for himself and Qyria (*sic*), his wife. (*CIJ* I² no. 681 = Scheiber no. 10 – 4th century CE(?))

At Mago on Minorca

Note that the authenticity of the work from which the following extract has been taken, purportedly an eye-witness account by Severus, Bishop of Minorca *c.* 417 CE, of the recent, miraculous conversion of the Jews of that island to Christianity, is not accepted by all. While E.D. Hunt ('St Stephen in Minorca – an episode in Jewish-Christian relations in the early 5th century AD', *JThS* n.s. 33 (1982), 106-23) accepts Severus' letter as substantially genuine and believes it provides evidence of an exceptional quality for social relations between Christians and Jews in the early fifth century, B. Blumenkrantz (*Les Auteurs chrétiens latins du moyen âge sur les juifs et le judaïsme* (Paris, 1963), pp. 106-10) thinks that it is a 7th-century forgery. For further extracts from it detailing the conversion itself, see **VI.61**.

(VI.19) The Jewish community (at Mago) greatly relied on the authority and power of a certain Theodorus, who, by virtue of both his wealth and his (public) honours was the leading man of the time not only among the Jews but even the Christians of that town. For while with the former he was a Doctor of the Law and – to use their term – a Father of Fathers (*pater patrum*), in the municipality he enjoyed total immunity from curial obligations, had already held the high office of *defensor* (*civitatis*)[16] and now (417-18 CE) was the town's *patronus*. (Severus Majoricensis, *Epistola de Iudaeis* 4 = *PL* 41.823)

3. JEWISH INVOLVEMENT IN ROMAN CULTURAL
AND RELIGIOUS LIFE

Although it may reasonably be inferred from certain poems of Martial that Jews enjoyed the public leisure facilities of Rome and were active on the literary scene there (see, for instance, *Epigrams* 7.82 for a Jewish singer/actor at the palaestra and *Epigrams* 11.94 for an anonymous circumcised poet), evidence for the involvement of real, as opposed to fictional, Jews in Roman cultural and religious life is severely limited, as the meagre evidence presented in this section shows.

(a) Jews on the Roman stage

(VI.20) Having arrived safely at Dikaiarchia, which Italians call Puteoli, I formed a friendship with Alityros. He was an actor (*mimologos*), who was a special favourite of Nero and a Jew by birth. Through him I gained the acquaintance of Poppaea, the wife of Caesar ... (Josephus, *Vita* 16)

(VI.21) To M(arcus) Aurel[ius] Py[lades], son of ..., of the tribe Ter(etina), from Scythopolis (Bet She'an in Judaea), the first *pantomimus* of his time[17] in ... and esteemed by [the Emperors Valerian] and Gal[lien]us[18] ... from the province of [Juda]e[a ... after] the death of his father Iud[a;[19] also a de]curion of the cities of Ascalon and Damascus. To him, the second order of the Augustales[20] (have set up this statue) not only in memory of his father but on account of [his own] consummate skill, all the citizens equally demanding it ... (*CIL* XIV Supp. no. 4624 = Noy I no. 15 – Ostia; 3rd century CE)

(b) A Jewish devotee of the Mother-Goddesses
in Cisalpine Gaul

(VI.22) To the Iunones.[21] Annia Iuda,[22] freedwoman of Lucius, has fulfilled a vow on behalf of her family. (*CIJ* I no. 77*; not included by Noy – Brescia; undated)

4. ROMAN CULTURAL INFLUENCE ON THE JEWS

(a) The civic sphere

(i) The importance attached to the tenure of community office

So great was the prestige that attached to office-holding in Roman society, that a common feature of civic and funerary monuments set up in honour of the socially and politically prominent was an inscribed record, often detailed, of the dedicatee's public career. Although the Jews of Judaea never engaged in this practice, their Diasporan counterparts, to a limited extent, did. Many Roman Jews, for example, cite on their tombstones their last, and therefore most senior synagogal office (for examples, see Chapter II § 2 *passim*) and a few, in clear imitation of their Gentile neighbours, list the principal community offices (*honores*) they had held.

(VI.23) To Stafylus, *archon* and *archisynagogus*, who has held all the public offices.[23] Restituta, his wife, has set up (this stone) to a well-deserving (husband). In peace your sleep. (*CIJ* I no. 265 = Noy II no. 322 – Rome; 3rd-4th century CE(?))

(VI.24) Eternal home. Here lies Eupsychos, *archon* twice, *archon of all honour* and *phrontistes*. In peace his sleep. Aged 55. (*CIJ* I no. 337 = Noy II no. 164 – Rome; 3rd-4th century CE(?))

(VI.25) Here lies Domnos, Father of the Community (*synagoge*) of the Vernaculi, *archon* thrice and *phrontistes* twice. In peace his sleep. (*CIJ* I no. 494 = Noy II no. 540 – Rome; 3rd-4th century CE(?))

(ii) The appointment of children to community offices

A marked feature of Diasporan, as opposed to Judaean/Palestinian, Jewish inscriptions, is the appearance in the former of infant office-holders. In epitaphs found in the Jewish catacombs of both Rome and Venosa, we come across children, some as young as two or three years old, designated as *archons*, *mellarchons* (i.e. archons-elect), *grammateis* and even (one late example only) *archisynagogoi*. Directly parallel to these young Jewish officials are the frequently attested child decurions (local councillors) of municipal Italy. The model for both is Roman – a common way of acknowledging the status of the 'better' families of the community was to award their young scions conspicuous public honours.

(VI.26) Here lies Bitalio, *grammateus*, who lived for 7 years and 14 days. In peace his sleep. (Noy II no. 255, combining *CIJ* I nos. 99 and 180 – Rome; 3rd-4th century CE(?))

(VI.27) Marcus Cuyntus* Alexus, *grammateus* of the Augustesians (and) *mellarchon* of the Augustesians,[24] aged 12 years. (*CIJ* I no. 284 = Noy II no. 547 – Rome; 3rd-4th century CE(?))

(VI.28) Here lies Sikoulos Sabeinos, *mellarchon* of the Volumnesians, aged 2 years (and) 10 months. (*CIJ* I no. 402 = Noy II no. 100 – Rome; 3rd-4th century CE(?))

(VI.29) Here lies Iokathinos, *archon*, a child (*nepios*). (*CIJ* I² no. 120 = Noy II no. 337 – Rome; 3rd-4th century CE(?))

(VI.30) Tomb of Kallistos, child (and) *archisynagogos*. Aged 3 years (and) 3 months. In peace his sleep. (*CIJ* I no. 587 = Noy I no. 53 – Venosa; 5th century CE)

(b) The social sphere – Jews as clients and patrons

Central to Roman society was *clientela* (clientship), the formal relationship between weak and strong, under which services (*officia*) rendered by the former compelled the performance by the latter of *beneficia* (lit. kindnesses). Liberated slaves enjoyed a cliental relationship with their former owners (now their patrons), in whose homes they frequently continued to live; and among commonly attested features of that relationship are (i) the provision by the patron/ess of burial facilities for the household's freedmen and freedwomen and (ii) *their* naming in his/her honour the associations they formed for social and religious purposes. The centrality of clientship and patronage to Roman society was such that no one residing at Rome itself and in areas where Roman influence was strong could remain unaffected by it. In addition to the evidence cited in this section for Jews playing either a cliental or patronal role, note should also be taken of the patronal connotations of the synagogal titles Father and Mother of the Community, for which see **II.68-75**.

Jews as clients of Julius Caesar

(VI.31) At the height of the public mourning (in Rome, for Julius Caesar), a multitude of foreigners went around lamenting, each one in his native manner. Conspicuous were the Jews, who night after night swarmed around the funeral-pyre.[25] (Suetonius, *Iulius* 84.5 = Stern II no. 302)

A Jewish client of Libanius

(VI.32) To the Patriarchs (*sic*).[26] I am all too conscious of the fact that Theomnestos who is the subject of this letter has performed many deeds in compliance with my wishes. Although I have not repaid him for these favours until now, I have discovered a way of doing so through this letter, which he requested and I have consented to write, in the belief that I am not altogether despised by you. There were those who said that I was, and even tried to prove it. Mindful of your many and great deeds, I could not, however, be persuaded. Grant me a favour, then, and do not disturb the old age of Theomnestos, who wants to remain settled rather than be perpetually travelling.[27] You must not fear that I shall ask many favours, for not many days of life perhaps remain to me. I pray that he will obtain the greater boon, which is to remain. If there is anything that prevents that, I ask for the second best, that he may see his native country again (and that) as soon as possible. (Libanius, *Epistulae* 1097 = Stern II no. 501)

Jewish associations named after Roman patrons

The three associations listed here, the communities (*synagogai*) of the Augustesians, Agrippesians and Volumnesians, are thought to have been formed originally by Jewish members of the households of (respectively) the emperor Augustus, his right-hand man, Marcus Agrippa and Herod the Great's friend, Volumnius, a procurator in Syria in 8 BCE. For other inscriptions relating to these congregations, see **II.20**; **35**; **71**; **VI.27** (Augustesians); **II.24** (Agrippesians); **VI.28**; **VII.30** (Volumnesians).

(VI.33) Here lies Annis*, *gerousiarch* of the Community (*synagoge*) of the Augustesians. In peace his sleep. (*CIJ* I no. 301 = Noy II no. 96 – Rome; 3rd-4th century CE(?))

(VI.34) Here lies Zosimos, (*archon*) for life of the Community (*synagoge*) of the Agrippesians. In peace his sleep. (Rest of text omitted.) (*CIJ* I² no. 503 = Noy II no. 549 – Rome; 3rd-4th century CE(?))

(VI.35) Here lies Flabios Sabeinos, (*archon*) for life of the Community (*synagoge*) of the Volumnesians. In peace their (*sic*) sleep. (*CIJ* I² no. 417 = Noy II no. 163 – Rome; 3rd-4th century CE(?))

Provision of burial facilities by Jewish patrons

(VI.36) [The community?] of the Jews living [in the colony of Ostia?] who from [the proceeds of a collection?] have acquired a plot of land for G(aius) Iulius Iustus, [*gerusiarch*], to construct a tomb on, [have presented it] to him [on the motion?] of Livius Dionysius, *Father*[28] and [...]nus, *gerusiarch* and Antonius ... [(*archon*) for?] life, in their year (of office), with the unanimous agreement of the *gerusia*. [G(aius) Iulius Iu]stus, *gerusiarch*, has built (the tomb) for himself [and his wife], his freedmen and freed-women, and their descendants. Width: 18 feet; depth: 17 feet. (*CIJ* I no. 533 = Noy I no. 18 and Plate X – from Castel Porziano, near Ostia; 2nd century CE(?))

(VI.37) Rufina, Jewess (and) *archisynagogos*,[29] has built the tomb for her freedmen and house-born slaves. No one else has the right to bury anyone else (in it). If anyone dares to do so, he shall give to the most holy treasury 1,500 denarii and 1,000 to the *ethnos*[30] of the Jews. A copy of this inscription has been deposited in the record office. (*CIJ* II no. 741 = *IK* Smyrna no. 295 – no earlier than the 3rd century CE)

(VI.38) To Niketas, the proselyte, a worthy and well-deserving man, Dionysias, his patroness (*patrona*), has set up (this memorial). (*CIJ* I no. 256 = Noy II no. 218 – Rome; 3rd-4th century CE(?))

(VI.39) Felicitas, a proselyte for 6 years by the name Peregrina,[31] who lived for 47 years. Her patron (*patronus*)(has set this up) to a well-deserving woman. (*CIJ* I² no. 462 = Noy II no. 62 – Rome; 3rd-4th century CE(?))

(c) The funerary sphere

(i) Use of the epithet benemerens (well-deserving)

In the heavy Jewish use of this, the most favoured of all Latin funerary epithets, we see a clear endorsement of a key Roman value, for *benemerens* reflects the stress placed by the Romans on the performance and reward of duty. (See van der Horst, *Ancient Jewish Epitaphs* p. 63, n. 6, citing Kajanto.) In the Jewish epitaphs from Rome *benemerens* occurs more often than any other epithet, Greek or Latin. In four instances it is even transliterated into Greek! Of the many examples available only a few are presented here. For others, see, inter alia, **VI.8-10; 23; 38-9**.

(VI.40) Iulius Iuda has set up (this memorial) to his well-deserving wife Iulie Maria, with whom he lived for 25 years. (*CIJ* I² no. 636 = Noy I no. 11 – Centumcellae in Etruria; 2nd-4th century CE(?))

(VI.41) Iulia Afrodisia has set up (this stone) to Aur(elius) Hermias her well-deserving husband and she begs and requests that a place may be reserved for her so that she may be placed with her husband when her time comes.[32] (*CIJ* I no. 220 = Noy II no. 378 – Rome; 3rd-4th century CE(?))

(VI.42) Cocotia, also called Iuda, has set up (this memorial) to my (*sic*) well-deserving brother Abundantius, who grew up with me and worked alongside me. He lived for 18 years. In peace his sleep. (*CIJ* I² no. 206 = Noy II no. 217 – Rome; 3rd-4th century CE(?))

(VI.43) Ch... (has set up this memorial) to his wife Gargilie Eufraxia, who lived for 19 years, 3 months (and) 12 days. To a well-deserving woman, who did not deserve this (i.e. death).[33] (*CIJ* I no. 237 = Noy II no. 258 – Rome; 3rd-4th century CE(?))

(ii) Use of the pagan formula D(is) M(anibus) – to the Departed Spirits

What significance, if any, this pagan funerary formula possessed for the small number of Jews who used it, we cannot say. It certainly reflects the influence on them of the Roman environment, where its occurrence was extremely frequent.

(VI.44) To the Departed Spirits of Septima Maria, a Jewess, who lived for 18 years, Actia Sabinilla, her mother (has set up this memorial.) (*CIJ* I² no. 678 = Scheiber no. 7 – Soklos, Pannonia; undated)

(VI.45) Sacred to the Departed Spirits of Iudas ... (Le Bohec, no. 12 – Segermes in the province of Africa Proconsularis; late 3rd century CE)

(VI.46) To the Departed Spirits of Iulia Victoria, a Jewess ... (Le Bohec, no. 71 – Cirta in Numidia; 2nd-3rd century CE)

(VI.47) To the Departed Spirits. To Fofos (?),[34] a well-deserving son (?), who lived for 2 years (and) 7 months. In peace his (or her) sleep. (*CIJ* I no. 464 = Noy II no. 608 – Rome; 2nd-3rd century CE(?))

(VI.48) To the Departed Spirits. P(ublius) Claudius Aciba[35] has erected this for himself. (*CIJ* I no. 76*; not listed by Noy – Puteoli)

(iii) A Jewish metrical epitaph in Latin

This elaborate poem is the only example known to us of a Jewish metrical epitaph in Latin. For Jewish metrical epitaphs in Greek, see **II.26** and **V.65-7**.

(VI.49) Here lies Regina, covered by the tomb her husband has set up, (a monument) such as reflects his love. After twice ten years, she had spent with him a year and fourth months with eight days remaining.[36] Again she will live (and) return to the light again, for she can hope that she will rise to the life promised as a real assurance (interpretation of text uncertain here) to the worthy and pious, since she has earned possession of an abode in the hallowed land (= (?) Paradise). This, your piety will have guaranteed for you, this, your chaste life, this, your love for your family, this, your observation of the Law (and) the merit of your marriage, whose fair reputation was your care.[37] Because of these achievements the future is something for which you must have hope. From these, too, your sorrowing husband searches for solace. (*CIJ* I² no. 476 = Noy II no. 103 – Rome; 2nd century CE(?))

5. JEWISH INTERACTION WITH CHRISTIANS IN THE ROMAN WEST

As in the East, so in the Roman West there is little evidence for relations between Jews and Christians (of pagan origin) in the period before Constantine. While the more plentiful source material from the second half of the fourth and the early fifth century CE testifies mainly to the growing tension between the two groups, it also indicates that peaceful forms of interaction were still possible.

(a) Co-operation between Jews and Christians

(i) Intermarriage, adultery and general socialising

The Canons of the Council of Elvira in Spain, which date from around 300 CE, provide our only evidence here. From the necessity the Church felt to ban inter-marriage and general socialising and punish Christians who engaged in adulterous relationships with Jews, we must conclude that such practices did take place. How prevalent they were is impossible to say.

(VI.50) If heretics have refused to join the Catholic Church, then Catholic girls are not to be given to them in marriage; nor are they to be given to either Jews or heretics, for the reason that there can be no fellowship between a believer and an unbeliever. If Christian parents offend against this prohibition, it is decreed that they must abstain from communion for a period of five years. (Council of Elvira, Canon 16 = Mansi II, col. 8)

(VI.51) If any cleric or lay Christian has eaten with the Jews, it is decreed that he shall be banned from holy communion, in order to force him to mend his ways. (Council of Elvira, Canon 50 = Mansi II, col. 14)

(VI.52) If any married Christian commits adultery with a Jewess or a pagan, he is to be denied communion. If he is exposed by a second party, he (i.e. the offender) shall be able, after a period of five years and the performance of the lawful penance, to participate in the communion of the Lord's day.[38] (Council of Elvira, Canon 78 = Mansi II, col. 18)

(ii) Interaction between Christians and Jews
in religious matters

(VI.53) It is decreed that landowners are to be warned that they are not to allow their crops, which they have received through the favour of God, to be blessed by the Jews, lest they render our blessings invalid and weak. If anyone presumes to do such a thing after this prohibition, he is to be completely excommunicated. (Council of Elvira, Canon 49 = Mansi II, col. 14)

(VI.54) Let no bishop forbid any pagan or heretic or Jew to enter the Church and hear the word of God as far as the Mass of the Catechumens. (Council of Carthage IV, Canon 84 = Mansi III, col. 958)

(iii) Scholarly collaboration between Jews and Christians

The need felt by serious Christian scholars to know the exact wording of the original Scriptures meant that they had to turn to the Jews for instruction in the Hebrew language, access to Hebrew manuscripts and advice about textual inter-pretation. While there is no *Diasporan* evidence for the first of these activities, the letters of Jerome and Augustine throw a fitful light upon the other two.

(VI.55) Jerome to the most blessed bishop, Damasus.[39] After I received the letter from Your Holiness, I immediately summoned a secretary and instructed him to take down my words. While he was getting himself ready for the task, I was conjuring up in my mind what my voice was going to utter. At the very moment when I was going to set my tongue and he his hand in motion, suddenly in burst a Jew carrying a lot of scrolls which he had borrowed from the synagogue[40] on the pretext that he was going to read them. There and then he said, 'Here's what you asked for.' I dithered and did not know what to do, but he so rushed and terrified me that, abandoning everything else, I flew to the job of transcribing them. That I have been doing right up to the present time. (Jerome, *Epistulae* 36.1)

(VI.56) For when a certain brother bishop of ours (Augustine is writing to Jerome in 403 CE) had begun to read your translation (from the Hebrew) in the church over which he was presiding, he created a bit of a stir with a word that you had put in the Book of Jonah (lit. the prophet Jonas), for it was quite different from what was engrained in the mind and memory and had been sung so many times by successive generations. Such a rumpus broke out among the congregation, with the Greeks in particular stirring things up with accusations and charges of falsification, that the bishop was compelled – it was the city of Oea (in Tripolitania) – to ask the Jews to bear witness (to the correctness of Jerome's translation). Was it through ignorance or malice that they replied that what the Hebrew texts contained was what both the Greeks and Latins believed and asserted?[41] (Augustine, *Epistulae* 71, 3.5)

(iv) Christian use of Jewish magical expertise

For other passages relating to the practice of magic by Jews, see **II.127-30** and **V.98**.

(VI.57) We (Augustine is referring to himself) have discovered that at the colony of Uzali also, which is adjacent to Utica, many remarkable miracles have been effected through the same martyr (i.e. St Stephen). His shrine there was established by Bishop Evodius long before any in our city (i.e. Hippo Regius) but there is no practice of issuing reports there (about miracles) – or rather, there wasn't, for perhaps one has started now. For when we were there recently, we encouraged Petronia, a woman of great distinction, to issue, subject to the permission of the above-mentioned bishop of the place, a report which might be read in public and she has most obediently complied. She has been miraculously cured there of a serious and protracted debilitating illness, for which all the treatments of the doctors had been of no avail. In this report she has put down material about which I cannot be silent, even though I am under pressure to hasten on to the topics which form the proper subject of (lit. drive on) this work.

She said that she had been persuaded by a certain Jew to place a ring on a band made of hair which she was to wear around her body under all her clothes next to her skin. The ring was to contain, beneath its gem, a stone that had been found in the kidney of an ox. Having girdled herself with this would-be cure, she started on her journey to the shrine of the holy martyr. She had left Carthage and stopped over at her estate which is bounded by the river Bagrada. On rising to continue her journey, she saw that ring lying at her feet and in wonder inspected the band of hair by which it had been tied on. When she discovered that it was in its original state, tied, with the knots completely firm, she suspected that the ring had cracked and fallen off. When that too was found to be completely intact, she assumed that she had somehow received from such a great miracle a pledge of her future healing. And so, untying the band, she threw it, together with the ring, into the river. (Augustine, *City of God* 22.8)

(b) Conflict between Jews and Christians

(i) *Christian disruption of synagogal worship*

Good evidence for such disruption is provided by an episode from the early life of Callistus, who ended up as bishop of Rome in 217 CE. A slave of Carpophorus, a Christian in the imperial household, Callistus had been set up by his master in a banking business at Rome. Having embezzled both the money entrusted to him by Carpophorus, as well as the investments of certain other Christians, he had attempted to run away but been caught. As our story opens, he languishes in prison ...

(**VI.58**) In due course, as generally happens, certain brethren approached Carpophorus and begged him to release the runaway slave from punishment. Callistus admitted, they alleged, that he had money deposited (to his credit) with certain people. Carpophorus, inasmuch as he was a devout man, said that he was indifferent about his own money but worried about the deposits (of others). For many were in tears as they told him that it was because of the front that he had provided that they had entrusted to Callistus the money they had entrusted to him. Carpophorus was convinced and gave orders for Callistus' release. The latter, not having anything to pay back and not being able to run away since a watch was being kept over him, thought up a scheme for (encompassing his own) death (as a Christian martyr). Pretending to go as if to his creditors, he hurried on the Sabbath to the synagogue where the Jews were assembled and, standing up, disrupted their proceedings. Because they had been disturbed by him, they dragged him off with insults and blows to Fuscianus, the Prefect of the City (of Rome *c.* 185-6 CE). (In response to the latter's questioning), they answered as follows: 'Although the Romans have permitted us to read in public our ancestral laws, this man has prevented this, by coming upon us (and) disrupting our proceedings with his claim that he is a Christian.' While Fuscianus was at his tribunal and reacting with displeasure at the Jews' allegations against Callistus, someone went and told Carpophorus what was going on. Hastening to the Prefect's tribunal, he cried out, 'I beg you, Fuscianus, my Lord, do not believe him. He is not a Christian but looking for an opportunity to die (a martyr's death), since he has embezzled a great deal of my money, as I will demonstrate.' The Jews considering this a ruse – they thought that by this pretext Carpophorus was seeking Callistus' release – denounced him to the Prefect with even greater hostility. Moved by them, he scourged Callistus and sentenced him to the mines of Sardinia. (Hippolytus, *Elenchos* 9.12.5-9)

(ii) Destruction of synagogues by Christians

As in the East, so in the Roman West, the accession to power of hardline orthodox emperors led to the rapid deterioration in relations between Christians and Jews. Symptomatic of this is the destruction of synagogues, which, by 397 CE, had become such a problem that a widespread crack-down on the practice was ordered by the imperial authorities. Besides the individual cases noted here and in (iii) below, synagogues are known to have been either destroyed or converted into churches during this period at Dertona in northern Italy and Tipasa in Mauretania. For details, see J.E. Seaver, *Persecution of the Jews in the Roman Empire (300-438)* (Lawrence, Kansas, 1952), pp. 45-6.

(VI.59) Surely it was for that reason (vindicating the rights of the Jews) that Maximus[42] was undone? When he had heard, before the time set for his expedition, that a synagogue had been burnt at Rome, he had sent an edict to Rome as if he were the vindicator of public order. As a result, the Christian populus (of Rome) said, 'No good will come of this for him. The king has become a Jew ...' If that was said about his words, what will be said about your actual avenging (of the destruction of a synagogue)?[43] (Ambrose, *Epistulae* 40.23 = *PL* 16, col. 1109)

(VI.60) The same two Augusti (Arcadius and Honorius) to Anatolius, Praetorian Prefect of Illyricum. Your excellent authority is to order the governors to meet, so that they may understand and know that the assaults of those who attack the Jews must be repelled and their synagogues remain in their customary peace. Given on the 15th day before the Kalends of July at Constantinople during the consulship of Caesarius and Atticus. (*Codex Theodosianus* 16.8.12 = Linder no. 25 – 17 June, 397 CE)

(iii) Inter-communal violence and the forcible conversion of Jews on Minorca

On the authenticity of the document from which the following extracts have been taken, see introduction to **VI.19**.

(VI.61) From the town of Iamo there gathered for the expedition (to Mago, a town on the other side of the island) a crowd of Christ's servants who were thought to be residents of the town itself. With such eagerness did they overcome the hardships of the difficult journey that they traversed the thirty miles with greater satisfaction than if they had been invited to a dinner party at some delightful suburban villa. And so we arrived at Mago. Immediately I despatched some clergymen, announced my arrival to the Jews and demanded that they do me the honour of coming to the holy church. They, however, sent back a message which we did not expect. They announced that they were obliged not to enter the church on that day, out of fear, I believe, that they might be polluted. For it was the Sabbath, they said, and if they so acted, they would mar its celebration. A second request was then sent – if they preferred, they were to await me at the synagogue, since entry into the church seemed a pollution; in no way were they being compelled by us to perform a servile act on the Sabbath day but an honorable debate would take place about the Law ... (Since the Jews did not like that suggestion either and proceeded to prevaricate mightily, the Christians decided to force the issue.)

And so we began to proceed towards the synagogue and as we advanced along the street we sang a hymn to Christ through sheer joy. The psalm, which the Jews also took up and chanted with remarkable satisfaction over and over again, was this: 'Their memory perishes with a mighty din and the Lord remains for ever!' (*Psalm* 9.6-7). But before we arrived at the synagogue, certain Jewish women, at God's order, I believe, audaciously took the initiative and started to hurl enormous rocks down on us from a higher place, with the intention, of course, of provoking us to violence. Wonderful to relate, although these fell like hail-stones upon the dense mass of people, not only did they fail to strike any of us but they did not even make contact! At this point that terrible lion deprived his sheep of a little of their mildness. For, despite our protests, everybody started to grab a stone. Totally ignoring the warnings of their shepherd (i.e. Bishop Severus himself), they all decided unanimously, out of Christian zeal, rather than anger, that they must use their horns to attack the wolves. That this was done, however, at the nod of Him who alone is the Good Shepherd, admits of no doubt. Finally so that He should not appear to have engineered a bloody victory for His flock, not one of the Jews pretended, not even out of malice, as is their custom, that he had been in the least bit hurt. (After singling out for mention an incident in which a Christian slave was accidently struck on the head by another stone-throwing Christian, Severus briefly describes how the fracas ended.) And so after the Jews had surrendered and we had taken possession of the synagogue, no one stole anything from it or even thought of doing so. With the exception of the Scriptures and the silver, fire consumed the entire structure and its fittings. We took away the sacred Scriptures lest they should sustain any damage at Jewish hands(!) but the silver we returned to them so that there should be no complaints either about our plunder or their losses. After the synagogue had been destroyed while the Jews looked on dumbfounded, we made our way back to the church singing hymns. Giving thanks to the author of our victory, we poured out prayers and asked that the Lord should take by storm the true haunts of perfidy and the dark hearts of the unfaithful should be overwhelmed by light.

(The rest of the letter is largely taken up with those processes, the result of which was, first, the (largely forced) conversion to Christianity of five hundred and forty of the Jews of Mago and, second, the re-building of the synagogue as a church. As the final sentence of Severus' narrative, quoted below, shows, that was mainly at Jewish expense and with Jewish labour.)

First of all the Jews demolished the foundations of the synagogue and then they not only contributed money for the construction of the new basilica but even carried the stones (for it) on their shoulders. (Severus Majoricensis, *Epistola de Iudaeis*, 9, 10 and 20 (extracts only) = *PL* 41.824-5 and 832)

(c) Epigraphic evidence for the conversion of Jews to Christianity

(VI.62) Tomb of the innocent Istablicus, also called Donatus. His own brother Peregriniu(s), also called Mosattes, has erected it. Formerly Jews.[44] (Le Bohec, no. 75 – Sitifis, Mauretania; undated)

(VI.63) Here reposes Peter, also called Papario, the son of Olympius the Jew, and the only member of his family who has deserved to attain the grace of Christ. He was buried with due honour in this sacred hall (*aula*) one day before the Ides of July (i.e. on 14 July) in the IVth indiction. (*CIJ* I² no. 643a = Noy I no. 8 – Grado, north Italy; probably the first half of the 5th century or earlier)

(VI.64) [Tomb of Anasta?]sius, formerly called Iuda,[45] ... Ides of September. (*CIJ* I no. 2 = Noy II no. 530 – Rome; 4th-5th century CE(?))

VII

Pagans and Judaism: academic and real-life responses

The impact made by the Jews on the Greeks and Romans is dramatically illustrated by both the vast numbers of references to them in Greek and Latin literature and the many pagans (most of them epigraphically attested) who had dealings of one kind or another with the synagogue. The greater part of this section is given over to the latter, as the evidence for them is scattered, not easy of access and in some cases not translated into English. Since the pagan literary evidence has been collected and exhaustively commented upon by Stern in his *Greek and Latin Authors on Jews and Judaism*, it will receive very little coverage here. To give some idea, however, of how Jewish matters were handled by those writers, two examples of their work, both ethnographic, are presented below. The first, from Strabo's *Geography*, is one of the few favourable treatments of Judaism to survive from Graeco-Roman antiquity. The second, an excerpt from Tacitus' famous digression on the Jews on the eve of the fall of Jerusalem in 70 CE, represents the much commoner, largely negative, view of the Jews and Judaism, which was disseminated vigorously by Graeco-Egyptian scholars such as Apion.

1. TWO ACADEMIC VIEWS OF THE JEWS AND JUDAISM

(VII.1) But though there is this mix (of peoples living in Judaea), the most prevalent of the accredited reports about the Temple at Jerusalem declares that the Egyptians are the ancestors of the people now called Jews. For one of the Egyptian priests, a certain Moses, who held a part of what is called Lower Egypt, left there for here (i.e. Judaea), through discontent with the prevailing situation. With him there departed many of those who honour the Divine. For he said and taught that the Egyptians, as well as the Libyans, were mistaken in representing the Divine as a wild beast or domestic animal. And the Greeks were wrong too in beating out (divine) images in the shape of man. For God is the single and sole entity that embraces all of us and the earth and the ocean – the thing we call heaven and cosmos and the nature of matter. Who, with any sense, would dare to fabricate an image resembling one of the creatures among us? There should be an abandonment of all image-production. Instead, people should set aside a sacred precinct and a worthy sanctuary and pay honour without a statue. Those who have good dreams should practise incubation on their own behalf and that of the rest of the people.[1] Those who lived with restraint and justice should always expect from the Divine some benefit or gift or sign, but the rest should have no expectations.

With such arguments as these, Moses convinced many men of sound judgement and he led them away to this place, where the settlement of Jerusalem now is. He easily gained possession, since the place was not the object of envy, nor such as to be keenly fought over. For it was rocky, and, while it was itself well-off for water, the land immediately around it was poor and waterless and the ground within sixty stades stony. At the same time, he used for his defence not weapons but sacrifices and the Divine. For he was resolved to seek out a seat for It and and he undertook to make available worship and a ritual of such a nature that participants would not be troubled by either expenses or divine possessions or other strange, magical happenings. Having gained a high reputation on this account, he put together no ordinary polity. All the people round about willingly came over to him because of his dealings with them and the promises he made.

His successors for some time adhered to the same practices. They acted justly and were truly Godfearing. But then, first of all superstitious men were appointed to the priesthood and then tyrannical ones.[2] From the superstition there arose the abstinences from foods, which are still habitual with them, and the circumcisions and the excisions and other such customs,[3] and from the tyrannies, the bands of robbers ... (Strabo, *Geography* 16.34-7 = Stern I no. 115)

(VII.2) To retain his hold over the people for ever, Moses established rites that were new and quite contrary to those practised by other mortals. To the Jews, everything is profane which we hold in reverence and what is permissible with them is abhorrent to us. They dedicated in their inmost sanctuary an image of the animal through whose guidance they had terminated their wandering and thirst. A ram was sacrificed, in derision, as it were, of Ammon. And they sacrifice bulls too, because the Egyptians worship Apis. Because the disease to which pigs are prone once disfigured them, out of mindfulness of that disaster they abstain from (the flesh of) that animal.[4] They still bear witness with frequent fasts to a long famine of long ago and, as proof of the haste with which the grain was seized, no raising agent is used in Jewish bread.[5] They say that they decided to rest on the seventh day because that was the day that brought an end to their struggles. However, because indolence was so attractive, they then gave over to idleness the seventh year as well ...[6]

These rites, however they were established, are maintained through their antiquity but the rest of the (Jews') customs are sinister and abominable and owe their vigour to their depravity. For Jewish wealth has increased because the very worst among other peoples, after spurning their ancestral religions, have channelled tribute and contributions to Jerusalem;[7] further, because their (the Jews') group loyalty is so strong, they are always quick to show compassion (towards one another)[8] but towards everybody else they display only enmity and hate. In dining and sleeping, they keep themselves strictly apart and, despite the strong proclivity of their race to lust, they abstain from sexual relations with foreign women. Among themselves, however, everything goes. They decided to circumcise their genitals, so that by this difference they might be distinguished from other peoples.[9] Those who go over to their ways observe the same practice and they are barely initiated before they start despising the gods, disowning their native land and holding cheaply their parents, children and brothers.[10] To the increase of their own numbers, however, considerable attention is paid: it is a crime to make away with any issue[11] and they consider that the souls of those who die in battle or through capital punishment are immortal. Hence their passion for procreation and their contempt of death. Like the Egyptians, they bury the body rather than cremate it. There is the same concern and the same belief about the nether world but as far as celestial matters are concerned, they are quite different. The Egyptians venerate a host of animals and composite images but the Jews conceive of a sole divinity and that with the mind alone. They consider profane those who, from mortal materials, fashion images of the gods to look like men. In their opinion, that supreme and eternal being cannot be copied and will not perish. And so, they set up no images in their cities, still less in their temples. This flattery is not paid to kings, nor this honour to emperors. Because their priests used to chant together to the accompaniment of flute and drums and wreath themselves with ivy and a golden vine was found in the Temple, some have thought that they worshipped father Liber (i.e. Dionysos/Bacchus), the conqueror of the East. But there is no similarity whatsoever between the two cults. For Liber has instituted rites that are festive and joyous but the customs of the Jews are ridiculous and mean. (Tacitus, *Histories* 5.4-5 = Stern II no. 281)

2. PAGANS SYMPATHETIC TO JUDAISM

Literary texts of the first century indicate that significant numbers of Gentiles were interested in, and sympathetic towards, Judaism. While many of these people did no more than adopt the more conspicuous customs of their Jewish neighbours (e.g. Sabbath-observance), others, particularly in the eastern half of the Roman empire, enjoyed a close association with the local synagogue, whose benefactors they often became. What technical term, if any, there was in the first century for the members of this second category is not known. However, by the third, they are regularly referred to in inscriptions as *Theosebeis* (Godfearers). Although our evidence does not permit us to determine what the Godfearers believed or what the precise nature of their association with the synagogue was, it is generally agreed that they probably formed a very heterogeneous group. While some may have sought no more than the prestige that flowed automatically from being seen to be a public benefactor, for others Judaism's moral code may have been the magnet that attracted them to the synagogue. Conceivably it was from their ranks that at least some of the proselytes known to us (see next section) were drawn. For good general discussions of the Godfearers, see J. Reynolds and R. Tannenbaum, *Jews and Godfearers at Aphrodisias* (Cambridge, 1987), pp. 48-66; Trebilco, *Jewish Communities*, pp. 145-66; Feldman, *Jew and Gentile*, pp. 342-82 and 569-70 and I. Levinskaya, *The Book of Acts in its Diaspora Setting = The Book of Acts in its First Century Setting* 5 (Grand Rapids, Michigan, 1996), chs 4-7.

(Levinskaya's valuable study only became available to me after the completion of the MS of this sourcebook and so has not been utilised in any of my discussions.)

(a) Gentiles broadly sympathetic to Judaism

Aristius Fuscus, poet and friend of Horace

(VII.3) While he (an anonymous bore who had waylaid Horace on the Sacred Way at Rome and was pestering him for an introduction to Maecenas) was going on like this, who should appear but Aristius Fuscus, a good friend of mine,[12] who knew him only too well. We stop. We exchange pleasantries: 'Where have you come from?' 'Where are you going?' I begin to pluck at his cloak and squeeze his arm, which was utterly unresponsive, nodding and winking hard for him to rescue me. The cruel joker laughed and pretended not to notice. My blood boiled over. 'You said there was something you wanted to talk to me about in private.' 'Oh, I remember, but I'll speak about it at a better time. Today's the thirtieth Sabbath.[13] Do you want to offend the circumcised Jews?' 'I have no religious objection.' 'But I have. I'm weaker than you, one of the crowd.[14] Pardon me. I'll speak with you some other time.' (Horace, *Satires* 1.9.60-72 = Stern I no. 129)

Publius Petronius, Roman governor of Syria in 41 CE

(VII.4) He possessed, so it seems, some rudiments of Jewish philosophy and religion. He had picked them up a long time before either from his zeal for learning or after governing territories in which Jews are numerous in all the cities, namely, Asia and Syria, or because he was mentally disposed, through some voluntary, instinctive and spontaneous inclination, towards what is worthy of serious attention. (Philo, *Legatio ad Gaium* 245)

Judaizers in Syria and elsewhere

(VII.5) The whole of Syria was in the grip of terrible confusion. Every city was divided into two camps.[15] Safety for one lay in taking pre-emptive strikes against the other. They passed their days in bloodshed and their nights, which were even worse, in fear. For though the Syrians in each city thought they had rid themselves of the Jews, they viewed the Judaizers[16] with suspicion. While they held off summarily exterminating this ambivalent and intermingled element, they feared these people as much as if they were complete foreigners. (Josephus, *Jewish War* 2.463)

(VII.6) Moreover, among the masses a great enthusiasm for our religious observances took hold long ago. There is not one city, Greek or barbarian, nor a single nation, to which our custom of observing the Sabbath as a day of rest from work has not spread and where the fasts and the lighting of the lamps and many of our usages with regard to food are not observed. (Josephus, *Contra Apionem* 2.282)

(b) Sympathetic Gentiles at the synagogue

(VII.7) Because the later (Seleucid) kings continued to treat the Jews of Antioch in the same (i.e. favourable) manner, they grew in number and adorned their sanctuary[17] with elaborate and costly offerings. All the time they were attracting to their rituals a large number of Greeks, whom they had, to a certain extent, incorporated in their own community.[18] (Josephus, *Jewish War* 7.45)

(VII.8) Meanwhile, the people of Damascus, learning of the catastrophe that had befallen the Romans,[19] were eager to eliminate the local Jews. And inasmuch as they had long had them cooped up in the gymnasium – an action prompted by suspicion – they thought this undertaking would be very easy. However, they feared their wives, all of whom, with a few exceptions, had gone over to the Jewish religion.[20] And so their greatest efforts were devoted to keeping them in the dark. (Josephus, *Jewish War* 2.560-1)

(VII.9) Some of them (i.e. members of the Sabbath congregation in the synagogue at Thessalonica) were persuaded. Among those who threw in their lot with Paul and Silas were a large number of the Greeks who were worshipping (*sebomenon*) and many of the women of standing. (*Acts of the Apostles* 17.4)

(c) Inscriptions referring to Godfearers (*theosebeis*) who appear to have been formally associated with their local Jewish community

(VII.10) ... I emancipate in the prayer-house Elpias, son(?) of my house-bred slave, on condition that he is untroubled and unassailed by all my heirs. The sole stipulation is that he is to attend the prayer-house regularly. The guarantor (of this agreement) is the community (*synagoge*) of the Jews and Godfearers (*theo<n>sebon*).[21] (*CIJ* I² no. 683a = *CIRB* no. 71 – Panticapaeum; 2nd century CE)

(VII.11) God the Helper, who puts [food] on our plate.[22]
Those listed below from the Society of the Law-Lovers, also known as Those who Continuously Offer Praise, in order to alleviate suffering(?), have built (this) memorial for the community (*plethos*) out of their own resources.
Iael, *prostates*,
with her/his son Iosoua*, *archon*

Theodotos, *palatinos*, with
his son Hilarianos
Samuel, *archi(dekanos?)*, proselyte
Ioses*, son of Iesse
Beniamin, psalm-singer
Ioudas, the contented one
Ioses*, proselyte
Sabbatios, son of Amachios
Emmonios, Godfearer (*theosebes*)
Antoninos, Godfearer (*theosebes*)
Samouel, son of Politianos
Eioseph*, son of Eusebios, proselyte[23]
And Eioudas*, son of Theodoros
And Antipeos, son of Hermes
And Sabathios, the sweet one (?)
[And?] Samouel, envoy, priest[24]
(*SEG* 36 (1986) no. 970 = Reynolds and Tannenbaum, p. 5, Face a –
Aphrodisias in Caria; 3rd century CE(?))

The following inscription is an acephalous donor(?)-list from 3rd (?) century CE
Aphrodisias, carved on the same block of marble as the previous entry but on a
different face of the stone. Though clearly relating to the same Jewish community,
it is not certain whether this text, the first few lines of which are lost, is a
continuation of the previous entry or not. (See Reynolds and Tannenbaum, pp.
19-24.) What is virtually certain is that the first half of it consists of Jews and the
second of *theosebeis* (Godfearers). The text is important for illustrating how
numerous the latter could be in any one community and from what a wide social
range they could be drawn. Both this and the previous entry are the subject of
intense ongoing debate. Apart from Reynolds and Tannenbaum's edition of these
texts, the following articles are to be noted: P.W. van der Horst, 'Jews and
Christians in Aphrodisias in the light of their relations in other cities of Asia
Minor', *Nederlands Theologisch Tijdschrift* 43 (1989), pp. 106-21; M.H. Williams, 'The Jews and Godfearers inscription from Aphrodisias – a case of Patriarchal interference in early 3rd century Caria?', *Historia* 41 (1992), 297-310; H.
Botermann, 'Griechisch-jüdische Epigraphik: zur Datierung der Aphrodisias-
Inschriften', *ZPE* 98 (1993), 184-94.

(VII.12)
[Iose]ph, son of Zenon
[Ze]non, son of Iakob; Manases*, son of Ioph (Job?)
Ioudas, son of Eusebios
Heortasios, son of Kallikarpos
Biotikos; Ioudas, son of Amphianos
Eugenios, goldsmith
Praoilios; Ioudas, son of Praoilios
Rouphos*; Oxycholios, old man (the elder?)
Amantios, son of Charinos; Myrtilos
Iako*, shepherd;[25] Seberos*

Euodos; Iason, son of Euodos
Eusabbathios, greengrocer; Anysios
Eusabbathios, foreigner; Milon
Oxycholios, the younger
Diogenes; Eusabbathios, son of Diogenes
Ioudas, son of Paulos; Theophilos
[I]a[k]ob, also called Apellion; Zacharias, retailer(?)
[Le]ontios, son of Leontios; Gemellos
[Io]udas, son of Acholios; Damonikos
Eutarkios, son of Ioudas; Ioseph, son of Philer(iphos?)
Eusabbathios, son of Eugenios
Kyrillos; Eutychios, bronze-(smith?)
Ioseph, confectioner; Rouben, confectioner
Ioudas, son of Hortasios; Eutychios, poulterer
Ioudas, also called Zosi(mos?); Zenon, rag-dealer
Ammianos, dealer in horse-fodder (?); Ailianos, son of Ailianos
Ailianos, also called Samouel; Philanthos
Gorgonios, son of Oxycholios; Heortasios, son of Achilleus
Eusabbathios, son of Oxycholios; Paregorios
Heortasios, son of Zotikos; Symeon, son of Zen(on?)

And such as are *theosebeis* (Godfearers). Zenon, city councillor
Tertullos, city councillor; Diogenes, city councillor
Onesimos, city councillor; Zenon, son of Longi(nos?), city councillor
Antipeos, city councillor; Antiochos, city councillor
Romanos, city councillor; Aponerios, city councillor
Eupithios, purple merchant; Strategios
Xanthos; Xanthos, son of Xanthos
Aponerios, son of Aponerios; Hypsikles, son of Mel(iton?)
Polychronios, son of Xanthos; Athenion, son of Ai(lianos?)
Kallimorphos, son of Kal(limorphos?); Ioun(ios?) Balos(?)
Tychikos, son of Tychikos; Glegorios, son of Tychikos
Polychronios, son (?) of Bel(?); Chrysippos
Gorgonios, coppersmith (?); Tatianos, Oxy(cholios?)
Apellas, son of Hege(mon?); Balerianos, maker of wooden tablets?
Eusabbathios, son of Hed(ychroos?); Ma(rkos) Anikios (?), son of Attalos (?)
Hortasios, stone-carver; Brabeus
Klaudianos, son of Kal(limorphos?); Alexandros, son of (?)
Appianos, son of (?); Adolios, mincemeat-maker
Zotikos, armlet-maker (?); Zotikos, Egyptian-dance performer (?)
Eupithios, son of Eupithios; Patrikios, coppersmith
Elpidianos, athlete (?); Hedychrous
Eutropios, son of Hedychrous; Kallinikos
Balerianos, treasurer (?); Heuretos, son of Athenag(oras)
Paramonos, maker of images (?)
Eutychianos, fuller; Protokopios, money-changer (?)

Prounikios, fuller; Stratonikos, fuller
Athenagoras, carpenter
Meliton, son of Amazonios
(*SEG* 36 (1986) no. 970 = Reynolds and Tannenbaum, pp. 6-7, Face b)

(d) Inscriptions referring to Godfearers (*theosebeis*) who were benefactors of the synagogue

Although the word *theosebes*, which characterises all the people in this section, has sometimes been taken as no more than an epithet meaning pious, it more likely that it is the technical term Godfearer. In donor inscriptions, for which see B. Lifshitz, *Donateurs et fondateurs dans les synagogues juives* (Paris 1967), *passim*, benefactors are generally characterised by their formal status within the Jewish and/or gentile community.

(**VII.13**) I, Capetolina,[26] a most illustrious woman[27] and a Godfearer, have made the whole platform (for the Torah?) and paved the steps with mosaics in fulfilment of a vow for herself (*sic*) [and?] my children and my grandchildren. Blessing! (*DF* no. 30 – Tralles in Caria; 3rd century CE)

(**VII.14**) I, Aur(elios) Eulogios, a Godfearer, have fulfilled my vow. (*DF* no. 17 – Sardis; 3rd or 4th century CE)

(**VII.15**) I, Aur(elios) Polyippos, a Godfearer, have made a vow and fulfilled it. (*DF* no. 18 – Sardis; 3rd or 4th century CE)

(e) Graeco-Roman builders of synagogues

(**VII.16**) When Jesus had finished speaking to the people, he went to Capernaum. A centurion there had a slave, whom he esteemed highly, who was ill and about to die. On hearing about Jesus, he sent some Jewish elders to him and asked him to come and save his slave. Approaching Jesus, they entreated him earnestly, with these words: 'He is worthy of this favour from you, for he loves our people (*ethnos*) and has built the synagogue for us.'[28] (*Gospel according to Luke* 7.1-5)

(**VII.17**) The prayer-house (lit. house) built by Ioulia Severa[29] P(oublios) Tyrronios Klados, *archisynagogos* for life, and Loukios, son of Loukios, *archisynagogos*, and Popilios Zotikos, *archon*, have repaired out of their own resources and the community funds. They have also embellished the walls and the ceiling with paintings and made safe the windows and carried out a general refurbishment. The community (*synagoge*) has honoured them with a gilded shield because of their virtuous conduct and their goodwill and zeal towards the community.[30] (*DF* no. 33 = Trebilco, *Jewish Communities* 3.2 – Akmonia; late 1st century CE)

3. PAGAN CONVERTS TO JUDAISM – THE PROSELYTES

For some Gentiles, simply being a benefactor of the synagogue or a fringe-member of the Jewish community was not enough. They converted outright to Judaism, undergoing in the process a name-change and, if male, circumcision. Despite the large claims of Josephus about the popularity of Judaism with Gentiles (**VII.6**) and the implication of Tacitus (**VII.2**) that Jewish proselytes were numerous, the number of converts known to us by name is very small. While that may be because such people saw no need to advertise their change of religious status or even feared to do so once circumcision had become illegal, an equally plausible reason could be that there were very few converts. Circumcision, a practice frequently mocked by Gentiles and from the time of Hadrian a capital offence, would have been a major stumbling block to male converts. We know from Josephus (**VII.18**) that the rigours of the Jewish Law acted as a deterrent to others. Given the poor quality of the evidence available to us, the extent of Jewish proselytism probably will always remain a matter of dispute. For two totally divergent modern views on the subject, see Feldman, *Jew and Gentile in the Ancient World*, ch. 9 and M. Goodman, *Mission and Conversion* (Oxford, 1994). Among older treatments, note M. Simon, *Verus Israel: a study of the relations between Christians and Jews in the Roman Empire (AD 135-425)*, translated from the French by H. McKeating (Oxford, 1986).

(a) General references to proselytes in literary sources

(**VII.18**) From the Greeks we are separated more by geography than institutions, with the result that we feel for them neither hate nor envy. Contrariwise, many of them have agreed to come over (*eiselthein*) to our laws. While some have abided by them, others, unable to endure their rigour, have withdrawn (*apestesan*) again.[31] (Josephus, *Contra Apionem* 2.123)

(**VII.19**) As Paul and Barnabas were leaving, they (the leaders of the synagogue at Pisidian Antioch) invited them to speak to them on these matters on the next Sabbath. When the congregation had dispersed, many of the Jews and proselytes[32] who were worshippers followed Paul and Barnabas. (*Acts of the Apostles* 13.42-3)

(**VII.20**) Some whose lot it was to have had a Sabbath-fearing father,[33] worship nothing but the clouds and the spirit of the heavens. They make no distinction between the flesh of a pig, from which their father abstained, and that of a human. In time they get themselves circumcised.[34] Habituated to despising the laws of Rome, they learn and observe and fear the Law of the Jews and all that Moses handed down in that arcane tome of his: not to point out the way except to a fellow believer (and) to lead only the circumcised to the sought-after fountain. The blame for all this lies with the father, for whom every seventh day was a day of idleness, entirely separated from the concerns of life.[35] (Juvenal, *Satires* 14.96-106 = Stern II 301)

(b) Named proselytes in literary sources

(VII.21) There was a Jew, a complete rogue, who had fled from his own country because he had been accused of breaking certain laws and feared punishment on that account. At that time, he was living in Rome, where he pretended to be an exegete of the Laws of Moses and their wisdom. He attached to himself three men who in all respects were like himself (i.e. just as corrupt as he was) and together they persuaded Fulvia, an aristocratic lady, who had become a proselyte and taken to visiting them regularly, to send purple and gold to the Temple in Jerusalem. Appropriating them for their own use, they put them towards their personal expenses, which had been the intention of their request in the first place. Saturninus,[36] the husband of Fulvia, at her instigation, appraised (the emperor) Tiberius, whose Friend[37] he was, (of the situation) ...[38] (Josephus, *Jewish Antiquities* 18.81-4)

(VII.22) During the time that Izates (son of the king of Adiabene) was staying at Charax Spasini (a small kingdom at the head of the Persian Gulf), a certain merchant, Ananias by name, visited the king's wives and taught them to worship God as the Jews traditionally did. It was through them that he came to know Izates and won him over. When the latter was recalled to Adiabene by his father, Ananias accompanied him, in response to his repeated requests. It so happened that Helena (the mother of Izates) too had similarly been taught by another Jew and converted to their laws ...

When Izates (who meantime had become king of Adiabene)[39] discovered that his mother was highly delighted with Jewish ways, he too was keen to convert to them. Thinking that he would not be a proper Jew unless he was circumcised, he was prepared to perform the deed. His mother, on learning of this, tried to stop him. She argued that he was endangering himself. He was a king, she said, and would cause much disgruntlement among his subjects, once they had discovered that he was keen on practices that were foreign and strange to them. They would not endure being ruled by a Jew. These were the arguments she produced and she did everything she could to stop him. He reported her words to Ananias, who agreed with the (king's) mother and threatened that he would leave him and go away if he did not obey. He said he was afraid that, if the business became universally known, he would run the risk of being punished for being personally responsible for these matters and for teaching the king things that were unseemly. He could worship God, he said, without circumcision, if he was completely resolved on zealously adhering to the ancestral practices of the Jews. That was more important than being circumcised. He said that God would pardon him for not performing the rite through force of circumstances and the fear inspired by his subjects. At that time the king was persuaded by these arguments. He had not, however, completely given up the desire. And later, another Jew, Eleazar by name, who came from Galilee and had a reputation for extreme rigour when it came to the ancestral practices, persuaded him to perform the act. For when he came to pay his respects and found the king reading the law of Moses, he said, 'You are unaware, O king, that you are committing the gravest offence against the laws and, through them, against God, for you must not just read the laws but rather do the things that are enjoined by them. How long will you stay uncircumcised? If you have not yet read the law on this point, read it now, so that you may know wherein your impiety lies.' On hearing this, the king put off the deed (no longer). Going into another room and summoning the doctor, he had the prescribed act carried out. Summoning his mother and his teacher Ananias, he made clear to them that the deed had been performed. They were filled with consternation and absolutely terrified that if the deed were proven the king might run the risk of losing his throne since his subjects would not endure being ruled by a man who was a devotee of alien practices and they themselves might be given the blame for it. God, however, was to prevent their fears from being realised. (Josephus, *Jewish Antiquities* 18.34-48)

(VII.23) Izates' brother Monobazus and his kinsmen, on seeing that the king had become the object of admiration among all men because of his piety towards God, conceived a desire to abandon their ancestral practices too and adopt those of the Jews.[40] (Josephus, *Jewish Antiquities* 18.75)

(VII.24) And they chose Stephen, a man full of faith and the Holy Spirit, and Philip, and Prochoros, and Nikanor, and Timon, and Parmenas, and Nikolaos, a proselyte from Antioch.[41] (*Acts of the Apostles* 6.5)

(VII.25) Hear also the very words that Irenaeus has written about the Septuagintal translation of the God-inspired scriptures. 'God, therefore, became man and the Lord himself saved us, giving us the sign of the virgin, but not, as some of those who dare to translate the Scriptures nowadays say, "Behold, *the young woman* shall conceive and bear a son."' This is how Theodotion of Ephesus has translated it and Aquila of Pontus,[42] both of them Jewish proselytes. The Ebionites follow them and say that he (i.e. Jesus) was begotten by Joseph. (Eusebius, *The History of the Church* 5.8.10)

(c) Some epigraphically attested proselytes

For proselytes at Aphrodisias, see **VII.11**.

(VII.26) (Bones of) Ioudas, son of Laganion, a proselyte.[43] (*CIJ* II no. 1385 – Jerusalem; 1st century BCE/CE)

(VII.27) Diogenes, a proselyte, son of Zenas. (Bagatti-Milik, no. 21 – Jerusalem; 1st century CE)

(VII.28) Salome, the proselyte. (Bagatti-Milik, no. 31 – Jerusalem; 1st century CE)

(VII.29) Sarra, proselyte, 18 years.[44] (*CJZC* no. 12 – Cyrene; Roman period)

(VII.30) Beturia Paulla, placed in her eternal home, who lived for 86 years and 6 months; a proselyte for 16 years by the name of Sara;[45] Mother of the Communities (*synagogarum*)[46] of Campus[47] and Bolumnius.[48] In peace her sleep. (*CIJ* I no. 523 = Noy II no. 577 – Rome; 3rd-4th century CE(?))

(VII.31) Eirene, a foster-child, a convert to Judaism through her father and mother, a Jewess (and) an Israelite,[49] has lived for 3 years and 1 day. (*CIJ* I no. 21 = Noy II no. 489 – Rome; 3rd-4th century CE(?))

(VII.32) Cresce(n)s Sinicerius, a Jew (and) a proselyte, (who) lived for 35 years, has fallen asleep. His mother has done for her sweet son what he should have done for me. 8 days before the Kalends of January (i.e. 25 December). (*CIJ* I no. 68 = Noy II no. 491 – Rome; 3rd-4th century CE(?))

(VII.33) Mannacius to his sweetest sister, C(h)rysis, a proselyte. (*CIJ* I no. 222 = Noy II no. 224 – Rome; 3rd-4th century CE(?))

4. OTHER ADHERENTS TO JUDAISM –
INSTANCES OF DISPUTED STATUS

Besides the adherents to Judaism listed above, there are in our sources individuals who either are described in terms that suggest they may have had some connection with Judaism or themselves use words and phrases that are open to the same implication. In such instances, this linguistic ambiguity makes precise classification impossible. In most cases, the people employing these terms presumably knew what they meant. For us, the loss of context makes their significance hard to determine. Sometimes, however, the ambiguity of the language may reflect a genuine ambiguity of status: many people on the boundaries of Judaism and Christianity or Judaism and paganism may have experienced genuine difficulty in defining their religious/cultural identity.

(a) Ambiguous instances of the epithet *theosebes*

Notoriously difficult to classify, in the absence of a clear link with the synagogue, are people described as *theosebes*. For the word, besides functioning as a *terminus technicus* for a Gentile synagogue-associate, can also be used simply as an epithet for any pious/godfearing person, be s/he pagan, Jewish or Christian.

(VII.34) Nero, having listened to them (the twelve Jewish delegates from Jerusalem), not only pardoned them for what they had done but allowed them to let the building stay as it was. He did this to gratify his wife,

Poppaea. For she, being a godfearing/Godfearing (*theosebes*) woman,[50] had pleaded on the Jews' behalf. Ten (of the delegates) she ordered to go (home) but Helkias (the Temple treasurer) and Ismaelos (the High Priest) she kept with her as hostages. (Josephus, *Jewish Antiquities*, 20.195)

(VII.35) Here lies Eparchia, *theosebes* (a Godfearer/godfearing),[51] who lived for 55 years (and) 6 days. (May) your sleep (be) among the good. (*CIJ* I² no. 228 = Noy II no. 207 – Rome, at the entrance to a Jewish catacomb but not actually inside it)

(VII.36) Agrippas, son of Phouskos*, from Phaena,[52] *theosebes* (God-fearer?).[53] (*CIJ* I no. 500 = Noy II no. 627(i), where the text is classified as not Jewish – Rome; 3rd-4th century CE(?))

(VII.37) *Euphro(s)yna theosebes chresta chaire* = (a) Euphro(s)yna, a Godfearer (and) an excellent woman. Farewell or (b) Euphro(s)yna, a pious (and) an excellent woman. Farewell.[54] (*CIJ* I² no. 731e – Rhodes; undated)

(b) *Metuens* and related phrases

Indisputable examples of the pagan usage of these terms make it hard to know whether people so described are fearers of a pagan deity such Jupiter or the Jewish God and, if the latter, whether as Jews, proselytes or *theosebeis*.

(VII.38) To the departed spirits of Maiania Homeris, a reverer of God/god (*d<a>e(um) m<a>etuenti*). (*CIJ* I² no. 524 = Noy II no. 626(iii), who does not consider the inscription to be Jewish – Rome; uncertain provenance)

(VII.39) Aur(elius) Soter and Aur(elius) Stephanus, sons, have set up (this monument) to Aur(elia) Soteria, the most conscientious of mothers (and) a reverer (*metuenti*) of the Jewish religion.[55] (*CIJ* I no. 642 = Noy I no. 9 – Pola; 3rd-5th century CE)

(c) 'Drifters into Jewish ways': Judaizers, proselytes or Christian converts?

(VII.40) And in the same year (95 CE), Domitian slaughtered, along with many others, Flavius Clemens the consul, even though he was his cousin and married to Flavia Domitilla, who herself was a kinswoman of the emperor. A charge of atheism had been brought against both. Many others who had drifted into Jewish ways[56] had been condemned for this, of whom some had been put to death and others deprived at least of their property. Domitilla was merely banished to Pandateria but Glabrio, who had been Trajan's colleague in the consulship (91 CE), was executed. The accusations against him included those which had been brought against many people and, specifically, that he fought (as a gladiator) against wild beasts. (Dio, *Roman History* 67.14.1-3 = Stern II no. 435)

(d) An adherent of 'a foreign superstition'

(VII.41) Pomponia Graecina, a woman of high rank (and) the wife of Aulus Plautius, whose triumph over the British I recorded earlier, was charged with foreign superstition[57] and referred to her husband for trial. Following ancient practice, he held the investigation which was to determine her fate and reputation before a family council and pronounced her innocent. (Tacitus, *Annals* 13.32.3-4 = Stern II no. 293)

(e) Ambiguous dedicatory language

Most of the examples in this section consist of dedications to the Most High God. The categorisation of such texts, of which there are large numbers in existence, is extremely problematic owing to the widespread use of the phrase by both Jews and pagans. While the former regularly applied it to Yahweh (e.g. II.133; IV.11), with the latter it was a common divine epithet, especially for Zeus/Jupiter. In many cases it is impossible to decide whether the dedicator was wholly Jewish, wholly pagan or a mixture of both.

Bi-partite inscription (here (a) and (b)) from a small marble altar:

(VII.42) (a) God, the Lord, who is for ever.
(b) Zopyros (has dedicated) to the Lord the altar and the lamp-holder with the lamp. (*DF* no. 12 – Pergamum; undated)

(VII.43) To God, Greatest and Highest, on behalf of Epitychia, also called Dionysia, and on behalf of her husband Harpochras and their children, in fulfilment of a vow. 2nd year of Caesar, Phaophi 6. (*CIJ* II no. 1532 (Jewish?) = *CPJ* III no. 1532 (not Jewish) = HN no. 116 (possibly Jewish) – Fayum, 29 BCE)

(VII.44) Theanos to God, the Most High, a vow.[58] (Trebilco, *Jewish Communities* 6.4.4 – Kos; 1st-2nd century CE)

(VII.45) Epiktetos has fulfilled his vow to God, the Most High. (*New Docs.* I no. 5(i) – Akmonia; Roman imperial period)

(VII.46) With good fortune. Aur(elia) Tatis, wife of Onesimos, blacksmith, together with her husband Onesimos, set up (this monument) from their own resources to the Most High God.[59] (*New Docs.* I no. 5(ii) – Akmonia; Roman imperial period)

(f) Ambiguous sepulchral language

(VII.47) Fabios Zosimos has made the sarcophagus and placed it on a holy site, which is before the city by the *sambatheion*[60] in the Chaldaean precinct alongside the public highway, for himself, so that he may be placed in it, and for his sweetest wife Aurelia Pontiane. No one else has the right to deposit anyone else in this sarcophagus. If anyone dares (to do so) or acts contrary to these stipulations, he shall pay to the city of the Thyateirans one thousand five hundred silver denarii, to the most holy treasury two thousand five hundred denarii (and) be liable besides to (punishment under) the law of tomb violation. Two copies of this inscription have been written, of which the other has been deposited in the public archives. This has been enacted in the most illustrious city of the Thyateirans, during the proconsulship of Katillios Seberos*, on the thirteenth of the month of Audnaios, by Menophilos, son of Ioulianos, public notary. (*CIJ* II no. 752 = *TAM* V.2, no. 1142; Thyateira; early 2nd century CE)

(VII.48) Year 338 (= 253-4 CE) Aelios Pancharios, also called Zotikos, has built the tomb during his lifetime for himself and his wife, Aelia Atalanta and their children. If anyone places another body in it, he shall have to reckon with God[61] and he shall give to the treasury five hundred denarii. (*CIJ* II no. 773 – Apamea in Phrygia)

(g) Ambiguous magical inscriptions

The combination of Jewish and pagan elements on most amulets, plus the fact that their ancient context in often unknown (of the two that figure here, one was a stray find in Sicily and the other a purchase on the antiques market in Damascus), means that it is usually impossible to know whether their original owners were adherents to Judaism or not. For a brief discussion of Jewish magic and magical texts, see P.S. Alexander in *HJPAJC* III, pp. 342-61.

(VII.49) I call upon Iao, Michael, Gabriel, Ouriel, Arbathiao, Abrathia, Adonai, Ablanathanalba, Sabaoth, Sesengenbarpharanges, Akrammachamari ... (astronomical signs) ... the Lords, Archangels, Gods and the Divine Characters. Drive away every evil and every ... and every ... to whom she has given birth ... from today and from now to all eternity ... (rest is unintelligible) (*CIJ* II no. 849 – Syria; 4th-6th century CE)

(VII.50) Delko, Ia, Dikon, Ia, Eska[...]seara, Ia, Michael, Ia, Gabriel, Ia, Iel, Ia, Raphael, Ia, Ouriel, you Eiliel, Ia, Tedchiel, Ia, Ouniel, Ia, Eistrael, Ia, Phoniphnael, Ia, Ia, Oth, Ia, Tibaoth, Ouriel, Ia, Tedchiel, Ia, Sei[lam]phiel, Ia, Tedchiel, Ia, Krou[...]thiel, Ia, Gibitiba, Ia, Chrouth[...], Ia, Seraphim, Msorthom (= (?) mesharethim = ministering angels), Ia, Arphellim, Ia, Maon, Ia, Ra[kia?], Zboul, Ia, Arpheliem, Ia, Set<n>, Artemis. Flee from Iouda and all evil.. in the glory of the Holy God ...

(unintelligible letters) Sabaoth, Micha[el], Gabriel (unintelligible) Guard Thybes the bearer (of this amulet). Iouda, the Holy Law ... (rest is unintelligible) (Noy I no. 159 – Sicily; 3rd-5th century CE)

5. SYNCRETIST CULTS

From the reign of Augustus down to the fourth century, there are scattered references in our sources to religious groups which, while displaying certain Jewish features (mainly respect for the Sabbath and worship of the Most High God), were clearly not wholly Jewish. Whether they were comprised mainly of Judaizing pagans or paganizing Jews cannot be determined. The final group in this section, the *Caelicolae*, is thought by some to have been a Judaeo-Christian-pagan sect. Although the only 'cell' certainly known to us was in north Africa, the cult may have been more widely spread. Imperial rulings against it, the source of most of our information, had application throughout the western provinces.

(a) A pagan association of Sabbath observers?

(VII.51) ... son of Ammonios, convener (*synagogos*) ... for the Sambathic association, [in the year ...] of Caesar (Augustus?), Phamenoth 7. (HN no. 26 – Naucratis; 30 BCE – 14 CE)

(b) The *Sabbatistai* of Cilicia Tracheia

(VII.52) Decree of the Companions and the Sabbatistai who have gathered through the goodwill of the god Sabbatistes. No one is to render invalid the inscription they have carved. If anyone does, purification ceremonies must be held for him. If anyone wishes to dedicate an offering, let him dedicate an offering. Protos proposed that (A)i(th)ibelios the *synagogeus*[62] be crowned. As to the dedications in the temples and the inscriptions on the stelai and dedications, let no one erase them or damage them or change (?) them. If anyone sins against the god Sabbatistes, either by doing something or omitting to do something, he shall pay to the god Sabbatistes and the Sabbatistai 100 denarii and to the city 100 denarii and to the dynast[63] 100 denarii. Be this stele an oath (for everyone) in the like manner: thou shalt not reveal the day.[64] The priest is to apportion for the maintenance of the place the offerings made to the god. (*OGIS* II no. 573 – 1st century CE)

(c) Worshippers in Cappadocia of the Most High God

(VII.53) He (Gregory is speaking of his father *c*. 374 CE) was a shoot from a root that is not to be praised. It was – and I am not ashamed of his early history since I have confidence in his later career – not naturally disposed towards piety nor was it planted in the house of God. It was altogether strange and peculiar, in that it was a mixture of two utterly opposed elements – Greek illusion and legal trickery. While eschewing some parts of each, it was composed of others. Although they reject idols and sacrifices, they worship fire and lamps. Despite revering the Sabbath and being fastidious about certain foods, circumcision they do not hold in honour. The name of these benighted souls is *Hypsistarioi*. Their sole object of worship is the All-Powerful One (*Pankrator*).[65] (Gregory of Nazianzus, *Funebris in patrem* 5 = *PG* 35, cols. 989-92)

(**VII.54**) Let us examine the words which follow: 'In every way and absolutely He is one; in the same respect and in the same manner He remains a single entity.' If he (i.e. Eunomius) is speaking about the Father, with this even we are in agreement ... If, then, these words refer to the Father, let him not fight with the decree of piety, since he is in agreement with the Church on this point, for he who concedes that the Father is always the same and is one and alone, confirms the argument of piety. He sees in the Father the Son, without Whom the Father cannot exist or be spoken of. But if he is imagining some other god besides the Father, let him go and talk to Jews or the so-called *Hypsistianoi*.[66] They have this difference with the Christians – they concede that the one whom they call *Hypsistos* or *Pankrator* is God but they do not accept that he is the Father. But if the Christian does not believe in the Father, he is not a Christian. (Gregory of Nyssa, *Contra Eunomium* 2 = *PG* 45, cols. 481-4)

(d) Bosporan synods of the Most High God

From Tanais near the mouth of the Don and north-east of the Sea of Azov several dozen inscriptions of 2nd-3rd century date have survived relating to the cult of the Most High God. Although the cultists themselves do not have Jewish names, many features of their worship – e.g. the titles *presbyteros* and *synagogos*, and the 'name' accorded their deity – reveal Jewish influence. Who the cultists and what their rituals were is disputed. The terms in which they describe themselves and make their dedications – namely Fearers of the Most High God (*sebomenoi theon hypsiston*) to Good Luck (*agathe tyche*) and God the Most High (*theos hypsistos*) – point in the direction of Judaizing pagans. Only two of these thiasic lists are included here. The appearance of the same cultists in many of these inscriptions means that little doubt attaches to most of the restored names in the documents below.

(**VII.55**) To Good Luck.
To God the Most High, for a vow.
In the reign of King Tiberios Ioulios Rheskouporis, the Friend of Caesar and the Friend of Rome, the Pious, (the) newly admitted brethren who worship the Most High God around (name lost), the Elder (*presbyteros*), have set up the stele inscribed with their names. Phannes, son of Am...razmes, (next name and patronymic lost), Herakleides, son of [A]ttas, Phorera[nos, son of Euios(?)], Ardinzianos, son of Chrysippos, Pharn[akes, son of Pharnakes?], Psycharion, son of Phidanoi, Ompsa[lakos, son of Pha]zinames, Menios, son of Herm[es... Ath]enodoros,

son of Phazin[ames] ... (*IOSPE* II no. 450 = *CIRB* 1285 – Tanais; early 3rd century CE)

(VII.56) To Good Luck.

To the Most High God who listens, the synod around the Most High God and the priest (*hiereus*) Chophrasmos, son of Phorgab[a]kes and the convener (*synagogos*) Rhadamophourtos, son of Tryphon and the *philagathos*,[67] Demetrios, son of Herakleides and the *paraphilagathos*, Euios, son of Rhodon and the gymnasiarch, Thiagaros, son of Antisthenes and the *neaniskarches*,[68] Chariton, son of Makarios and the rest of the cult members (*thiasotai*) (have made the following dedication). Zenon, son of [Pha]nnes, Antimachos, son of Pasion, Eunoikos, son of Eunoikos, [Gor]gias, son of Pha[rnak]ion, Thalamos, son of Pitopharnakes, Asandros, son of Thaumastos, [I]talorhas[p]os, son of Herakleides, Arathes, son of Phidanoi, Phannes, son of Dadas, Pateis, son of Alkimos, Proxenos, son of Basileides, Kadanakos, son of Nauages, Zabargos, son of Char[i]ton, Apollonios, son of Apollonios, Dadas, son of Pappos, Pharnakes, son of Herakleides, Charaxs[t]os, son of Pharnakes, X[egodis?], son of Achaimenes, Oxardozis, son of Eubarnak[es, Z]orthines, son of Phaz[imanes], Ardarakos, son of Tryphon, Bassos, son of B[assos?], Demetrios, son of [Anti]machos, Sambation, son of Gorgi[as]. (The remaining thirty or so names and the date have been omitted as they are rather fragmentary.) (*IOSPE* II no. 446 = *CIRB* no. 1278 – Tanais; 2nd-3rd century CE)

(e) The *Theosebeis* of Phoenicia and Palestine

(VII.57) You admit, do you not, that the Midianite was foreign and barbarous? For he was not from the root of Abraham. He was, in some manner or other, a priest and an acolyte of the voluntary cult that was observed at that time throughout the land. On the one hand, they worshipped, as many tell us and as they themselves thought, the Highest God, as, of course, did Melchisedek.[69] But they also, apparently, acknowledged other gods too and they counted among their number, alongside Him, the choicest works of creation – namely, the earth and sky, the sun and moon, and the more remarkable of the stars. The slippage and error in that matter was an ancient fault but it has persisted right up to the present day. For certain people in Phoenicia and Palestine, who call themselves *Theosebeis*, still hold these crazy beliefs. In religion they follow a middle course, inclining wholeheartedly neither to the ways of the Jews nor those of the Greeks but are tossed and torn between the two.[70] (Cyril of Alexandria, *De Adoratione in Spiritu et Veritate* 3.92-3 = *PG* 68, col. 281)

(f) The *Caelicolae* (lit. worshippers of Heaven)

(VII.58) The same two Augusti (Honorius and Theodosius II) to Iovius, the Praetorian Prefect. In some manner or other a new and criminal superstition has appropriated for itself the unheard-of name, *Caelicolae*. If those people have not returned to the worship of God and the veneration of Christ by the end of the year, let them know that they too are to be restrained by the laws by which we have ordered heretics to be bound. For it is a certainty that whatever differs from the faith of the Christians is contrary to the Christian Law. Some people, forgetful of their life and justice, dare to treat the law in such a way that they force some Christians to adopt the foul and loathsome name of Jews. Although those who have admitted this will have been condemned under the laws of the Emperors of old, nonetheless we have no regrets about warning again and again that those who have been initiated into the Christian mysteries are not to be compelled, after (abandoning) Christianity, to take hold of the Jewish perversity, which is alien to the Roman empire. If someone believes that this should be attempted, we order that the instigators of the deed, together with their accomplices, suffer the penalty stipulated in former laws. For assuredly it is more serious than death and more cruel than slaughter if anyone of the Christian faith is polluted by Jewish incredulity. We, therefore, order ... (text corrupt) ... (and) decree ... that, if anyone attempts to contravene this law, he is to know that he is to be charged with treason. Issued on the Kalends of April at Ravenna in the consulship of the two Augusti, Honorius for the 8th time and Theodosius for the 3rd. (*Codex Theodosianus* 16.8.19 = Linder no. 39 – 1 April, 409 CE)

(**VII.59**) The next day he (Fortunius, bishop of Tubursi in Africa) came to see me himself and we began to discuss the matter again. I could not, however, stay long with him, as the ordination of a bishop required my departure from the place. I had already sent a messenger to the leader of the *Coelicolae*, of whom I had heard that he had introduced a new baptism among them and, by this impiety, led many astray. I intended, so far as my limited time allowed, to confer with him. (Augustine, *Epistulae* 44 – c. 398 CE)

Notes

I. The Jewish Diaspora in the Hellenistic and early Roman imperial periods

1. Strabo was writing at the time of Augustus (31 BCE – 14 CE).

2. Note that this comment, by a Greek author from Asia Minor, is not entirely friendly.

3. *Apoikiai*, the word used by Philo here, conjures up a picture of deliberate, 'government-led', Greek-style colonisation. There is no evidence that the Jerusalem authorities ever behaved in such a manner.

4. The Greek verb used here (*katoikountes*) indicates that they were settlers, not pilgrims. So, correctly, E. Haenchen, *The Acts of the Apostles* (Oxford, 1971), p. 168, n. 7.

5. Presumably there would have been other Jewish prisoners of war in Pompey's triumphal procession. For the triumph of Titus in 70 CE, seven hundred were selected, apart from the Jewish leaders themselves. See Josephus, *Jewish War* 7.118.

6. Apart from the prisoners who were brought in to grace the triumphs of Pompey and Sosius in 63 and 37 BCE respectively, some may also have come in 53 BCE, after the revolt of Pitholaos. See Smallwood, *Jews under Roman Rule*, p. 131.

7. After the fall of Taricheae in Galilee in 67 CE, Vespasian had despatched 6,000 Jewish prisoners to Greece to labour on the cutting of the Corinthian canal. See Josephus, *Jewish War* 3.539-40.

8. Probably in 70 CE, when the city was taken by Titus. Subsequently, as the name Claudia shows, Aster (Heb. Esther) was liberated, probably by her freedman husband, a former slave of either the emperor Claudius or Nero.

9. Earlier stated to have been Hadrian for the second time and Rusticus. Chronogically the *Chronikon* is seriously confused here. While the insurrection alluded to (i.e. that of Bar Kochba) probably started in the spring of 132 CE (Smallwood, *Jews under Roman Rule*, p. 141), Hadrian's second consulship was in 118 CE and that of P. Dasumius Rusticus in 119 CE.

10. Gaius Sentius Saturninus. For his daughter-in-law, the Jewish proselyte, Fulvia, see **VII.21**.

11. His name was Zamaris, for whom see also **III.3**.

12. This settlement, the so-called Land of Onias or Jews' Camp, is referred to several times by Josephus and also attested epigraphically (**V.65**). For Vespasian's closure of the temple there after the First Jewish War, see **IV.49**.

13. On this expulsion and other disciplinary measures of Claudius against the Jews of Rome, see **II.144** and **IV.47**.

14. For the trouble they caused there, see **II.142**.

15. Just how threatened Josephus' life was is demonstrated by the attacks mounted on him even while enjoying imperial protection at Rome. See *Vita* 424-5 and T. Rajak, *Josephus* (London, 1983), p. 194.

16. Modern scholars doubt this claim. See introductory discussion at Chapter

V § 1. There is no doubt, however, that Jews were widely used as settlers in the new Hellenistic foundations of the East.

17. It is not certain from which Antioch Debbora hailed. Calder (*MAMA* VII, p. x, n. 1) argues against nearby Antioch in Pisidia on the grounds that 'metrical epitaphs of this type, detailing place of birth and place of burial, regularly stress distance and contrast.' He suggests that the missing word at the beginning of the epitaph may be *Karidos* (of Karia). If correct, then Debbora's place of birth would have been Antioch on the Maeander.

18. A Greek city on the Campanian coast, otherwise known as Puteoli. Before the time of Claudius it functioned as a port for Rome. For its flourishing Jewish community, see also **I.74** and **VI.20**.

19. All the people in this list are Jews. Barnabas and Saul, originally from Cyprus and Cilicia respectively, had recently come from Jerusalem. Manaen, who had been brought up with Herod Antipas, ruler of Galilee and Peraea from 4 BCE to *c.* 39 CE, was from Judaea.

20. Jerusalem here is a plausible restoration from Ἱερ....υμίτα. For Niketas, son of Jason, a Jerusalemite at Iasos and Judaean Jews at Smyrna, see **V.18-19**.

21. Which of the many cities called Laodicea is indicated here, we cannot tell.

22. Whether this was Tripolis in Syria, Asia Minor or Libya is impossible to determine.

23. See **V.43** for a Jew at Rome actually from Caesarea in Palestine.

24. Note that firm evidence for Jews in Africa (apart from Egypt and Cyrene) only starts in the second century CE.

25. See H.J. Leon, *The Jews of Ancient Rome* (Philadelphia, 1960), pp. 135-6.

26. Roman client ruler of Judaea between 4 BCE and 6 CE. A son of Herod the Great.

27. P. Quinctilius Varus, Roman governor of Syria and the official with ultimate control over Judaea.

28. Roman emperor from 14-37 CE. For this expulsion, see also **IV.45**.

29. The Delta quarter is generally believed to have been located in north-eastern Alexandria, on the coast to the east of Cape Lochias. Cf. Josephus, *Contra Apionem* 2.33. Jewish tombs have been found in the area. See *CIJ* II nos. 1427-8 = HN nos. 1-2.

30. This area had been officially made over to them by the Ptolemies (Josephus, *Jewish War* 2.488). His contradictory assertion that the donor was Alexander the Great (*Contra Apionem* 2.35) should be taken with a pinch of salt.

31. Text uncertain at this point. For the reading adopted here, see *CIJ* I², *Proleg.*, p. 26.

32. Despite the variation in spelling, it is customary to associate this congregation, most of the evidence for which comes from one of the Jewish cemeteries near the Subura, with that district. See Leon, *Jews of Rome*, pp. 152-3. For this congregation, see also **II.29**.

33. Thought to be a mocking reference to the Jewish tax, for which see **IV.50-68**.

34. The Jewish identity of this man has been inferred primarily from his patronymic, which was greatly favoured by Jews in Egypt. For other Jewish weavers, see **I.83** (at Nearda in Babylonia) and **II.143** (a Palestinian refugee in Cyrene).

35. Thought by Tcherikover (*CPJ* I, *Proleg.*, p. 17) to have been a professional musician.

36. These events occurred during the racial inrest of 38 CE, for which, inter alia, see also **I.56** and **79**; **V.31** and **80**.

37. This man was probably the younger son of Alexander the *alabarch* (**I.74**) and hence the brother of Tiberius Iulius Alexander, the later prefect of Egypt, for whom, see primarily **IV.30-4**.

38. Other documents in this dossier (*CPJ* II no. 419a, c and e) reveal dealings by Alexander in skins, lime-wood and cords.

39. For the payment by this man of the Jewish tax in 80 CE, see **IV.53**.

40. For the payment by this man of the Jewish tax in 95 CE, see **IV.60**. Tcherikover suggests (*CPJ* I, *Proleg.* p. 54) that he may have been a trader.

41. The term denotes a man qualified to work as an advocate by virtue of having passed through all the normal stages of higher education. Euthalis is one of three Jewish examples known. For the others, see **I.95** and *DF* no. 74 (Sepphoris in Galilee; 5th century CE).

42. Jewish silk merchants are also attested at the Mesopotamian city of Edessa, which lay on the Silk Route to China. See H.J.W. Drijvers, 'Jews and Christians at Edessa', *JJS* 36 (1985), pp. 89 and 94.

43. Possibly in the employ of the city. For a 5th-century Jewish *archiatros* at Venosa, see Noy I, no. 76, formerly *CIJ* I no. 600.

44. For other examples of this term, see **II.22-4**. For *scholastikos*, see n. 41 above.

45. Notwithstanding the commandment against making images of living things (*Exodus* 20.4), representational art (*zographia*, for which see *DF* no. 20 from Sardis) was permitted among the Jews, providing that its purpose was purely decorative. The best examples of it are the murals found in the synagogue at Doura-Europos. For these, see, E.R. Goodenough, *Jewish Symbols in the Greco-Roman Period* IX-XI (New York, 1964).

46. The title of this congregation has been taken to indicate that originally it was founded by lime-burners but other interpretations are possible. See Leon, *Jews of Rome*, pp. 142-4. For other inscriptions referring to this congregation, see **II.33** and **69**.

47. One of the few references to local Jewish archives. For another, see **II.83**.

48. This is one of the earliest references anywhere to a Jewish prayer-house (*proseuche*). For another, see **IV.1**.

49. On the multi-functional role of the synagogue, see especially **II.1-18**.

50. In the parallel account in Josephus, *Jewish Antiquities* 12.107, the phrase 'all the Jews' is found.

51. On this phrase, see now Lüderitz in *SEJE*, pp. 183-225, who argues persuasively that *politeuma* here must designate not the whole Jewish community but a much smaller body, possibly a council of the great and good.

52. On this, the so-called Eumeneian Formula, see **VII.48** (note). For other examples, see **V.68** and **73**.

53. For the interpretation of the text here, see Robert in *Hellenica* 11-12 (1960), p. 261, n. 1.

54. In **I.101**, this community is referred to as a *katoikia*. Either we have a change in terminology here or a case of loose usage.

55. An oblique reference to his construction of the *whole* synagogue. This inscription was probably over the entrance door, which would have faced east-wards towards Jerusalem.

56. Interpreted by Lifshitz (*DF* no. 31 – comm. ad loc.) as a cultic club *within* the Jewish community but the sense is not altogether clear. For other instances of *synodos* in a Jewish or Judaizing context, see **II.16** and **VII.56**.

II. Life inside the Jewish Diasporan community

1. Probably of the Torah portion in the synagogue, like Jesus in the *Gospel according to Luke* 4.16-20.

2. For a psalmodist at 3rd (?) century Aphrodisias, see **VII.11**. On the attraction to non-Jews of the synagogal liturgy and especially its music, see John Chrysostom, *Adversus Iudaeos* 1.7.

3. Such structures have been attested in a number of synagogues – e.g. at Antioch (*IGLS* III no. 70) and Caesarea Maritima (*DF* no. 66). They were used principally for the communal feasting that took place regularly on the Sabbath eve, the New Moon and at festival times. Private dining clubs, as in **II.8**, may also have used them.

4. Probably one of the Patriarchs of the House of Hillel in Galilee, for whom, see **III.76-80**, rather than a local official. On this point and the inscription generally, M. Hengel, 'Die Synagogeinschrift von Stobi', *ZNTW* 57 (1966), pp. 145-83 is fundamental.

5. The identity of this individual, whose name has become rather scrambled in transmission, is uncertain.

6. Some critics prefer to read Paros (in the Cyclades) here.

7. For Jewish charitable activities, see **II.103-5** and **VII.2**.

8. The passage describes an imaginary confrontation in a slum district of Rome, such as the Subura.

9. On the equation of synagogues with temples and the theft of Jewish sacred monies from them as sacrilege, see also **IV.3** and **28**.

10. Generally taken to be a reference to a synagogue.

11. The allusion is to the corporal punishment inflicted by synagogal authorities in the Diaspora probably in the earliest phase of Paul's apostolic work.

12. By the Romans, as in *Acts of the Apostles* 16.22.

13. Usually quoted only in part (*synagogae Iudaeorum fontes persecutionum*) and construed as a generalised allusion to Jewish persecution of Christians, this passage actually refers to the corporal punishment inflicted on the early apostles by the synagogal authorities. See F. Millar, *JRS* 56 (1966), p. 234 (review of W. Frend's *Martyrdom and Persecution in the Early Church*).

14. On this title, see introductory discussion at **II.35**.

15. Although the *prostates* both here and in the previous entry is sometimes claimed to be a legal officer who defended the community's interests, that is unlikely, as the Greek terms used for the individuals who habitually fulfilled that rôle were quite different. For further discussion, see M.H. Williams, 'The structure of Roman Jewry re-considered', *ZPE* 104 (1994), pp. 138-9.

16. Although some have thought that Sanbati(o)s was the president of an old man's club, it seems preferable to view him as the chairman of the local *gerousia* (lit. 'council of old men'). While the former institution is nowhere attested in our sources, the latter is frequently. For *palaios* as an epithet for Jews, see **V.30** and Reynolds and Tannenbaum, p. 132.

17. The rather high-flown language of this metrical epitaph makes interpretation of the word *politarchon* difficult. Although some have suggested that it is no more than a fancy rendering of *archon*, Abramos' age suggests he was probably the president of the community council. The archonship (see next section) tended to be held by men in their twenties and thirties. For a general discussion of the office of *politarch*, see G.H.R. Horsley, 'Appendix – The Politarchs' in D. Gill and C. Gempf (eds), *The Book of Acts in its Graeco-Roman Setting* II (Michigan, 1994), pp. 419-31.

18. Probably Leontopolis and some other Jewish settlement nearby. See HN ad loc.

19. Probably the same as the Community (*synagoge*) of the Vernaculi, for which see Leon, *Jews of Rome*, pp. 154-7.

20. Possibly an allusion to *Proverbs* 10.7, for whose rendition from Hebrew into Greek, see **V.42-4**.

21. For another example of this combination of offices, see *DF* no. 66 (Caesarea; 6th century). Whether the man, described in **VI.23** as having been both *archon* and *archisynagogos*, held those offices concurrently or in succession, is not clear.

22. The term used here by the plaintiff, a woman who may or may not be a Jewess, is the common Greek term for a temple warden, which, in origin, probably meant sweeper. It is not wholly certain, of course, that the Jews of Alexandrou Nesos themselves actually used this term for their 'verger'.

23. Not attested in any Diasporan source, but quite likely to have been a regular function of the Diasporan synagogal assistant, was his handing of the scroll to the reader of the Torah portion in the synagogue on the Sabbath. For this, see *Gospel according to Luke* 4.16-20.

24. Frey's interpretation of the text has been followed here in preference to that of Noy.

25. On *laos* (people) as a common term for Jewish community, see **I.109-12**.

26. So translated by both Frey and Lifshitz. See *CIJ* and *DF* ad loc.

27. Probably a reference to the Jewish military settlement at Leontopolis, for the foundation of which see **I.20**.

28. Strabo is describing the situation in the period immediately before the radical shakeup of 11/12 CE, when the more collective type of leadership, described in **II.77-8**, was established by the Romans.

29. Generally assumed to be the same official as Strabo's *ethnarch* in **II.76**.

30. The reference is to the Feast of Tabernacles in 38 CE. For this festival, see **II.134-6**.

31. The *archons* here are the same men as the thirty-eight council members in **II.77**.

32. Libanius is writing here to his old friend, Priscian, now the governor of Palestine, about the Jews of Antioch.

33. Thought to be an elaborate reference to the Jewish Patriarch. See Stern, comm. ad loc.

34. Though not admitted by Noy, there is a real possibility that this pupil was a girl. Other pieces of evidence suggest that learning (of the Law) on the part of women was both admired (next entry) and expected, at least in some families. The name Eumathia (lit. a good learner) found in an epitaph at Beth She'arim (*BS* II no. 113) could well reflect parental aspirations for their daughter.

35. A translation of *talmid hakham* – rabbinical scholar. The term points to the presence of a Bet ha-Midrash at Rome, such as the 2nd-century academy of Mattithiah ben Heresh, mentioned in bT, *Sanhedrin* 32b. Only at Dabbura in the Golan has a Bet Midrash been attested epigraphically in Roman times. For the inscription: Eli'ezer ha-Qappar. This is the school (Bet Midrash) of the Rabbi, see D. Urman, 'Jewish inscriptions from Dabbura in the Golan', *IEJ* 22 (1972), pp. 21-3.

36. The classification of this metrical text as Jewish is largely based upon this phrase.

37. For another example of this epithet, see **II.5**. For the name Philonomios, see *MAMA* III no. 751 and M.H. Williams, 'The Jewish Community of Corycus – two more inscriptions', *ZPE* 92 (1992), pp. 249-50.

38. Besides this epithet, for which see also the next entry and **II.100**, note also its variant, *philentolios*, at **II.53** and the name Entolios, at *CIJ* II no. 1438 = HN no. 5.

39. For the *observantia legis* of another Roman Jewess, see **VI.49**.

40. An alternative reading here is M(arkos) A<u>r(elios) Moussios. See L. Robert, *Hellenica* 11-12 (1960), pp. 381-4.

41. The prestige that still attached to the priesthood even at this late date emerges clearly from this text. The main claim to fame of the deceased was that her daughter had married a priest.

42. Cicero is addressing a Roman jury during the trial of L. Valerius Flaccus in 59 BCE and referring to the Jews of Rome. For their numbers about three quarters of a century later, see **I.52-4**.

43. On *laos* as a Jewish community term, see **I.109-12**.

44. For other Thessalian epitaphs with this valedictory message, see *CIJ* I², nos. 702-8 and *Hellenica* 3 (1946), pp. 103-4.

45. This epithet is found only here.

46. This epithet is found only here.

47. A distinctly Jewish epithet, found only here.

48. 18 July – the anniversary of the heavy defeat of the Romans by the Gauls on the banks of the river Allia in 390 BCE.

49. On the probable Antiochene provenance of this homily, see W.A. Meeks and R.L. Wilken, *Jews and Christians in Antioch in the First Four Centuries of the Common Era* (Missoula, Montana, 1978), p. 42, n. 65.

50. Persius' words conjure up the slum tenements in the Subura or Transtiberinum which would have housed the vast majority of the Roman Jews in his day.

51. The allusion here is to two key elements of the Sabbath supper, namely fish and wine. The poverty of the Jews is further emphasised by the reference to earthenware (= poor man's crockery) and the tail of the tuna (a notoriously cheap cut). See R.A. Harvey, *A Commentary on Persius* (Leiden, 1981), comm. ad loc. For an exhaustive discussion of this passage, see W. Horbury, 'Herod's Temple and Herod's Days' in W. Horbury (ed.) *Templum Amicitiae, Essays on the Second Temple presented to Ernst Bammel* (Sheffield 1991), pp. 103-49.

52. The general misapprehension among the Romans that the Sabbath was a fast day surfaces again in Petronius, Fr. 37 and Martial, *Epigrams* 4.4.7 = Stern I nos. 195 and 239. Perhaps there was a confusion with the Day of Atonement.

53. A distinguished jurist of the first half of the 3rd century CE.

54. Although the emperor Antoninus Pius (138-161 CE) did not rescind his predecessor's ban on circumcision, he did soften its impact. At some point in his reign, both the Jews and others for whom circumcision was of ritual significance, were granted exemption from it.

55. The general context of this passage indicates that the purpose of Pius' rescript was to prevent Jews from circumcising their Gentile slaves. Repeated rulings by Rome on this issue (e.g. next document) reveal the ineffectiveness of official policy in this matter.

56. Banishment to an island and confiscation of property.

57. For similar rulings of the years 335, 339 and 384 CE, see Linder nos. 10; 11 (= **IV.71**) and 17.

58. I have omitted from my translation here the probably interpolated word *politai*, meaning citizens of Sardis.

59. An unexpected word, given that the temples at Jerusalem and Leontopolis were the only places at which Jews offered sacrifices then. Probably it represents a misapprehension on the part of the city authorities about the nature of Diasporan Judaism.

60. See **IV.26** for another reference to Jewish foodstuffs.

61. And hence immune from slaughter. Cf. Juvenal, *Satires* 6.159-60 –

(Judaea), where ... a long-established clemency allows pigs to reach old age (*ubi ... vetus indulget senibus clementia porcis*).

62. The delegation, of which Philo himself was a member, was visiting Rome *c.* 40 CE in connection with the ethnic troubles that had erupted in Alexandria in 38 CE.

63. An allusion to the expulsion of the Jews and the suppression of the cult of Isis in 19 CE, for which see **I.53-4** and **IV.45**.

64. Presumably there had been a real danger that Seneca's Pythagorean-inspired vegetarianism might be confused with Jewish abstention from pork and so render him liable to (false) prosecution and punishment.

65. A Greek doctor of medicine and sceptical philosopher, possibly of the 2nd century CE.

66. And then Roman governor of the island.

67. The thirty-one angels invoked here probably correspond to the maximum number of days in the months of the solar calendar. See Kotansky, art. cit., p. 269.

68. Thought to be a reference to *Yom Kippur*. On this and the Septuagintal language of this epitaph, see P.W. van der Horst, *Ancient Jewish Epitaphs* (Kampen, 1991), p. 149.

69. The reference is to the summary arrest for treason of A. Avillius Flaccus, the then governor of Egypt.

70. In the coincidence between Flaccus' downfall and the non-celebration of the Feast of Tabernacles, Philo sees the hand of God at work. God had intervened and saved the Jews at the precise moment when, because of Flaccus, their fortunes had reached their nadir.

71. Apparently celebrants of this seven day festival habitually passed the night without sleep. See Stern, *CPJ* ad loc.

72. Whether the membership of the two craft guilds mentioned here was wholly Jewish, wholly pagan or a mixture of the two is disputed. For discussion, see Trebilco, *Jewish Communities*, pp. 178-9 and 261.

73. Haman's effigy, which the Jews burned every Purim, was tied to a cross, in memory of his crucifixion.

74. For Purim junketings which tragically got out of hand, see **V.91**.

75. The meaning of this phrase is disputed. While Musurillo (ad loc.) suggests there may be an allusion to the Passover, R. Lane Fox, *Pagans and Christians* (Penguin Books, 1988), pp. 486-7, argues at some length that the reference is to the celebration of Purim in 250 CE.

76. Opposite the harbour at Alexandria. For the translation of the Septuagint there, see **V.41**.

77. i.e. taking up arms on behalf of Ptolemy VI's widow, Kleopatra, against the usurper, Ptolemy (later VIII, Euergetes II) Physkon in 145 BCE.

78. Although many of the details here are clearly apocryphal (an even more fanciful version of these events, this time located in the reign of Ptolemy IV Philopator, is to be found in 3 *Maccabees* 5-6), there is no reason to doubt that the Jews of Alexandria did celebrate an annual festival of thanksgiving for divine deliverance from some impending catastrophe.

79. Usually taken as an allusion to the dissension created among the Jews of Rome by Christian missionising.

80. Dated by the 5th-century Christian historian Orosius in *Adversus Paganos* 7.6.15 to the ninth year of Claudius' reign – i.e. 49 CE. For two named victims of this expulsion, see **I.21**.

81. For some epigraphic Godfearers, see **VII.10-15**.

82. For this office, see **II.56-63**.

83. Although the Christian community at Corinth had many non-Jewish members, the leadership in its early days was largely Jewish. Apollos, for instance, was a Jew of Alexandria. See **I.32**.

84. The Aramaic nickname of the Apostle, Simon Peter.

III. Diasporan Jews and the Jewish homeland

1. Probably located on Mt Ophel, where this stone was found.

2. Needed for purificatory purposes. See introductory note at **II.39**.

3. For Herod's establishment of this Babylonian Jew as puppet-ruler in the toparchy of Batanaea, see **I.19**.

4. For her conversion to Judaism, intense piety and burial in Jerusalem, see **III.18; 20; 36(a)** and **(b); VII.22**.

5. From the rest of the passage it is clear that what Philo is actually talking about here is the half-shekel Temple tax.

6. On the difficulties and dangers of the route, see Philo, *Legatio ad Gaium* 216.

7. L. Valerius Flaccus was governor of the Roman province of Asia in 62 BCE.

8. Among the Jews listening to the case against Flaccus. Their presence in the crowd is alluded to earlier in the speech.

9. This person is not otherwise known.

10. Lit. fruits. Generally thought to be a reference to tithes set aside for payment to priests in Jerusalem. See S. Safrai in S. Safrai and M. Stern (eds), *The Jewish People in the First Century I* (Assen, 1974), pp. 201-2.

11. Possibly the same man as in **III.37**.

12. For other examples of this additional levy by Rome, see **IV.52-3** and **55-8**.

13. Josephus has just been describing M. Licinius Crassus' seizure from it in 55 BCE of several thousand talents of silver and large quantities of gold.

14. Probably a reference to the Godfearers, for some epigraphic examples of whom see **VII.10-15**.

15. The reference is to the assault by Mithridates VI of Pontus on the Roman province of Asia in 88 BCE.

16. The gate of Nikanor. See **III.16**.

17. Alexander the *alabarch*, brother of Philo of Alexandria and father of Tiberius Julius Alexander, for whom, see **I.74** and **IV.30**.

18. Probably the Corinthian gate mentioned in **III.15**.

19. Other interpretations of the Hebrew here are (i) Nikanor, son of Alexas and (ii) Nikanor, the Alexandrian.

20. Even if not a Jew, the dedicator must have been, at the very least, a Godfearer. See B. Isaac, 'A donation for Herod's Temple' in *IEJ* 33 (1983), p. 90.

21. From the findspot, it has been suggested by Isaac, art. cit. (n. 20), p. 89 that this may well have been of the southern courtyard of the Temple.

22. For these pious converts to Judaism from the royal family of Adiabene, see also **III.6; 20; 36a** and **b; VII.22-3** and L.H. Schiffman, 'The conversion of the Royal House of Abiabene (*sic*) in Josephus and Rabbinic sources' in L.H. Feldman and G. Hata (eds), *Josephus, Judaism and Christianity* (Leiden, 1987), pp. 293-312.

23. i.e. the Christians. Although the context here is Christian, the people involved were mainly Jews.

24. On the motives for her journey to Jerusalem from Adiabene, see **III.6**.

25. King of Adiabene and, like his mother, a Jewish proselyte. For his conversion, see **VII.22**.

26. Adiabenian military support is also to be deduced from *Jewish War* 6.356.

27. This is not the only interpretation of this sentence. Some think that, not one, but as many as five different congregations of Diasporan Jews may be indicated here. See Haenchen, *Acts of the Apostles*, p. 271, n. 1. The freedmen (Lat. *libertini*) would have been one-time Roman slaves.

28. Mother of the emperor Nero. If it was in Rome that Theodotos served her, as suggested by Hachlili at *BASOR* 235 (1979), p. 46, then clearly he must have returned to Judaea on his liberation. From other inscriptions in the family burial chamber it emerges that Theodotos was this man's slave-name, his Hebrew name being Nath[an]el, which, of course, has the same meaning as Theodotos – i.e. given by God. See R. Hachlili, 'The Goliath family in Jericho: funerary inscriptions from a first century AD Jewish monumental tomb', *BASOR* 235 (1979), pp. 33 and 46-7.

29. While Hillel's Babylonian origin is not in dispute, (for further information about him, see *HJPAJC* II, pp. 363-7), the details given here about his age are clearly fanciful. For a full discussion of the passage, see J. Neusner, *The Rabbinic Traditions about the Pharisees before 70* (Leiden 1971), Part I, pp. 220-1.

30. Possibly connected with the pious royal proselyte family from Adiabene, for whom, see nn. 4 and 22 above. For the despatch by king Izates of his five sons to Jerusalem so that they could get a thorough grounding in the Hebrew language and Jewish culture, see Josephus, *Jewish Antiquities* 20.71.

31. Ananel's priesthood lasted for only a few months in 37 BCE.

32. Nothing further is known about either Abba or Mattathiah.

33. Probably from northern Mesopotamia. See Puech, *Rev. Bib.* 90 (1983), p. 519.

34. For the so-called monuments of Helena, see Josephus, *Jewish War* 5.119 and 147.

35. Inscriptions, written (respectively) in Estrangela and Aramaic, from an ossuary, thought to be that of Queen Helena of Adiabene, which was found in the Tomb of the Kings at Jerusalem. If that is correct, Sarah will have been her conversion name. For name-change on conversion, see **III.37a-c**; **VI.39**; **VII.30**.

36. It is impossible to know which of the several towns of that name in the eastern Mediterranean is meant here.

37. It is not clear whether Mesopotamian or Egyptian Babylon is meant.

38. Part of Cyrenaica.

39. Gk. *lamprotatos* = Lat. *clarissimus* – a Roman honorific title.

40. Both the names found in the epitaphs in this burial hall, as well as the language of one of them (Palmyrene), reveal that its occupants originally came from Palmyra. For discussion, see Lifshitz, *BS* II, pp. 5-6.

41. The date given here has been the subject of much debate. Some would emend it to one hundred and *forty*-eight (of the Seleucid era), thus giving this (forged?) document a date of 164 BCE, the year of the cleansing of the Temple – the subject of this letter.

42. The feast indicated here is Hanukkah, the eight-day festival inaugurated in 164 BCE to celebrate the purification of the Temple three years to the day after its desecration by Antiochus IV Epiphanes. The festival is also sometimes referred to as the Festival of Lights or the Feast of the Dedication of the Temple.

43. If correct, this would give this rather confusing document a date of 143/2 BCE. For a full discussion of this and the preceding entry, see E. Bickermann, 'Ein jüdischer Festbrief vom Jahre 124 v. Chr (II *Macc*.1,1-9)' in *Studies in Jewish and Christian History* II (Leiden, 1980), pp. 136-58.

44. A reference to the troubles in Judaea of the early 160s BCE.

45. A reference to the Festival of Lights (Hanukkah), for which see n. 42.

46. Of the several possible dates here, 114/3 BCE is generally thought to be the most likely. See Tcherikover in *CPJ* I, p. 46, n. 119 and *HJPAJC* III, p. 506.

47. Also known as Letter of Purim or the Book of Esther. The reading of this is the central event of the annual festival of Purim, for which see **II.138**.

48. Date of, inter alia, the destruction of the Temple. See M. *Taanith* 4.6.

49. For a similar accusation against the Jerusalem authorities, see Eusebius, *In Isaiam* 18 = *PG* 24, col. 213.

50. The overseas travels of these four rabbis (in the 90s CE?) are frequently mentioned in Talmudic sources. For a list, see Smallwood, *Jews under Roman Rule*, p. 383, n. 99.

51. For criticism of the historicity of this passage, see T. Zahavy, *The Traditions of Eleazar ben Azariah* (Missoula, Montana, 1977), p. 132.

52. This anecdote appears, with minor variations, in a number of places – e.g. jT, *Pesahim* 34a; bT, *Pesahim*, 53a; bT, *Bezah* 23a. Note that the variant cited here contains a historical impossibility: while Thaddeus (otherwise known as Todos and Theodosios) flourished in the 2nd century CE, Simeon ben Shetah, who is alleged to have rebuked him, lived in the first half of the first century BCE. On the problems of using the Todos/Theudas material as historical evidence, see L.V. Rutgers, *The Jews in Late Ancient Rome: Evidence of Cultural Interaction in the Roman Diaspora* (Leiden, 1995), p. 204.

53. Probably Judah IV (fl. 385-400 CE)

54. Hazzans. For a specific bearer of this office, see **II.66**.

55. Of the officials mentioned here, only the *apostoloi* performed this function.

56. A reference to their abolition of the *aurum coronarium* in 399 CE, for which, see previous entry.

57. Thus far the text is in Hebrew. The remainder of it is in Latin. For a full discussion of it, see F. Millar, 'The Jews of the Graeco-Roman Diaspora between Paganism and Christianity, AD 312-438' in J. Lieu, J. North and T. Rajak (eds), *The Jews among Pagans and Christians* (London, 1992), pp. 97-9.

58. Just conceivably the Old Testament patriarchs (i.e. Abraham, Isaac and Jacob) but more probably the ruling dynasty of Hillel in Galilee, whose power and prestige were at their zenith at this time. For an invocation of Patriarch's authority in the 3rd century, see **II.7**.

59. For other Godfearers, see **VII.10-15**.

IV. Jewish interaction with Greek and Roman authorities

1. An important Nilotic customs post (Strabo, *Geography* 17.800), which the Jews may have either manned or guarded. For Jewish river guards on the Nile, see Josephus, *Contra Apionem* 2.64 and **IV.10**.

2. Possibly Cleopatra VII (51-30 BCE) and Caesarion, her son by Julius Caesar, thus giving a date to this inscription of 37 BCE.

3. Their identity is uncertain, some arguing for Cleopatra VII and Caesarion (44-30 BCE), others for Zenobia and Valballathus of Palmyra who ruled Egypt between 269-71 CE.

4. Whether this was Ptolemy III Euergetes I (246-222 BCE) or Ptolemy VIII Euergetes II Physkon (145-116 BCE) is uncertain.

5. This is the only example known to us of a synagogue being awarded this privileged status. There are, however, numerous examples of pagan temples in Ptolemaic Egypt being so honoured. To infringe the inviolability of a such place was to be guilty of sacrilege.

6. The First Jewish War (66-73/4 CE).

7. About 54 gallons, if LSJ is correct in estimating a *metretes* at 9 gallons.

8. Possibly an army paymaster.

9. The standard Ptolemaic rate of interest. For other examples of Jews lending at interest to each other, see below **V.56-7**.

10. Tcherikover (*CPJ* ad loc.) suggests that it may have been a shop in the military camp at Herakleopolis.

11. The large size of the land-holdings of these men, over 50 acres each, suggests they enjoyed a high rank within their cavalry unit.

12. See n. 8 above.

13. He belonged to the lowest grade of court officials.

14. As in the previous document, the Jews here are engaging in (entirely legitimate) extra-curricular activities.

15. For this, see **I.20**.

16. The word used is non-specific *hegemon* (leader).

17. Stated by Horsley, *New Docs* 4, p. 201 to be a Gentile but there seems no reason why he should not be considered Jewish.

18. Identified by Tcherikover (*CPJ* I, pp. 230-1) with the high-flying Jewish apostate, Dositheos, son of Drimylos, mentioned in 3 *Maccabees* 1.3. For his cultic rôle, as High Priest of the deified Alexander, see **V.51**.

19. This official headed one of the two branches of the royal secretariat.

20. The name proclaims the Jewish origin of this official. It was not used by Gentiles. Although neither the position nor the identity of Onias can be established, both the tone and content of the letter indicate that he was an official of high status.

21. For the name, see previous note.

22. The name Joseph indicates that this teller in a government chaff-bank was a Jew.

23. The name, the Greek equivalent of Nathaniel and Mattithiah (Matthew), makes it virtually certain that this manager of the royal bank at Koptos was a Jew.

24. The name proclaims a Jew.

25. The date of this episode is 38 CE. For the honorary Jewish decree which Augustus ordered to be set up in the Temple of Rome and Augustus at Ancyra, see **IV.28**.

26. The name of the dedicator and the apparent reference to his family were inscribed over an erasure perhaps as much as a century after the main body of the text was carved.

27. Impossible to identify what this object was.

28. Joint rulers of the Roman Empire between 198 and 209 CE. The second is more commonly known as the emperor Caracalla.

29. Julia Domna, the mother of Caracalla and his younger brother, Geta. She was awarded the title, Mother of the Camps in 195 CE.

30. Lifshitz's restorations of this text in *CIJ* I² are accepted here in their entirety. For a similar but slightly later dedication to Septimius Severus and his sons in Palestine, see *CIJ* II no. 972. For another Pannonian example, see **IV.42**.

31. He had been sent by the Senate to recruit two legions in the province of Asia for the war against Julius Caesar. See Caesar, *Civil Wars* 3.4.

32. Other citations of this ruling give the Kalends of July. See, for instance, Josephus, *Jewish Antiquities* 14.234 and 237.

33. A misapprehension on Philo's part. Handouts of cash were intermittent.

34. Whether the fragments belong to the same edict or not is disputed.

35. In the Temple at Jerusalem. The most frequently attested of these is the Temple tax, paid annually by all adult Jewish males. For this, see **III.7-8**.

36. So that they might have a ready supply of water for ritual purposes. On this, see **II.39** and **III.2**.

37. In the original text, the precise amount would have been stated.

38. A numeral has fallen out of the text here.

39. The Greek reads *andronos* – a banqueting hall or lounge. These are attested in many synagogues. See **II.7**.

40. Consul in 8 BCE; proconsul of Asia in 2-3 CE.

41. For other passages illustrating Christian attacks on synagogues, see **V.92-4** and **VI.59-61**.

42. The dates of Tiberius' governorship are uncertain. Smallwood, *Jews under Roman Rule*, p. 257, suggests 46-8 CE.

43. See **I.74** and **III.15**.

44. So thorough had the assimilation of Tiberius Alexander been that Tacitus does not think of him except in Roman terms.

45. To Gnaeus Domitius Corbulo, the Roman commander-in-chief of the war against Tiridates, the king of Armenia.

46. Only in inscriptions, such as this, and papyri (*CPJ* II no. 418c, not quoted here) does Tiberius Alexander's full Roman name appear. It is not known when his Prefectship of Egypt started. Certainly he was already in post by the beginning of the Jewish War (66 CE).

47. 69 CE. The edict itself, which is too long to be quoted here, was issued in 68 CE.

48. According to *Jewish War* 6.237, he was a kind of quarter-master general.

49. This papyrus fragment has been taken by some scholars as evidence that Tiberius Julius Alexander was rewarded for his services to the Flavians by being given the command of the Praetorian Guard at Rome. For discussion, see Fuks, *CPJ* ad loc.

50. Previously held by the father of Tiberius Julius Alexander (**I.74**). Possibly the post involved superintending the collection of customs duties on the eastern (i.e. Arab) side of the Nile.

51. On this ostrakon we have a Jew (note the Hebrew patronymic) collecting a state tax from other Jews. For proof of the Jewish identity of the latter, see, inter alia, **IV.56**.

52. For these important officials who managed the state granaries, see S.L. Wallace, *Taxation in Egypt from Augustus to Diocletian* (Princeton, 1938), pp. 36-8.

53. The Jewish identity of Ioses, Isakis and Eleazaros is revealed by their names.

54. From the time of the emperor Diocletian (284-305 CE), the term denoted an employee in one of the two financial departments of the state: *sacrae largitiones* and *res privatae*. For another possible example, see **VII.11**.

55. Best seen as referring to Leontios. For arguments that he came from Palmyra, see Lifshitz, *BS* II, pp. 38-40.

56. Another may have been the Jewish *ducenarius* from Seleukeia on the Kalykadnos, mentioned in **V.10**. Other (still unpublished) inscriptions from the Sardis synagogue mention assistants at the record office and a count. For a general description of these, see Trebilco, *Jewish Communities*, pp. 48-9.

57. i.e. a centurion. For a 1st century legionary, see **VI.7**.

58. Possibly the town of that name in Upper Egypt. Until the 4th century CE, a Roman legion was garrisoned there.

59. On this unit, see now D. Woods, 'A note concerning the *Regii Emeseni Iudaei*', *Latomus* 51 (1992), pp. 404-7.

60. The Roman magistrate concerned with foreigners.

61. On this interpretation of the text, see E.N. Lane, 'Sabazius and the Jews in Valerius Maximus: a re-examination', *JRS* 69 (1979), pp. 35-8. Others, less plausibly, have taken the passage in its unemended state as evidence for a pagan-Jewish syncretistic cult devoted to the worship of Yahve-Sabazius.

62. A puzzling phrase, at odds with the non-sacrificial nature of Diasporan Judaism.

63. This clause refers only to the cult of Isis. For a more detailed account of the measures taken against it, see Josephus, *Jewish Antiquities* 18.65-80.

64. Actually just Sardinia (see **I.53-4**), at that time highly malarial.

65. As the date of this fragment is uncertain, it cannot be automatically assumed that Dio is referring to the same expulsion as Suetonius in **IV.45** and Josephus and Tacitus at **I.53-4**. Possibly there was more than one Jewish expulsion under Tiberius, just as there were repeated attempts in the early years of his reign to expel astrologers. See Williams, art. cit., pp. 767-8.

66. At the foot of the Alban Mount, just sixteen miles south-east of Rome.

67. Whether this ancient commentary on the line, 'a man well fitted to beg at the wheels of Arician chariots', is referring to any of the expulsions mentioned above, or one otherwise unknown, cannot be determined.

68. Trouble in Egypt caused by refugees of an extremist bent from the war in Judaea. On them, see **I.22**.

69. For its erection, see **I.20**.

70. And of both sexes from the age of three. See **IV.52**. This represented an extension of the tax: previously only male Jews between the ages of twenty and fifty years had been liable.

71. An official dealing with tax liability.

72. An area of Arsinoe in the Fayum in Egypt.

73. The equivalent of the Egyptian month Pachon, for which see Appendix 3.

74. Note that slaves, too, were liable to the tax. For some examples, see *CPJ* II nos. 206-7 and 218.

75. This is the last year for which individual tax receipts have been found at Apollinopolis/Edfu. By then, Egyptian Jewry was in revolt (**V.83**).

76. Presumably the Jewish Patriarch is meant.

77. The end of the Bar Kochba revolt in 135 CE. Eusebius is writing in the 4th century.

78. It is the Roman Senate that is being addressed here.

79. Cf. **II.119-21**.

80. Obligatory public offices, the expenses of which had to be borne by the holder.

V. The Jews among the Greeks

1. A coastal town in Cilicia, lying to the west of Korykos, in whose necropolis this epitaph was found.

2. Septimius Severus and Caracalla; the date must lie between 198 and 209 CE, the period of their joint rule.

3. This was the area of the city later occupied by the Forum of Valens. In the late fifth century (491 CE), a synagogue in the south of the city, thought to have been named after the same Asabinos, was burned down in hippodrome-related riots. See **V.29** and Downey, *Antioch*, p. 499, n. 120.

4. A *ducenarius* was a medium-ranking Roman official. Quite possibly this Jew had been a financial procurator. For another, see **IV.40**.

5. Probably Cilician Seleukeia on the Kalykadnos just along the coast from Korykos.

6. For this unique (for a Jewish inscription) expression of belief in astral immortality, see van der Horst, *Ancient Jewish Epitaphs*, pp. 123-4 and 138-9.

7. Probably the father of the Pegasios in **V.6**.

8. Of the Actian era = 59/60 and 60/61 CE.

9. The name indicates a Jew.

10. It is from the reference to these curses (they are 'written' in *Deuteronomy* chs 27-9) that the Jewish identity of Titus Flavius Alexander is generally inferred. (For a recent challenge to this view, see, however, J.W. van Henten with A. Bij de Vaate, 'Jewish or non-Jewish? Some remarks on the identification of Jewish inscriptions from Asia Minor', *Bibliotheca Orientalis* 53 (1996), pp. 16-28.) For further examples of the curses from Deuteronomy, see next entry and **V.70**.

11. On the duties associated with the offices held by this high-flying Jew, see Trebilco, *Jewish Communities*, pp. 63-4.

12. It is from this reference to Deuteronomy that the Jewish identity of this monument is generally inferred.

13. On these offices, see Trebilco, *Jewish Communities*, pp. 63-4.

14. The name Simon suggests that this envoy was a Jew. See introductory discussion at **V.21**. For a Jewish envoy from Perge at Aphrodisias, see **VII.11**.

15. Niketas' patronymic and place of origin suggest that he may well have been a Jew. Jason was a common name among Jews, probably because in its Ionic form, Ieson, it sounded like Jesus (Iesous).

16. And thus apostates. For this interpretation, see, among others, Smallwood, *Jews under Roman Rule*, p. 507 and Feldman, *Jews and Gentiles*, p. 83. For a different interpretation, see A.T. Kraabel, 'The Roman Diaspora: six questionable assumptions', *JJS* 33 (1982), p. 455.

17. The precise constitutional significance of this phrase is disputed. On one interpretation, Jason's intention here was to secure a city charter for the Jerusalemites and then re-name the community 'the city of the Antiochenes in Jerusalem'.

18. The broad-brimmed felt hat worn by ephebes everywhere and hence considered their badge.

19. For another piece of literary evidence for Jews at the theatre, see **V.99**.

20. One of the organised, colour-coded supporter-groups that frequented the various hippodromes of the Graeco-Roman world. Though attested occasionally in the early Roman imperial period, they only attained prominence in the Byzantine era and then mainly in the great cities of the east, such as Constantinople and Antioch.

21. Confirmed by Suetonius, *Gaius* 55.

22. A mistake for Petronius, for whom, see **VII.4**.

23. For Asabinos, see also **V.9**.

24. The central Jewish council at Alexandria, for the creation of which by the emperor Augustus, see **II.77**.

25. Chief magistrates of the Alexandrian Jewish community (**II.78**).

26. The significance of this unique term remains elusive.

27. Of which era? If the Ptolemaic or Actian, then the date of this text would be either 41 BCE or 24/5 CE but if the Berenican, then the date is harder to fix, as it is not known for certain when that began. For arguments for a date of 68/7 BCE for the Berenican era and 13 BCE for our document, see M. Baldwin Bowsky, 'M. Tittius Sex. F. Aem. and the Jews of Berenice (Cyrenaica)', *AJPh* 108 (1987), pp. 503-5.

28. For other evidence for the Feast of Tabernacles in the Diaspora, see **II.134-6**.

29. Possibly as a legate of the Roman governor of the province of Crete and Cyrene. See Baldwin Bowsky, art. cit. (n. 27 above), 499-500.

30. On the possible meaning of this difficult term, see note accompanying **I.104**.

31. Argued by Lüderitz, *SEJE*, p. 213, to indicate a council chamber or *bouleuterion* (apparently *amphitheatron* can describe any structure which had seats for spectators in either an oval or a U-shape) and by L.I. Levine, 'The Second Temple Synagogue: the formative years' in L.I. Levine (ed.) *The Synagogue in late Antiquity* (Philadelphia Pennsylvania, 1987), pp. 13-14, the synagogue itself.

32. This formula apparently was borrowed from local Greek practice – see *SEJE*, p. 219, n. 96.

33. Altogether uncertain. For a 1st century BCE date for this document, see Lüderitz, *SEJE*, p. 211.

34. For this phrase and the terms *politeuma* and amphitheatre, see the commentary on the preceding text.

35. For this honour, see also **I.105**. For the award of a golden shield to community benefactors, see **VII.17**.

36. The privilege of a front seat. In the synagogue, the place of honour was where the Torah was located. See Horsley, *New Docs.* I, p. 111.

37. Actions of this nature were very common among the Greeks. See A.H.M. Jones, *The Greek City from Alexander to Justinian* (Oxford, 1940), pp. 247, 286-7 and 359-60.

38. For a similar making over to the community of a private tomb, see **V.68**.

39. The court official in charge of entertainment – *Letter of Aristeas* 182-3.

40. The translators were also seventy-two in number. On the annual festival on Pharos which celebrated the completion of the translation, see **II.140**.

41. One of the few explicit references to God in Jewish inscriptions. For others, see **I.25** and **33**; **II.133**; **IV.11**. For *Pronoia* (Forethought/Providence), a frequent euphemism for God, see Trebilco, *Jewish Communities*, pp. 49-50 (discussion of the eleven, still unpublished, Sardian inscriptions in which the term appears).

42. For this interpretation of the text, see Lifshitz, *DF* ad loc.

43. That Theudotos had deliberately come to the Temple of Pan to give thanks for his safe return from the sea is incontrovertible. Whether the deity to whom he was rendering thanks was the Jewish god or Pan himself is disputed and not relevant here. The main point of interest is the visit of a Jew to a pagan temple apparently for a religious purpose.

44. This name has also been read, though with some hesitation, on a graffito inside the temple itself.

45. The obligation on a slave, whose manumission has been deferred, to remain in service for a stipulated time.

46. Since the king is Ptolemy III Euergetes I, the date here is 222 BCE.

47. The apostasy of this high-ranking Jewish official, for whom see also **IV.13**, is described in 3 *Maccabees* 1.3.

48. This name is probably a Hellenised form of Judah.

49. For this probably Jewish name, see introduction to **V.21**.

50. The government official in whose office the contract was drawn up.

51. Rare and valuable evidence for the physical appearance of Jews in Graeco-Roman antiquity.

52. For other Jewish priestesses (*hierisai*), see **II.97-8**. On the title and its implications, see introduction at **II.95**.

53. For this interpretation of this unusual bi-partite text, see van der Horst, *Ancient Jewish Epitaphs*, p. 145.

54. For the origins of this Jewish settlement near the apex of the Nile delta, see **I.20**.

55. Dositheos was probably the heir (and adopted son?) of Jesus. See HN ad loc.

56. The metre falters here and there may be a lacuna. In the rest of the epitaph no metrical pattern can be discerned, except 'by the friendly ear' (!). So Horbury, HN ad loc.

57. This line was added afterwards. Possibly Agathokles was Rachel's husband.

58. Either 215 or 295 CE. For discussion of this point in particular and the text in general, see L. Robert, *Hellenica* 11-12 (1960), pp. 409-12, who was the first to argue that it was Jewish.

59. Possibly a burial society.

60. Trebilco's translation here is wrong and should be ignored.

61. LSJ (Appendix) translate: *man-hole* in a grave-vault. This seems preferable to 'lair' at Trebilco, *Jewish Communities*, p. 62 and *SEJE*, p. 118.

62. The punctuation adopted here is that of Robert in *Hellenica* 11-12 (1960), p. 400, n. 1.

63. Although it would appear that this case is directly analogous to the one in **V.75**, it cannot be ruled out that Pontiana was a Greek proselyte to Judaism. For the use of the epithet 'Jew' in connection with proselytes, see **VII.31-2**.

64. A great-grandson of Herod the Great and the Hasmonaean princess, Mariamme, Tigranes had been recognised by the emperor Nero as king of Armenia. For other Herodian marriages with Gentiles, see Josephus, *Jewish Antiquities* 20.141-3 (Drusilla and Antonius Felix) and 20.145 (Berenice and M. Antonius Polemo). Both were daughters of Agrippa I.

65. The Gentile princess, Iotape, presumably forbade the circumcision of her sons.

66. The name is uncertain.

67. Probably an allusion to the Greeks' desecration of the Alexandrian synagogues in 38 CE through the installation of cult statues of the emperor Gaius (Philo, *In Flacc*. 41-3).

68. Games, organised by the heads of the gymnasia and their deputies, which were open only to those who possessed Alexandrian citizenship. That the Jews did not have that, the final clause of this sentence makes clear.

69. Thought to be an allusion to the Jews' metic status.

70. The reference is to the inter-communal violence that erupted all over Syria at the beginning of the First Jewish War.

71. For his response to the crisis, see **I.57**. For his career, see Chapter IV § 7 (a).

72. Something seems to have fallen out of the text here.

73. One of the Alexandrian envoys. His name presumably was introduced in an earlier, but now missing, part of this papyrus.

74. Some scholars believe, probably correctly, that Messianism was a potent factor in these badly documented and rather mysterious events. (See, for instance, W. Horbury, 'The beginnings of the Jewish revolt under Trajan' in H. Cancik, H. Lichtenberger and P. Schäfer (eds), *Geschichte – Tradition – Reflexion: Festschrift für Martin Hengel zum 70. Geburtstag* (Tübingen 1996), pp. 283-304.) Our sources, however, make no explicit reference to it. The repeated use by Eusebius in this passage of *stasis* and related words shows that he thought of it primarily as a faction-fight between Jews and Greeks which got out of hand.

75. For Greek fears of Jewish excesses at Alexandria, see the contemporary account of the historian Appian, who became caught up in the troubles there. Appian, *Arabicus Liber*, F19 = Stern II no. 348.

76. The locus of the imperial cult.

77. Other structures in Cyrene to suffer damage in the Jewish 'tumult' were a basilica, a temple to Hekate and several roads. See *CJZC* nos. 18; 21 and 24-5.

78. It is generally thought that the junketings here, which so tragically got out of hand, were part and parcel of the celebration of Purim. For this festival, see **II.138**.

79. Its identity is disputed. See Linder *ad loc*.

80. For the conversions of synagogues into churches at Stobi in Macedonia and Apamea in Syria, see Millar in Lieu, North and Rajak (eds), *The Jews among*

Pagans and Christians, pp. 100-1. For the conversion *c.* 412 CE of a synagogue at Edessa into a church dedicated to St Stephen, see the *Chronicon Edessenum* 51.

81. Another name for *Rosh ha-Shanah*, the Jewish New Year Festival, for which see **II.131**.

82. A reference to the Ten Days of Penitence which fell between the Feast of Trumpets and *Yom Kippur*, for which see **II.132-3**.

83. On the attraction to the Christians of Antioch of the synagogal liturgy and especially its music, see John Chrysostom, *Adversus Iudaeos* 1.7.

84. Evidence for the widespread recognition among the Christians of Antioch of Jewish medical (= (?) magical) expertise. For this, see Chapter II § 5 (d).

VI. The Jews among the Romans

1. The citizenship and other honours were in return for the signal services Antipater had rendered Caesar in the so-called *Bellum Alexandrinum* (Alexandrian War). According to Prof. J.A. Crook (personal communication), Caesar had made the grant of citizenship as dictator but had no legal right so to act.

2. The citizenship was for services rendered in the First Jewish War.

3. The allusion here is to the sale of citizenship under the emperor Claudius. On this passage, see A.N. Sherwin-White, *Roman Society and Roman Law in the New Testament* (Oxford, 1963), pp. 154-6.

4. Since we do not know how the citizenship came into Paul's family, we cannot establish his Roman name. That some Jews in Asia Minor were in possession of the Roman citizenship by the second half of the 1st century BCE is deducible from **IV.23**.

5. The citizenship of Queen Berenice and her father Agrippa I was through their descent from Julius Antipater, for whom see **VI.1**.

6. Son of Agrippa I, brother of the Berenice mentioned in the previous entry and great-great-grandson of the Antipater mentioned in **VI.1**.

7. lit. 'among friends'. For this informal manumission procedure, see J.A. Crook, *Law and Life of Rome* (1967), pp. 43-4.

8. Henceforth Paramone's full name would have been Aurelia Paramone and that of her son, Aurelios Iakob. For the large-scale enfranchisement of Jewish slaves at Rome, see **I.11**.

9. i.e. Matthew. The Jewish identity of this marine has been inferred from this name, which is not known to have been borne by Gentiles. His service with the navy would have commenced around 42 CE.

10. Paul's subsequent 'appeal unto Caesar' (not illustrated here, as he does not specifically mention in that context his Roman citizenship), was another privilege the Roman citizenship brought. In capital cases, Roman citizens, unlike other inhabitants of the Roman Empire, could always demand that their case be heard by the Emperor, a more impartial judge.

11. i.e. that which resulted from the ruling of the Severans, for which, see **V.8**.

12. i.e. having to perform curial liturgies.

13. Text here not wholly certain. See Linder ad loc.

14. The basic meaning of the word is not in doubt: LSJ see it as the straight equivalent of *princeps civitatis* – *i.e.* leader of the community. But of which community was Caecilianus the leader – Volubilis as a whole or just its Jewish sub-group? The scholarly consensus favours the former but note that the latter has its advocates too – e.g. Horsley, *New Docs.* I p. 113.

15. Although this is how *principalis* is generally understood, note that Frey (*CIJ* ad loc.) took the term as the equivalent of *gerousiarch*, thus making Ioses the adminstrative head of the *Jewish* community.

16. The prime function of this official was to protect the poor and weak against injury by the rich and powerful in judicial and other matters. In 409 CE an (unsuccessful) attempt was made to restrict the office to orthodox Christians and in 438 CE Jews were specifically banned from holding it. For another Jewish holder of the post at Mago, see Severus Majoricensis, *Epistola de Iudaeis* 44 = *PL* 41.829.

17. For Jewish enthusiasm for pantomimic dancers, see also **V.99**.

18. Their joint rule lasted from 253-260 CE.

19. Pylades' patronymic establishes his Jewish origins. The name was not used by Gentiles.

20. A religious association, whose concern was the worship of the emperor and the imperial family. Whether Pylades and his father belonged to this pagan order is not made clear.

21. A trio of mother-goddesses. See C.B. Pascal, *The Cults of Cisalpine Gaul* (Brussels, 1964), pp. 117-32.

22. The name Iuda indicates that its bearer was probably in origin a Jewish slave.

23. *honoribus omnibus functus* – a stock phrase in the epitaphs of Romans of the curial class.

24. On the likely origin of this group title, see introductory note at **VI.33**.

25. For Caesar's patronage of the Jews, see Josephus, *Jewish Antiquities* 14.189ff. For the Jewish services which gave rise to it, see *Jewish Antiquities* 14.127-39.

26. Possibly the Jewish Sanhedrin is indicated here as well as the Jewish Patriarch himself.

27. It has been conjectured that Theomnestos may have been a Patriarchal envoy (*apostolos*). For the apostolate, see Chapter III § 9.

28. Possibly this is an abbreviation of the title *Father of the Community*.

29. For other female archisynagogues, and the significance of their titles, see **V. 32-3**.

30. Taken by *HJPAJC* III, p. 90 to designate the *local* Jewish community but it could just as easily be an oblique reference to the national authorities in Palestine. Cf. the Stobi inscription (**II.7**). In other inscriptions (**I.109**), the community at Smyrna is termed *laos*.

31. For further examples of name-change on conversion to Judaism, see **III.37** and **VII.30**.

32. The meaning of the final (incomplete?) clause is a little uncertain. Leon's interpretation (*Jews of Rome*, p. 296) is followed here.

33. *benemerenti set sic non merenti*. It is hard to capture in English the play on words here. (The use of *set* for *sed* is common in inscriptions of this date.)

34. The name is otherwise unknown and the gender of the deceased uncertain.

35. Probably this inscription should be classified as Jewish, Noy's rejection of it as such notwithstanding, as the name Aqiba was extremely common among Jews.

36. A rather complicated way of saying that they had been married for twenty-one years, three months and (approx.) three weeks!

37. For further passages illustrating these central Jewish values, see Chapter II § 4.

38. The Canon does not make clear how long a self-confessed adulterer is to be debarred from communion.

39. Bishop of Rome from 366-384 CE.

40. Presumably from the library of one of the many synagogues of Rome.

41. The dispute, mentioned also in *Epistulae* 75 and 82, centred on a Hebrew word, transliterated by Jerome as *ciceion*. While he, following Aquila's translation of the Bible, had translated it ivy, the LXX, with which the Greeks were more familiar, had rendered it gourd.

42. Magnus Maximus, Roman emperor of part of the West (Britain, Gaul and Spain) from 383-88 CE. He was defeated in the latter year by Theodosius, the emperor at whom Bishop Ambrose's harangue here is directed.

43. Ambrose here is trying to pressurise Theodosius into reversing his decision to punish a bishop who had ordered the destruction of a synagogue at Callinicum in Mesopotamia and have the synagogue itself rebuilt at the bishop's expense. For the episode, see **V.92**.

44. Their conversion to Christianity is indicated by the carving on their tomb of a crucifix.

45. Probably, but not certainly, a Jewish convert to Christianity.

VII. Pagans and Judaism

1. Incubation, a ritual attested at various pagan shrines, was not normally practised by the Jews. For the sole Jewish instance known to us, see **V.50**.

2. The Hasmonaeans are alluded to here.

3. Strabo's account of Jewish history after Moses is extremely compressed and rather misleading. Circumcision was not a priestly invention but of great antiquity and excision, the 'circumcision' of females, never practised by the Jews.

4. For the Jewish taboo on pork, see Chapter II § 5 (c).

5. A unique allusion, in pagan Greek and Latin texts, to the Passover and unleavened bread.

6. The only unambiguous reference in pagan literature to the sabbatical year; for Jewish observance of the Sabbath, see Chapter II § 5 (a).

7. For the gifts of Godfearers and proselytes to the Temple, see also **III.14** and **VII.21**.

8. For Jewish group solidarity, see Chapter II § 4 (c); for their charitable activities, see Chapter II § 4 (d).

9. For Tacitus, circumcision is just one more example of Jewish perversity. He shows no awareness of the religious significance of the act. For circumcision, see Chapter II § 5 (b).

10. For a similar charge against proselytes, see **VII.20**.

11. Sense requires that *agnatus*, the grandiose word (mockingly?) used by Tacitus here, should be translated offspring or issue. According to Jewish law, no child could be done away with (Chapter II § 4 (f)). Literally *agnatus* means a child born after the father has made his will and so, presumably, already named his heirs.

12. For other references to him by Horace, see *Odes* 1.22.4; *Satires* 1.10.83 and *Epistles* 1.10.1.

13. There has been much learned discussion about how to interpret this phrase, which has been seen as an allusion to (a) the celebration of the New Moon by the Jews and (b) the 30th Sabbath after the start of the Jewish year. Given the light-hearted nature of the poem, it seems preferable to follow those who see here a casual reference to the Jews' best known 'holiday' – namely the Sabbath. On this view, thirtieth has no religious significance, Horace having used the word (in Latin, *tricensima*) simply because it was prosodically convenient. For a full discussion of the passage, see L.H. Feldman, 'The enigma of Horace's thirtieth Sabbath' in *Studies in Hellenistic Judaism* (Brill, Leiden, 1996), pp. 351-76.

14. Whether Aristius Fuscus really was a Judaizer or not is irrelevant. What the passage illustrates is that casual Judaizing was a practice assumed to be so familiar to Horace's readership/audience that it could be made the subject of a joke.

15. Josephus is referring here to the racial conflict between Jews and Gentiles throughout Syria at the outbreak of the First Jewish War.

16. People whose lifestyle closely resembled that of the Jews.

17. The context suggests their synagogue is meant here; on the synagogue as a holy place, see **II.7** and **III.81-3**.

18. Josephus is speaking of the situation in the late 60s CE.

19. The defeat of Cestius Gallus at the hands of the Jews in 66 CE.

20. The Greek word used here, *threskeia* (cult), implies that it was the rituals of the synagogue that were the main attraction.

21. For a detailed discussion of this text, see H. Bellen, Συναγωγὴ τῶν Ἰουδαίων καὶ Θεοσεβῶν. Die Aussage einer bosporanischen Freilassungsinschrift (CIRB 71) zum problem der "Gottfürchtigen" ', *Jahrbuch für Antike und Christentum* 8-9 (1965-6), pp. 171-6.

22. The interpretation of the final word of the invocation, *patellado*[..], is uncertain and hence the subject of ongoing debate. G. Mussies at *SEJE*, p. 257 plausibly translates the line thus: 'May God the Helper provide meals.' For other (less likely) interpretations, see Reynolds and Tannenbaum, pp. 26-8.

23. This and the following three lines were at some point added to the original inscription by a different hand.

24. These words can only be detected beneath an erasure, the reason for which is uncertain. It may be that Samouel was wrongly described as a priest and put too low in the list. Conceivably the words 'Samouel, envoy, from Perge' which were crudely carved at some point down the left hand margin of the text alongside the names of the first ten donors relate to the same person and were an attempt to rectify these errors.

25. Possibly to be interpreted sheep-rearer. For other Jews on the land in Anatolia, see Mitchell, *Anatolia, Land, Men, and Gods in Asia Minor* II, p. 35.

26. Known from another Trallian inscription, this wealthy, aristocratic lady, whose full name was Claudia Capitolina, was married to one Roman senator and closely related to another. For the details, see Trebilco, *Jewish Communities*, pp. 157-8.

27. The Greek epithet used here, *axiolog(otate)* is the equivalent of Latin *illustrissima* and indicates Capitolina's high Roman status. Other Roman status indicators of this type are to be found at **II.61-2** and **III.56**.

28. Even if the centurion is fictional, the action attributed to him is entirely plausible, as **VII.17** shows.

29. Known also from coins and another Akmonian inscription, this aristocratic patroness of the Jews, whose son was a member of the Roman Senate under Nero, served also as the High Priestess of the imperial cult at Akmonia. For full details, see Trebilco, *Jewish Communities*, pp. 59-60.

30. For other examples of Greek-style honours and evergetist phraseology, see **I.105, V.35-7**.

31. From the verbs *eiselthein* and *apestesan*, it is clear (*contra* Trebilco, *Jewish Communities*, pp. 148-9) that Josephus is talking about conversion and apostasy here, not casual interest in Judaism.

32. One of the rare references in the *Acts of the Apostles* to proselytes. For another, see **VII.24**.

33. *metuentem Sabbata patrem* – i.e. the father is a Godfearer; for other instances of *metuens*, see **VII.38-9**.

34. The son undergoes full conversion and is thus a proselyte.

35. Juvenal's criticism of Judaism in this passage parallels that of Tacitus in **VII.2**.

36. His full name was Gaius Sentius Saturninus.

37. i.e. he was a member of the emperor's advisory council, the *concilium principis*. On this, see J. Crook, *Consilium Principis – Imperial Councils and Counsellors from Augustus to Diocletian* (Cambridge, 1955).

38. For the consequent expulsion of the entire Jewish community from Rome, see **I.53-4** and **IV.45**.

39. During the reign of the emperor Claudius (41-54 CE), to whom, on his accession, he sent some of his kinsmen as hostages. See Josephus, *Jewish Antiquities* 20.37.

40. For his benefactions to the Temple, see **III.18**.

41. Apart from Nikolaos, all the others in this list were Jews.

42. Both were active in the first half of the 2nd century CE. Their aim in translating the Scriptures was to provide Greek-speaking Jews with a more authoritative version of them than the Septuagint. For the use of Aquila's translation by the Jews of Rome, see **V.42** (introductory note) and **V.43-4**.

43. Note that this text is considered by some (e.g. Bagatti-Milik, p. 84) to be a modern forgery.

44. From her burial in a Jewish family grave, Lüderitz suggests, *CJZC* ad loc., that she may originally have been either a slave or a foundling.

45. For other examples of a name-change on conversion, see **III.37** and **VI.39**.

46. For this title, see **II.71-3**.

47. For this community, see **I.63** and **II.68**.

48. For the Volumnesians, see **VI.28** and **35**.

49. Although many interpretations of this inscription have been offered, Frey's in *CIJ*, which is followed here, seems to offer the fewest difficulties.

50. Since elsewhere in Josephus *theosebes* just means pious, it is unlikely that it is functioning as a *terminus technicus* here. See M.H. Williams, 'θεοσεβὴς γὰρ ἦν – the Jewish tendencies of Poppaea Sabina', *JTS* n.s. 39 (1988), 106-7.

51. Though taken by Frey (*CIJ* ad loc.) as a name and Leon (*Jews of Rome*, pp. 247 and 297) as the epithet god-fearing, *theosebes* here is surely more likely to be the technical term for Godfearer. It is, after all, the sole *Greek* word in an otherwise Latin inscription. For an analogous case from 4th-5th century Venosa, see *CIJ* I² no. 619a = Noy I no. 113.

52. In Trachonitis, a mountainous area north-east of Judaea.

53. His Trachonite origin suggests he may have been a member of the syncretist cult called the *Theosebeis*. On this, see § 5 (e) below.

54. If the translation offered in (b) is preferred, no connection with Judaism need be assumed.

55. This phrase, which is without parallel, has been interpreted as showing that the deceased was (a) a Jewess, (b) a proselyte and (c) a Judaizer. For the phrase Sabbath-fearing applied to a Godfearer, see **VII.20**.

56. For a full review of the various interpretations of this passage, see Stern, comm. ad loc.

57. Usually thought to have been either Christianity or Judaism.

58. The absence of the epithet Most High from the large number of identifiably pagan inscriptions on Kos, has led to the conclusion that Theanos in all probability was a Jew or a Judaizer. For the well-established Jewish community of Kos, see **I.3**.

59. It is uncertain whether the dedicators in this and the previous entry were purely pagan or pagans who had come under the influence of Akmonia's well-established Jewish community. For discussion, see Trebilco, *Jewish Communities* pp. 135-8, who inclines to the latter interpretation.

60. The meaning of this term is much disputed. Some see it as the direct equivalent of the *sabbateion* mentioned in Josephus, *Jewish Antiquities* 16.164

and conclude that a synagogue is indicated here and Fabios Zosimos was a Jew. Others connect the word with the Chaldaean Sibyl, Sambethe, and think that a pagan shrine (possibly belonging to Sabbath-worshippers) is indicated here. Whatever the truth, Jewish influence is unmistakeable: there was a strong tradition that the Chaldaean Sibyl was the daughter of Noah. See *HJPAJC* III, p. 623.

61. This is the so-called Eumeneian Formula, of which numerous examples have been found in Phrygia. Since it was used equally by Christians and Jews, it is impossible to determine the religious allegiance of Pancharios.

62. The president of the *Sabbatistai*. His name is Syrian.

63. Either Archelaus I, who ruled Cappadocia and parts of Cilicia between and 36 BCE and 17 CE, or his son Archelaus II. On the death of the former, the latter succeeded only to his Cilician territories, Cappadocia itself becoming a Roman province. See D. Magie, *Roman Rule in Asia Minor* I (Princeton, 1950), p. 494.

64. For the translation of this difficult sentence, I have followed Tcherikover in *CPJ* III, p. 53, n. 1, who interprets it thus: 'The day in question should be the holy day of the god Sabbatistes; whether Sabbath or some other day, we cannot know. "To reveal" the day does not mean the date of it, but its inner content, its mystery.'

65. Before converting to Christianity, Gregory's father had belonged to this Cappadocian sect.

66. Despite the slightly different term for the Highest-God worshippers here, it is clear from the details that follow that they must be equated with the *Hypsistarioi* of the previous entry.

67. lit. lover of goodness. The nature of his duties are unknown.

68. In charge of the youths (ephebes).

69. He was High Priest of the Most High God.

70. For a possible adherent, see **VII.36**.

Appendices

1. Main events mentioned in this sourcebook

Note that many of the dates are conjectural.

BCE

c. 320-301	Various Ptolemaic attempts to conquer Palestine.
300	Foundation of Antioch by Seuleukos I Nikator.
282-246	Translation of Septuagint allegedly begun at Alexandria during the reign of Ptolemy II Philadelphos.
c. 210-201	Antiochos III 'the Great' sends Jewish military colonists to Phrygia and Lydia from Mesopotamia.
175	Hellenising programme of Jason in Jerusalem begins and a gymnasium is established in the city.
170-168	Sixth Syrian War between Antiochos IV Epiphanes and Ptolemy VI Philometor.
167	Desecration of the Temple at Jerusalem by Antiochos IV Epiphanes.
164	Defeat of Seleucids by Judas Maccabaeus; re-dedication of the Temple; inauguration of the Festival of Hanukkah.
c. 162?	Foundation of the Temple at Leontopolis in Egypt by Onias.
c. 145?	Abortive attack by Ptolemy VIII Physkon on the Jews of Alexandria.
139?	Embassy of Simon Maccabaeus to Rome.
139	Expulsion of Jews from Rome.
116-101	Reign of Kleopatra III in Egypt. Prominent political role played by the Jewish generals, Onias and Helkias.
88	Mithridates VI of Pontus attacks Roman province of Asia. Jews of Asia Minor in consequence despatch their gold to Kos.
c. 86	Lucullus deals with the unrest in Cyrene.
63	Conquest of Judaea by Pompey.
62	Pompey's triumph over the Jews.
59	Jews present at trial in Rome of L. Valerius Flaccus, former governor of Asia.
55	Jews of Pelusium help the Romans with the restoration to throne of Ptolemy XII Auletes.
49	Ephesian Jews exempted by Rome from military service.
48/7	Jews help Julius Caesar in Alexandrine War.
43	Dolabella exempts Jews of Asia Minor from Roman military service.
37	Triumph of Sosius at Rome for the re-conquest of Judaea; the de facto reign of Herod begins; appointment and dismissal of the High Priest Ananel.
c. 24	Herod appoints as High Priest Simon, son of Boethus.
15	Herod in Asia Minor with Agrippa; uses influence to help the Jews of Asia Minor.
9-6	Herod settles Zamaris' Babylonian Jews, then at Antioch, in

	Batanaea as military colonists.
c. 5 **CE**	Travels of the False Alexander throughout the Mediterranean.
6	Deposition of the Judaean ethnarch Archelaus; Judaea becomes a Roman province.
10/11	Augustus re-organises Jewish local government at Alexandria; establishment there of a central *gerousia*.
19	Expulsion of the Jews from Rome by Tiberius.
c. 30-40	Conversion to Judaism of the royal house of Adiabene.
38	Trouble in Alexandria between Jews and Greeks.
39	Riots between Jews and Greeks at Antioch.
39/40?	Alexandrian delegations to Rome to petition Gaius/Caligula.
40	Gaius gives a brief and inconclusive hearing to the Alexandrian Jews.
41	Claudius closes the synagogues at Rome; in November rules on the dispute between Jews and Greeks in Alexandria.
c. 46-8	Tiberius Julius Alexander's governorship of Judaea.
c. 46-7	Famine in Judaea. Diasporan Jews send aid.
c. 46-8	Paul's first missionary journey; encounter with the Jewish magician, Bar-Jesus, on Cyprus.
c. 49	Claudius expels the Jews from Rome.
c. 49-52	Paul's second missionary journey; circumcision of Timothy at Lystra; Paul before Gallio's tribunal at Corinth.
c. 53-8	Paul's third missionary journey; Sons of Sceva at Ephesus.
c. 58-60	Paul's imprisonment in Judaea.
c. 60	Paul's appeal to Caesar and transfer to Rome.
63	Tiberius Julius Alexander involved in Corbulo's Armenian war.
64	Josephus goes on an embassy to Rome; establishes contact with Alityros, the actor, and Poppaea, the empress.
66	First Jewish War against Rome breaks out; rioting in Alexandria between Jews and Greeks suppressed by the then Prefect of Egypt, Tiberius Julius Alexander; conflict between Jews and Greeks at Antioch.
67	Fall of Taricheae in Galilee; Jewish prisoners despatched thence to Greece to work on the Corinthian canal.
69	Roman siege of the Temple at Jerusalem; Tiberius Julius Alexander brings troops from Egypt.
70	Fall of Jerusalem; destruction of the Temple; imposition by Rome of the Jewish Tax; tension between Jews and Greeks at Antioch.
c. 73	Unrest in Egypt and Cyrene caused by fugitives from Judaea; closure of the Temple at Leontopolis.
73/4	Capture of Masada; end of First Jewish War.
95	Domitian's punishes Romans who had 'drifted into Jewish ways'.
96	Reform by Nerva of the abuses associated with the *Fiscus Iudaicus*.
115-17	Revolts of Jews in Cyrene, Egypt and Cyprus.
132	Second Jewish War against Rome breaks out (i.e. the revolt of Bar Kochba).
135	End of Bar Kochba revolt; Jewish access to Jerusalem banned.
c. 138-55	Antoninus Pius relaxes the Hadrianic ban (date uncertain) on circumcision.
c. 156-7	Jews present at martyrdom of Polycarp in Smyrna.
c. 185-6	Callistus, the future Bishop of Rome, disrupts a synagogue service at Rome.

193	The emperor, Didius Julianus, builds the Plethrion in Antioch on land purchased from the Jew, Asabinos.
c. 200	Severus and Caracalla permit Jews to serve on city councils.
212	*Constitutio Antoniniana.*
c. 250	Jews at Smyrna witness the martyrdom of Pionius.
c. 300	Council of Elvira in Spain: attempts to ban social contacts between Jews and Christians.
321	Constantine regulates Jewish participation in local government in the West.
329-35	Various rulings of Constantine against Jewish proselytism, persecution of Jewish converts to Christianity, circumcision of non-Jewish slaves.
360	Council of Laodicea in Phrygia – attempts to outlaw contacts between Jews and Christians.
361	Jewish destruction of churches in Phoenicia and Alexandria.
364	Trouble within the Jewish community at Antioch; involvement of Libanius in the crisis.
386-7	John Chrysostom delivers his *Adversus Iudaeos* sermons at Antioch.
c. 388	Burning of a synagogue at Rome reprimanded by the emperor Maximus.
388	Burning of a synagogue at Callinicum on the Euphrates by local Christians; Theodosius I pressurised by Bishop Ambrose of Milan into condoning the incident.
393	Christian attacks on Jewish syagogues in the East.
397	Official attempts to curb Christian attacks on Jewish syagogues in the East.
399	Attempted abolition of *aurum coronarium* by Arcadius and Honorius.
404	Right of the Jewish Patriarch to collect *aurum coronarium* restored by the same two emperors.
408	The Roman authorities attempt to regulate Purim.
409	Imperial ruling against the Caelicolae.
c. 415	Jewish crucifixion of a Christian boy at Inmestar in Syria; conflict between Jews and Christians at Alexandria; Jews expelled from that city.
417-18	Forcible conversion of the Jews of Minorca.
418	Jews banned from the army and civil service.
423	Compensation to Jews for Christian damage to synagogues.

2. Select list of rulers

Ptolemies

NB Some of these dates are disputed.

BCE

Ptolemy, son of Lagos =	
Ptolemy I Soter	305-282
Ptolemy II Philadelphos	282-246 (sole reign)
Ptolemy III Euergetes I	246-222
Ptolemy IV Philopator	222-205/4
Ptolemy V Epiphanes	204-180
Ptolemy VI Philometor	180-145 (with a break)
Ptolemy VII Neos Philopator	145-144
Ptolemy VIII Euergetes II Physkon	145-116

Kleopatra III	116-101
Ptolemy IX Soter II Lathyros	116-80 (with breaks)
Ptolemy X Alexander I	110/9-88 (with breaks)
Ptolemy XI Alexander II	80
Ptolemy XII Neos Dionysos Auletes	80-51 (with breaks)
Ptolemy XIII	51-47
Ptolemy XIV	47-44
Ptolemy XV Kaisar (Caesarion)	44-30
Kleopatra VII Philopator	51-30 (with breaks)

Early Seleucids
(NB. Scholars are not unanimous about all of these dates)

	BCE
Seleukos I Nikator	305-281
Antiochos I Soter	281-261
Antiochos II Theos	261-246
Seleukos II Kallinikos	246-225
Seleukos III Soter	225-223
Antiochos III the Great	223-187
Seleukos IV Philopator	187-175
Antiochos IV Epiphanes	175-163
Antiochos V Eupator	163-162
Demetrios I Soter	162-150
Alexander Balas	150-145
Antiochos VI Epiphanes	145-142
Demetrios II Nikator	145-139
Antiochos VII Sidetes	139-129
Demetrios II Nikator	129-125

Roman Emperors, 27 BCE – 235 CE

Augustus	27 BCE – 14 CE
Tiberius	14-37
Gaius (Caligula)	37-41
Claudius	41-54
Nero	54-68
Year of the Four Emperors	69
Vespasian	69-79
Titus	79-81
Domitian	81-96
Nerva	96-98
Trajan	98-117
Hadrian	117-138
Antoninus Pius	138-161
Marcus Aurelius	161-180
Lucius Verus	161-169
Commodus	176-192
Pertinax	193
Didius Julianus	193
Septimius Severus	193-211
Caracalla	198-217
Geta	209-212

Macrinus	217-218
Diadumenianus	218
Elegabalus	218-222
Severus Alexander	222-235

Roman Emperors, 324 – 450 CE

Constantine I	324-337
Constantine II	337-340
Constans	337-350
Constantius	337-361
Julian	360-363
Jovian	363-364
Valentinian I	364-375
Valens	364-378
Gratianus	367-383
Valentinian II	375-392
Theodosius I	378-395
Arcadius	383-408
Honorius	394-423
Theodosius II	408-450

3. Egyptian months and their Julian equivalents

Thoth	Aug. 29 – Sep. 27
Phaophi	Sep. 28 – Oct. 27
Hathyr	Oct. 28 – Nov. 26
Choiak	Nov. 27 – Dec. 26
Tybi	Dec. 27 – Jan. 25
Mecheir	Jan. 26 – Feb. 24
Phamenoth	Feb. 25 – Mar. 26
Pharmouthi	Mar. 27 – Apr. 25
Pachon	Apr. 26 – May 25
Payni	May 26 – June 24
Epeiph	June 25 – July 24
Mesore	July 25 – Aug. 23
Epagomenal days	Aug. 24 – Aug. 28

4. Glossary of selected names

Listed in the left-hand column are the unusual name-forms, marked by an asterisk, that have appeared in the documents. Their standard form or, in the case of Hebrew names, their most common anglicised equivalent are listed on the right.

Hebrew names

Aster	= Esther	Eioudas	= Judas
Asther	= Esther	Eisakios	= Isaac
Beniames	= Benjamin	Iako	= Jacob
Eiako	= Jacob	Iakos	= Jacob
Eiakob	= Jacob	Iakoubis	= Jacob
Eioseph	= Joseph	Iakoumbos	= Jacob

Iesos	= Jesus	Matthaius	= Matthew
Iesous	= Jesus	Mniaseas	= Manasseh
Ionathas	= Jonathan	Naimia	= Nehemiah
Iosepos	= Joseph	Nemias	= Nehemiah
Ioses	= Joseph	Robes	= Reuben
Iosoua	= Joshua	Roubes	= Reuben
Ioudan	= Judas	Samaelos	= Samuel
Isak	= Isaac	Samoelis	= Samuel
Isakios	= Isaac	Samoes	= Samuel
Isakis	= Isaac	Samohil	= Samuel
Isas	= Isaac?	Samouelos	= Samuel
Ismaelos	= Ishmael	Saoulos	= Saul
Manases	= Manasseh	Shmuel	= Samuel
Mathios	= Matthew	Zonatha	= Jonathan

Greek names

Alypis	= Alypios	Teuphilos	= Theophilos
Alypos	= Alypios	Thedetos	= Theodotos
Amachis	= Amachios	Theudas	= shortened form
Dosas	= shortened form of		of Theodotos
	Dositheos	Theudes	= shortened form
Eusebis	= Eusebios		of Theodotos
Hermogenys	= Hermogenes	Theudotos	= Theodotos
Makedonis	= Makedonios	Zokles	= Diokles

Latin names

Aneis Geneiales	= Annius Genialis	Nebia	= Naevia
Annis	= Annius	Oursos	= Ursus
Cuyntus	= Quintus	Phouskos	= Fuscus
Datibos	= Dativus	Pomponis	= Pomponius
Dekmos Oualerios	= Decimus Valerius	Pouplis Katilis	= Publius Catilius
Elius	= Aelius	P(oplios)	= P(ublius)
Kailereina	= Celerina	Rout(ilios)	Rut(ilius)
Katillios Seberos	= Catillius Severus	Prokoulous	= Proculus
Krispeina	= Crispina	Roupheinos	= Rufinus
Kyntianos	= Quintianus	Rouphos	= Rufus
Kountos	= Quintus	Seberos	= Severus

Abbreviations

AE = *L'Année Épigraphique*

AJPh = *American Journal of Philology*

Bagatti-Milik = B. Bagatti and J.T. Milik, *Gli scavi del Dominus Flevit* I (Jerusalem, 1958)

BASOR = *Bulletin of the American Schools of Oriental Research*

BS II = M. Schwabe and B. Lifshitz, *Beth She'arim II: The Greek Inscriptions* (New Brunswick, N.J., 1974)

bT = Babylonian Talmud

CCL = *Corpus Christianorum Latinorum*

CIJ I = J-B. Frey, *Corpus Inscriptionum Iudaicarum* I (Rome, 1936)

CIJ I² = J-B. Frey, *Corpus Inscriptionum Iudaicarum* I, reprinted with a Prolegomenon by B. Lifshitz (New York, 1975)

CIJ II = J-B. Frey, *Corpus Inscriptionum Iudaicarum* II (Rome, 1952)

CIL = *Corpus Inscriptionum Latinarum*

CIRB = I. Struve, *Corpus Inscriptionum Regni Bosporani* (Leningrad, 1965)

CJZC = G. Lüderitz, *Corpus jüdischer Zeugnisse aus der Cyrenaika* (Wiesbaden, 1983)

CPJ = V.A. Tcherikover, A. Fuks and M. Stern, *Corpus Papyrorum Judaicarum* (3 vols, Cambridge, Mass., 1957-64)

DF = B. Lifshitz, *Donateurs et fondateurs dans les synagogues juives* (Paris 1967)

Fasola = U. Fasola, 'Le due Catacombe Ebraiche di Villa Torlonia', *RivAC* 52 (1976), 7-62

Goodenough, *Jewish Symbols* = E.R. Goodenough, *Jewish Symbols in the Greco-Roman Period* (13 vols, New York, 1953-68)

Hanfmann, *Sardis* = G. Hanfmann, *Sardis from Pre-historic to Roman Times* (Cambridge, Mass. and London, 1983)

HJPAJC = E. Schürer, *The History of the Jewish People in the Age of Jesus Christ*, revised by G. Vermes, F. Millar, M. Black and M. Goodman (3 vols, Edinburgh, 1973-87)

HN = W. Horbury and D. Noy, *Jewish Inscriptions of Graeco-Roman Egypt* (Cambridge, 1992)

HTR = *Harvard Theological Review*

IEJ = *Israel Exploration Journal*

IG = *Inscriptiones Graecae*

IGLS = *Inscriptions grecques et latines de la Syrie*

IK = *Inschriften griechischer Städte aus Kleinasien*

IOSPE = *Inscriptiones Antiquae Orae Septentrionalis Ponti Euxini Graecae et Latinae*

JJS = *Journal of Jewish Studies*

JQR = *Jewish Quarterly Review*

JRS = *Journal of Roman Studies*

JSJ = *Journal for the Study of Judaism*

JThS = *Journal of Theological Studies*

Le Bohec = Y. le Bohec, 'Inscriptions juives et judaïsantes de l'Afrique romaine', *Antiquités Africaines* 17 (1981), 165-207

Linder = A. Linder, *The Jews in Roman Imperial Legislation* (Michigan, 1987)

LSJ = H. G. Liddell, R. Scott and H. S. Jones, *A Greek-English Lexicon*[9] (Oxford, 1940)

M. = Mishnah (name of tractate follows)

MAMA = *Monumenta Asiae Minoris Antiqua*

Mansi II/III = G.D. Mansi, *Sacrorum conciliorum nova et amplissima collectio* II & III (Paris/Leipzig, 1901)

MPAT = J.A. Fitzmyer and D. Harrington, *A Manual of Palestinian Aramaic Texts* (Rome, 1978)

New Docs. I-V = G.H.R. Horsley, *New Documents Illustrating Early Christianity* (5 vols, MacQuarie University, 1981-9)

New Docs. VI = S.R. Llewelyn, *New Documents Illustrating Early Christianity* VI (MacQuarie University, 1992)

Noy I = D. Noy, *Jewish Inscriptions of Western Europe* I (Cambridge, 1993)

Noy II = D. Noy, *Jewish Inscriptions of Western Europe* II (Cambridge, 1995)

OGIS = *Orientis Graecae Inscriptiones Selectae*

PG = *Patrologia Graeca* (ed. Migne)

PL = *Patrologia Latina* (ed. Migne)

Puech = E. Puech, 'Inscriptions funéraires Palestiniennes: Tombeau de Jason et ossuaires', *Rev. Bib.* 90 (1983), 499-533

Rahmani = L.Y. Rahmani, *A Catalogue of Jewish Ossuaries in the Collections of the State of Israel* (Jerusalem, 1994)

REJ = *Revue des Études Juives*

Rev. Bib. = *Revue Biblique*

RIC II = H. Mattingly and E.A. Sydenham, *The Roman Imperial Coinage* II (London, 1926)

RivAC = *Rivista di Archeologia Cristiana*

Roueché = C. Roueché, *Aphrodisias in Late Antiquity* (London, 1989)

Reynolds and Tannenbaum = J. Reynolds and R. Tannenbaum, *Jews and Godfearers at Aphrodisias* (Cambridge, 1987)

Safrai and Stern = S. Safrai and M. Stern, *The Jewish People in the First Century* (2 vols, Assen, 1974-6)

Scheiber = A. Scheiber, *Jewish Inscriptions in Hungary* (Leiden, 1983)

SCI = *Scripta Classica Israelica*

SEG = *Supplementum Epigraphicum Graecum*

SEJE = J.W. van Henten & P.W. van der Horst (eds), *Studies in Early Jewish Epigraphy* (Leiden, 1994)

SHA = *Scriptores Historiae Augustae*

Stern = M. Stern, *Greek and Latin Authors on Jews and Judaism* (3 vols, Jerusalem, 1974-84)

TAM = *Tituli Asiae Minoris*

Trebilco, *Jewish Communities* = P. Trebilco, *Jewish Communities in Asia Minor* (Cambridge, 1991)

ZNTW = *Zeitschrift für die Neutestamentliche Wissenschaft*

ZPE = *Zeitschrift für Papyrologie und Epigraphik*

Bibliography

Bagatti, B. and Milik, J.T., *Gli scavi del Dominus Flevit* I (Jerusalem, 1958).

Baldwin Bowsky, M.W., 'M. Tittius Sex. F. Aem. and the Jews of Berenice (Cyrenaica)', *AJPh* 108 (1987), pp. 495-510.

Barclay, J.M.G., *Jews in the Mediterranean Diaspora* (Edinburgh, 1996).

Baron, S., *Social and Religious History of the Jews* I² (Columbia, 1952).

Bellen, H., Συναγωγὴ τῶν Ἰουδαίων καὶ Θεοσεβῶν. Die Aussage einer bosporanischen Freilassungsinschrift (CIRB 71) zum problem der "Gottfürchtigen"', *Jahrbuch für Antike und Christentum* 8-9 (1965-6), pp. 171-6.

Bickermann, E., *Studies in Jewish and Christian History* II (Leiden, 1980).

Bingen, J., 'Apamée de Syrie, IGLS IV 1319 (392 après J.-C.)', *ZPE* 109 (1995), p. 194.

Blumenkrantz, B., *Les Auteurs chrétiens latins du moyen âge sur les juifs et le judaïsme* (Paris, 1963).

Boterman, H., 'Griechisch-jüdische Epigraphik: Zur Datierung der Aphrodisias-Inschriften', *ZPE* 98 (1993), pp. 184-94.

Bowman, A., *Egypt after the Pharaohs* (Oxford, 1990).

Brooten, B., *Women Leaders in the Ancient Synagogues* (Chico, California, 1982).

Cohen, N., 'The names of the translators in the Letter of Aristeas: a study in the dynamics of cultural transition', *JSJ* 15 (1984), pp. 32-64.

Cohen, S.J.D., 'Epigraphical Rabbis', *JQR* 72 (1981), pp. 1-17.

Collins, J.J., *The Sibylline Oracles of Egyptian Judaism* (Missoula, Montana, 1972).

Collon, S., 'Remarques sur les quartiers juifs de la Rome antique', *Mélanges d'Archéologie et d'Histoire de l'École Française de Rome* 57 (1940), pp. 72-94.

Crook, J., *Consilium Principis – Imperial Councils and Counsellors from Augustus to Diocletian* (Cambridge, 1955).

Crook, J.A., *Law and Life of Rome* (London, 1967).

Di Stefano Manzella, I., 'L. Maecius Archon, centurio alti ordinis. Nota critica su *CIL* VI.39084 = *CIJ* I, 470', *ZPE* 77 (1989), pp. 103-12.

Downey, G., *A History of Antioch in Syria* (Princeton, 1961).

Drijvers, H.J.W., 'Jews and Christians at Edessa', *JJS* 36 (1985), pp. 88-102.

Fasola, U., 'Le due Catacombe Ebraiche di Villa Torlonia', *RivAC* 52 (1976), pp. 7-62.

Feldman, L., *Jew and Gentile in the Ancient World* (Princeton, 1993).

Feldman, L.H. and Hata, G. (eds), *Josephus, Judaism and Christianity* (Leiden, 1987).

Feldman, L.H., *Studies in Hellenistic Judaism* (Brill, Leiden, 1996).

Fraser, P., *Ptolemaic Alexandria* (3 vols., Oxford, 1972).

Frey, J-B., *Corpus Inscriptionum Iudaicarum* I (Rome, 1936), reprinted with a Prolegomenon by B. Lifschitz (New York, 1975), and II (Rome, 1952).

Goodenough, E.R., *Jewish Symbols in the Greco-Roman Period* III (New York,

1953); IX-XI (New York, 1964).

Goodman, M., *Mission and Conversion* (Oxford, 1994).

Goodman, M., 'Nerva, the *Fiscus Judaicus* and Jewish identity', *JRS* 79 (1989), pp. 40-4.

Hachlili, R., 'The Goliath family in Jericho: funerary inscriptions from a first century AD Jewish monumental tomb', *BASOR* 235 (1979), pp. 31-66.

Haenchen, E., *The Acts of the Apostles* (Oxford, 1971).

Hanfmann, G., *Sardis from Pre-historic to Roman Times* (Cambridge, Mass. and London, 1983).

Harvey, R.A., *A Commentary on Persius* (Leiden, 1981).

Hengel, M., 'Die Synagogeinschrift von Stobi', *ZNTW* 57 (1966), pp. 145-83.

Henten, J.W. van, with Bij de Vaate, A., 'Jewish or non-Jewish? Some remarks on the identification of Jewish inscriptions from Asia Minor', *Bibliotheca Orientalis* 53 (1996), pp. 16-28.

Henten, J.W. van, and Horst, P.W. van der (eds), *Studies in Early Jewish Epigraphy* (Leiden, 1994).

Horbury, W., 'Herod's Temple and Herod's Days' in W. Horbury (ed.), *Templum Amicitiae, Essays on the Second Temple presented to Ernst Bammel* (Sheffield 1991), pp. 103-49.

Horbury, W. and Noy, D., *Jewish Inscriptions of Graeco-Roman Egypt* (Cambridge, 1992).

Horbury, W., 'The beginnings of the Jewish revolt under Trajan' in H. Cancik, H. Lichtenberger and P. Schäfer (eds), *Geschichte – Tradition – Reflexion: Festschrift für Martin Hengel zum 70. Geburtstag* (Tübingen, 1996), pp. 283-304.

Horsley, G.H.R., 'Appendix – The Politarchs' in D. Gill and C. Gempf (eds), *The Book of Acts in its Graeco-Roman Setting* II (Grand Rapids, Michigan, 1994), pp. 419-31.

Horsley, G.H.R., *New Documents Illustrating Early Christianity* (5 vols., MacQuarie University, 1981-9).

Horst, P.W. van der, *Ancient Jewish Epitaphs* (Kampen, 1991).

Horst, P.W. van der, 'Jews and Christians in Aphrodisias in the light of their relations in other cities of Asia Minor', *Nederlands Theologisch Tijdschrift* 43 (1989), 106-21.

Hunt, E.D., 'St Stephen in Minorca – an episode in Jewish-Christian relations in the early 5th century AD', *JThS* n.s. 33 (1982), 106-23.

Ilan, T., 'New ossuary inscriptions from Jerusalem', *SCI* (1991-2), 149-59.

Isaac, B., 'A donation for Herod's Temple', *IEJ* 33 (1983), pp. 86-92.

Jones, A.H.M., *The Greek City from Alexander to Justinian* (Oxford, 1940).

Jones, A.H.M., *The Later Roman Empire* (Oxford, 1964).

Kasher, A., *The Jews in Hellenistic and Roman Egypt* (Tübingen, 1985).

Kotansky, R., 'Two inscribed Jewish Aramaic amulets from Syria', *IEJ* 41 (1991), pp. 267-81.

Kraabel, A.T., 'The Roman Diaspora: six questionable assumptions', *JJS* 33 (1982), pp. 445-77.

Kraemer, R., 'A new inscription from Malta and the question of women elders in the Diaspora Jewish communities', *HTR* 78 (1985), pp. 431-8.

Kraemer, R., 'On the meaning of the term "Jew" in Graeco-Roman inscriptions', *HTR* 82 (1989), pp. 35-53.

Lane, E.N., 'Sabazius and the Jews in Valerius Maximus: a re-examination', *JRS* 69 (1979), pp. 35-8.

Lane-Fox, R., *Pagans and Christians* (Penguin Books, 1988).

Lattimore, R., *Themes in Greek and Latin Epitaphs* (Urbana, Illinois, 1942).

Le Bohec, Y., 'Inscriptions juives et judaïsantes de l'Afrique romaine', *Antiquités*

Africaines 17 (1981), pp. 165-207.

Leon, H.J., *The Jews of Ancient Rome* (Philadelphia, 1960).

Levine, L.I. (ed.), *The Synagogue in Late Antiquity* (Philadelphia Pennsylvania, 1987).

Levinskaya, I., *The Book of Acts in its Diaspora Setting = The Book of Acts in its First Century Setting* 5 (Grand Rapids, Michigan, 1996)

Levinskaya, I.A. and Tokchtas'yev, S.R., 'The new Jewish manumission (*sic*) from Phanagoria (Crimea)', *Bulletin of Judaeo-Greek Studies* 13 (Winter 1993), pp. 27-8.

Lieu, J., North, J. and Rajak, T. (eds), *The Jews among Pagans and Christians* (London, 1992).

Lifshitz, B., *Donateurs et fondateurs dans les synagogues juives* (Paris 1967).

Linder, A., *The Jews in Roman Imperial Legislation* (Michigan, 1987).

Llewelyn, S.R., *New Documents Illustrating Early Christianity* VI (MacQuarie University, 1992).

Lüderitz, G., *Corpus jüdischer Zeugnisse aus der Cyrenaika* (Wiesbaden, 1983).

Lüderitz, G., 'What is the politeuma?', *SEJE*, pp. 183-225.

Magie, D., *Roman Rule in Asia Minor* (2 vols., Princeton, 1950).

Mansi, G.D., *Sacrorum conciliorum nova et amplissima collectio* (50 vols., Paris/Leipzig, 1901-27)

Mattingly H. and Sydenham, E.A., *The Roman Imperial Coinage* II (London, 1926).

Meeks, W.A. and Wilken, R.L., *Jews and Christians in Antioch in the First Four Centuries of the Common Era* (Missoula, Montana, 1978).

Mélèze Modrzejewski, J., 'Jewish law and Hellenistic legal practice in the light of Greek papyri from Egypt' in N.S. Hecht et al (eds), *An Introduction to the History and Sources of Jewish Law* (Oxford, 1996).

Mélèze Modrzejewski, J., *The Jews of Egypt from Rameses II to Emperor Hadrian*, translated from the French by Robert Cornman with a Foreword by Shaye J.D. Cohen (Edinburgh, 1995).

Mitchell, S., *Anatolia, Land, Men, and Gods in Asia Minor* (2 vols., Oxford, 1993).

Moehring, H., 'The *Acta pro Judaeis* in the *Antiquities* of Flavius Josephus: a study in Hellenistic and modern apologetic historiography' in J. Neusner (ed.), *Christianity, Judaism and Other Greco-Roman Cults: Studies for Morton Smith at Sixty* III (Leiden, 1975), pp. 124-58.

Musurillo, H., *The Acts of the Christian Martyrs* (Oxford, 1972).

Naveh, J. and Shaked, S., *Amulets and Magic Bowls: Aramaic Incantations of Late Antiquity* (Jerusalem and Leiden, 1985).

Neusner, J., *The Rabbinic Traditions about the Pharisees before 70* (3 pts., Leiden, 1971).

Nigdelis, M., 'Synagoge(n) und Gemeinde der Juden in Thessaloniki: Fragen auf grund einer neuen jüdischen Grabinschrift der Kaiserzeit', *ZPE* 102 (1994), pp. 297-306.

Noy, D., *Jewish Inscriptions of Western Europe* (2 vols., Cambridge, 1993 and 1995).

Pascal, C. B., *The Cults of Cisalpine Gaul* (Brussels, 1964).

Pucci Ben Zeev, M., 'Greek and Roman documents from Republican times in the *Antiquities*: what was Josephus' source?', *SCI* 13 (1994), pp. 46-59.

Puech, E., 'Inscriptions funéraires palestiniennes: tombeau de Jason et ossuaires', *Rev. Bib.* 90 (1983), pp. 499-533.

Rahmani, L.Y., *A Catalogue of Jewish Ossuaries in the Collections of the State of Israel* (Jerusalem, 1994).

Rajak, T. and Noy, D., 'Archisynagogoi: office, title and social status in the Greco-Jewish synagogue', *JRS* 83 (1993), pp. 75-93.

Rajak, T., *Josephus* (London, 1983).

Rajak, T., 'Was there a Roman charter for the Jews?', *JRS* 74 (1984), pp. 107-23.

Reynolds, J. and Tannenbaum, R., *Jews and Godfearers at Aphrodisias* (Cambridge, 1987).

Roueché, C., *Aphrodisias in Late Antiquity* (London, 1989).

Rutgers, L.V., 'Roman policy towards the Jews: expulsions from the City of Rome during the first century CE', *Classical Antiquity* 13 (1994), pp. 56-74.

Rutgers, L.V., *The Jews in Late Ancient Rome: Evidence of Cultural Interaction in the Roman Diaspora* (Leiden, 1995).

Safrai, S. and Stern M., *The Jewish People in the First Century* (2 vols., Assen, 1974 and 1976).

Scheiber, A., *Jewish Inscriptions in Hungary* (Leiden, 1983).

Schürer, E., *Geschichte des jüdischen Volkes im Zeitalter Jesu Christi*[4] (3 vols., Leipzig, 1901-9).

Schürer, E., *The History of the Jewish People in the Age of Jesus Christ*, revised by G. Vermes, F. Millar, M. Black and M. Goodman (3 vols., Edinburgh, 1973-87).

Schwabe, M. and Lifshitz, B., *Beth She'arim II: The Greek Inscriptions* (New Brunswick, N.J., 1974).

Seaver, J.E., *Persecution of the Jews in the Roman Empire (300-438)* (Lawrence, Kansas, 1952).

Sherwin-White, A.N., *Roman Society and Roman Law in the New Testament* (Oxford, 1963).

Simon, M., *Verus Israel: A Study of the Relations between Christians and Jews in the Roman Empire (AD 135-425)*, trans. by H. McKeating (Oxford, 1986).

Smallwood, E.M., *Philonis Alexandrini Legatio ad Gaium* (Leiden, 1961).

Smallwood, E.M., *The Jews under Roman Rule from Pompey to Diocletian* (Leiden, 1976).

Stern, M., *Greek and Latin Authors on Jews and Judaism* (3 vols., Jerusalem, 1974-84).

Strubbe, J.H.M., 'Curses against the violation of the grave' in *SEJE*, pp. 70-127.

Tcherikover, V.A., Fuks, A. and Stern, M., *Corpus Papyrorum Judaicarum* (3 vols., Cambridge, Mass., 1957-64).

Thompson, L.A., 'Domitian and the Jewish tax', *Historia* 31 (1982), pp. 329-42.

Trebilco, P., *Jewish Communities in Asia Minor* (Cambridge, 1991).

Wallace, S.L., *Taxation in Egypt from Augustus to Diocletian* (Princeton, 1938).

Urman, D., 'Jewish Inscriptions from Dabbura in the Golan', *IEJ* 22 (1972), pp. 16-23.

Williams, M.H., 'Domitian, the Jews and the "Judaizers" – a simple matter of *cupiditas* and *maiestas*?', *Historia* 39 (1990), pp. 196-211.

Williams, M.H., 'Palestinian Jewish personal names in Acts', in R. Bauckham (ed.), *The Book of Acts in its Palestinian Setting = The Book of Acts in its First Century Setting* 4 (Grand Rapids, Michigan, 1995), pp. 79-113.

Williams, M.H., 'The expulsion of the Jews from Rome in AD 19', *Latomus* 48 (1989), pp. 765-84.

Williams, M.H., 'The Jewish community of Corycus – two more inscriptions', *ZPE* 92 (1992), pp. 248-52.

Williams, M.H., 'The Jews and Godfearers Inscription from Aphrodisias – a case of Patriarchal interference in early 3rd century Caria?', *Historia* 41 (1992), pp. 297-310.

Williams, M.H., 'The structure of Roman Jewry re-considered', *ZPE* 104 (1994), pp. 129-41.

Woods, D., 'A note concerning the *Regii Emeseni Iudaei*', *Latomus* 51 (1992), pp. 404-7.

Zahavy, T., *The Traditions of Eleazar ben Azariah* (Missoula, Montana, 1977).
Zuckermann, C., 'Hellenistic politeumata and the Jews: a reconsideration', *SCI* 8-9 (1985-8), pp. 171-85.

Concordance of sources

Bold numbers refer to the sources in this book.

1. Literary texts

A. Pagan

Cicero, *Pro Flacco* 28.66-9, **II.99**, **III.9**
Cleomedes, *On the circular motion of celestial bodies* 2.1.91, **II.10**
Dio, *Roman History* 57.18.5a, **IV.46**; 60.6.6, **IV.47**; 66.4.1-4, **III.22**; 66.7.2, **IV.50**;
    67.14.1-3, **VII.40**; 68.32.1-3, **V.84**
Diodorus Siculus 40.3.8, **II.109**
Hecataeus, *see* Diodorus Siculus
Horace, *Satires* 1.9.60-72, **VII.3**
Julian (emperor), *see* Sozomenus
Juvenal, *Satires* 3.10-16, **I.62**; 3.290-6, **II.11**; 14.96-106, **VII.20**
Libanius, *Epistulae* 1097, **VI.32**; 1251, **II.80**
Libanius, *Orationes* 47.13, **I.86**
Macrobius, *Saturnalia* 2.4.11, **II.123**
Ovid, *Remedia Amoris* 217-20, **II.112**
Persius, *Satires* 5.179-84, **II.115**
Petronius, *Satyricon* 102.13-14, **II.118**
Plutarch, *Life of Pompey* 45.5, **I.10**
Scholium on Juvenal, *Satires* 4.117, **IV.48**
Seneca, *Epistulae Morales* 95.47, **II.116**; 108.22, **II.125**; *see also* Augustine, *City of God* 6.11
Sextus Empiricus, *Hypotyposes* 3.222-3, **II.126**
Strabo, *Geography* 16.34-7, **VII.1**; *see also* Josephus, *Jewish Antiquities* 14.114-15
Suetonius, *Iulius* 84.5, **VI.31**
Suetonius, *Augustus* 76.2, **II.117**
Suetonius, *Tiberius* 36, **IV.45**
Suetonius, *Claudius* 25.4, **II.144**
Suetonius, *Domitian* 12.2, **IV.66**
Tacitus, *Annals* 2.85.5, **I.54**; 13.32.3-4, **VII.41**; 15.28.3, **IV.31**
Tacitus, *Histories* 5.4-5, **VII.2**
Valerius Maximus 1.3.3, **IV.44a**; **IV.44b**

B. Judaeo-Greek

Esther, LXX supplement, **III.66**
Josephus, *Contra Apionem* 1.32-3, **III.23**; 2.44, **I.17**; 2.53-5, **II.141**; 2.123, **VII.18**;
    2.202, **II.110**; 2.282, **VII.6**; 2.283, **II.103**
Josephus, *Jewish Antiquities* 4.115-16, **I.2**; 12.119, **I.24**; 12.120, **IV.4**; 12.148-53,
    I.18; 13.284-5, **IV.8**; 14.110-13, **III.14**; 14.114-15, **I.4**; 14.117, **II.76**; 14.213-16,

C. Talmudic

D. Christian

1 *Corinthians* 1.10-12, **II.146**
2 *Corinthians* 11.24-25, **II.17**
Council of Carthage IV, Canon 84, **VI.54**
Council of Elvira, Canon 16, **VI.50**; 49, **VI.53**; 50, **VI.51**; 78, **VI.52**
Council of Laodicea, Canon 37, **V.95**; 38, **V.96**
Cyril of Alexandria, *De Adoratione in Spiritu et Veritate* 3.92-3, **VII.57**
Epiphanius, *On the Heresies* 30.11, **III.76**
Eusebius, *In Isaiam* 18, **III.77**
Eusebius, *The History of the Church* 4.2, **V.83**; 4.6.3, **IV.69**; 5.8.10, **VII.25**
Gospel according to Luke 7.1-5, **VII.16**
Gregory of Nazianzus, *Funebris in patrem* 5, **VII.53**
Gregory of Nyssa, *Contra Eunomium* 2, **VII.54**
Hippolytus, *Elenchos* 9.12.5-9, **VI.58**
Jerome, *Epistulae* 36.1, **VI.55**
Jerome, *In Ieremiam* 31.15, **I.13**
Jerome, *In Zachariam* 11.4-5, **I.16**
John Chrysostom, *Adversus Iudaeos* 1.1, **V.97**; 1.3, **II.15**; 1.6, **I.66**; 8.6, **V.98**
John Chrysostom, *Si esurierit inimicus* 161, **II.114**
John Malalas, *Chronographia* 206, **I.64**; 244, **V.28**; 261, **I.65**; 290, **V.9**
John Malalas, *Excerpta de insidiis* 166-7, **V.29**
Justin Martyr, *Apologia* 77, **IV.70**
Justin Martyr, *Dialogus cum Tryphone* 17.108, **III.72**
Martyrdom of Pionius, 3.6, **II.139**
Martyrdom of Polycarp 12.1-13.1, **V.89**
Origen, *Epistola ad Africanum* 14, **IV.68**
Pseudo-Chrysostom, *De nativ. S.Ioannis* in *PL* Supp. I, col. 564, **II.27**
Severus Majoricensis, *Epistola de Iudaeis* 4, **VI.19**; 9, 10 and 20 (extracts only), **VI.61**
Socrates, *Ecclesiastical History* 7.13, **V.99**; 7.16, **V.91**
Sozomenus, *History* 5.16.5, **II.105**
Tertullian, *Scorpiace* 10, **II.18**

2. Inscriptions

AE, 1990, no. 823, **IV.42**
Bagatti-Milik, no. 9, **III.44a**; no. 13a, **III.40**; no. 21, **VII.27**; no. 31, **VII.28**
BASOR 187 (1967) 29, **II.2**; 235 (1979) 33, **III.28**
BS II no. 11, **III.61**; no. 61, **IV.39**; no. 66, **II.98**; no. 92, **I.85**; no. 100, **III.57**; no. 111, **III.63**; no. 137, **III.60**; no. 141, **II.79**; no. 147, **III.55**; no. 148, **III.62**; no. 164, **III.56**; no. 171, **III.54b**; no. 172, **III.54a**; no. 173, **III.54c**; no. 203, **III.58**; no. 221, **III.59**
Bulletin of Judaeo-Greek Studies 13 (Winter, 1993), p. 27, **I.106**
CIJ I no. 2, **VI.64**; I no. 9, **II.21**; I no. 21, **VII.31**; I² no. 22, **I.61**; I² no. 25, **I.47**; I² no. 47, **VI.14**; I no. 68, **VII.32**; I no. 76*, **VI.48**; I no. 77*, **VI.22**; I no. 85, **II.37**; I no. 86, **V.44**; I no. 88, **I.63**; I² no. 99, **VI.26**; I² no. 100, **II.23**; I no. 109, **I.98**; I² no. 111, **II.92**; I no. 113, **II.86**; I² no. 119, **V.63**; I no. 120, **VI.29**; I no. 121, **II.43**; I no. 125, **II.107**; I no. 132, **II.93**; I no. 140, **II.29**; I no. 145, **II.44**; I no. 146, **II.46**; I no. 147, **I.43**; I no. 148, **II.49**; I no. 149, **II.45**; I no. 152, **V.64**; I² no. 166, **II.72**; I no. 172, **II.65**; I no. 180, **VI.26**; I no. 190, **II.87**; I no. 201, **V.42**; I no. 203, **II.104**; I² no. 206, **VI.42**; I no. 209, **VI.8**; I² no. 210, **I.97**; I² no. 215, **II.88**; I no. 217, **VI.9**; I no. 219, **VI.10**; I no. 220, **VI.41**; I no. 222, **VII.33**; I² no. 228, **VII.35**; I no. 237, **VI.43**; I no. 256, **VI.38**; I no. 265, **VI.23**; I² no. 277, **II.31**; I² no. 283, **II.131**; I no. 284, **VI.27**; I² no. 296, **I.45**; I no. 301, **VI.33**; I no. 304, **I.99**; I² no. 315, **II.97**; I

no. 319, **II.68**; I no. 321, **II.102**; I^2 no. 324, **II.38**; I^2 no. 333, **II.84**; I no. 337, **VI.24**; I no. 347, **II.96**; I^2 no. 358, **V.62**; I^2 no. 362, **I.48**; I^2 no. 363, **II.108**; I no. 365, **II.24**; I no. 368, **II.20**; I no. 370, **V.43**; I no. 374, **II.136**; I no. 383, **II.58**; I^2 no. 384, **II.33**; I^2 no. 391, **II.34**; I no. 397, **II.32**; I no. 398, **II.36**; I no. 402, **VI.28**; I^2 no. 408, **I.46**; I^2 no. 416, **II.35**; I^2 no. 417, **VI.35**; I no. 456, **II.48**; I no. 457, **II.28**; I^2 no. 462, **VI.39**; I no. 464, **VI.47**; I^2 no. 470, **II.82**; I^2 no. 476, **VI.49**; I^2 no. 482, **II.94**; I no. 494, **VI.25**; I no. 496, **II.71**; I no. 500, **VII.36**; I no. 502, **I.49**; I^2 no. 503, **VI.34**; I^2 no. 508, **II.89**; I no. 509, **II.100**; I no. 523, **VII.30**; I^2 no. 524, **VII.38**; I no. 530, **IV.25a-b**; I no. 531, **I.60**; I no. 532, **IV.65**; I no. 533, **VI.36**; I^2 no. 537, **II.69**; I^2 no. 538, **II.30**; I^2 no. 556, **I.14**; I no. 561, **II.19**; I no. 587, **VI.30**; I^2 no. 636, **VI.40**; I^2 no. 639, **II.73**; I no. 640, **IV.43**; I no. 642, **VII.39**; I^2 no. 643a, **VI.63**; I^2 no. 650, **III.80**; I^2 no. 662, **I.112**; I^2 no. 663, **II.51**; I^2 no. 677, **IV.42**; I^2 no. 678, **VI.44**; I^2 no. 678a, **IV.22**; I^2 no. 680, **VI.13**; I^2 no. 681, **VI.18**; I^2 no. 681b, **I.96**; I^2 no. 683, **II.14**; I^2 no. 683a, **VII.10**; I^2 no. 690, **V.53**; I^2 no. 690a, **V.54**; I^2 no. 692, **II.55**; I^2 no. 694, **II.7**; I^2 no. 696, **I.40**; I^2 no. 696b, **V.34**; I no. 697, **V.76**; I^2 no. 701, **II.101**; I^2 no. 709, **I.9**; I^2 no. 710, **I.8**; I no. 711, **V.55**; I^2 no. 711b, **V.50**; I no. 715, **I.37**; I^2 no. 715a, **I.35**; I^2 no. 715b, **II.85**; I^2 no. 715d, **I.38**; I^2 no. 715f, **I.39**; I^2 no. 720, **II.74**; I^2 no. 721a, **I.36**; I^2 no. 721c, **V.23**; I^2 no. 722, **II.63**; I^2 no. 723, **II.40**; I no. 725, **II.133**; I^2 no. 727, **I.33**; I^2 no. 731c, **V.33**; I^2 no. 731e, **VII.37**; I^2 no. 731f, **II.50**; I^2 no. 731g, **I.100**; II no. 736, **III.87**; II no. 738, **V.37**; II no. 739, **II.75**; II no. 741, **VI.37**; II no. 742, **V.19**; II no. 744, **II.61**; II no. 745, **I.90**; II no. 746, **II.95**; II no. 748, **V.26**; II no. 749, **V.18**; II no. 752, **VII.47**; II no. 754, **III.81**; II no. 755, **V.24**; II no. 756, **V.32**; II no. 757, **V.39**; II no. 760, **V.15**; II no. 764, **VI.11**; II no. 768, **V.72**; II no. 770, **V.14**; II no. 772, **I.27**; II no. 773, **VII.48**; II no. 774, **V.71**; II no. 775, **I.101**; II no. 776, **I.110**; II no. 777, **II.137**; II no. 786, **V.5**; II no. 788, **V.10**; II no. 790, **I.89**; II no. 791, **V.69**; II no. 798, **II.4**; II no. 800, **II.25**; II no. 803, **II.62**; II no. 804, **III.84**; II no. 805, **II.66**; II no. 814, **I.87**; II no. 829, **II.52**; II no. 831, **III.86**; II no. 845, **III.85**; II no. 849, **VII.49**; II no. 873, **I.88**; II no. 902, **III.46**; II no. 910, **III.47**; II no. 918, **II.41**; II no. 920, **IV.41**; II no. 925, **III.48**; II no. 928, **III.49**; II no. 930, **III.50**; II no. 931, **III.24**; II no. 934, **III.51**; II no. 950, **III.52**; II no. 954, **III.53**; II no. 1006, **IV.39**; II no. 1010, **I.85**; II no. 1011, **III.57**; II no. 1024, **III.61**; II no. 1107, **II.98**; II no. 1138, **III.63**; II no. 1227a, **III.38a**; II no. 1227b, **III.38b**; II no. 1230, **III.31**; II no. 1233, **III.41**; II no. 1256, **III.16**; II no. 1284, **III.42**; II no. 1385, **VII.26**; II no. 1388, **III.36b**; II no. 1390, **III.43**; II no. 1404, **III.2**; II no. 1414, **III.45**; II no. 1419, **I.84**; II no. 1432, **IV.2**; II no. 1440, **IV.1**; II no. 1441, **II.22**; II no. 1442, **I.103**; II no. 1443, **IV.11**; II no. 1444, **V.38**; II no. 1449, **IV.3**; II no. 1450, **I.105**; II no. 1453, **V.58**; II no. 1468, **V.59**; II no. 1476, **V.60**; II no. 1511, **V.66**; II no. 1513, **V.67**; II no. 1514, **V.61**; II no. 1530, **V.65**; II no. 1531, **IV.9**; II no. 1532, **VII.43**; II no. 1537, **V.47**; II no. 1538, **V.48**

CIL XIV Supp. no. 4624, **VI.21**

CIL XVI Diploma no. 8, **VI.7**

CIRB no. 70, **II.14**; no. 71, **VII.10**; no. 1123, **V.53**; no. 1126, **V.54**; no. 1278, **VII.56**; no. 1285, **VII.55**

CJZC no. 6, col. II, **V.1**; no. 7a, right hand column, lines 39ff, **V.21**; no. 7c, line 13, **V.2**; no. 8, **V.13**; no. 12, **VII.29**; no. 17, **V.87**; no. 23, **V.88**; no. 29b, **III.44a**; no. 35, **III.44b**; no. 36, **V.16**; no. 70, **V.36**; no. 71, **V.35**; no. 72, **I.107**

CPJ III no. 1530a, **II.26**; III no. 1532, **VII.43**; III no. 1532a, **I.102**

DF no. 1, **II.63**; no. 2, **II.40**; no. 4, **I.33**; no. 9, **II.74**; no. 10, **II.7**; no. 12, **VII.42**; no. 13, **V.37**; no. 14, **II.75**; no. 16, **II.61**; no. 17, **VII.14**; no. 18, **VII.15**; no. 22, **I.92**; no. 23, **I.91**; no. 24, **V.11**; no. 25, **V.12**; no. 26, **V.6**; no. 28, **III.81**; no. 29, **V.32**; no. 30, **VII.13**; no. 31, **I.111**; no. 32, **III.82**; no. 33, **VII.17**; no. 35, **V.45**; no. 38, **II.62**; no. 39, **III.84**; no. 40, **II.66**; no. 49, **I.87**; no. 55, **V.46**; no. 58, **II.52**; no. 59,

III.86; no. 79, **III.2**; no. 83, **III.87**; no. 85, **II.60**; no. 100, **I.107**; no. 101, **II.51**
Fasola, fig. 11, **II.90**
Hanfmann, fig. 268, **I.93**; fig. 272, **IV.40**
Hellenica 11-12 (1960) 260, **I.109**; 392-4, **V.73**
HN no. 13, **IV.2**; no. 22, **IV.1**; no. 24, **II.22**; no. 25, **I.103**; no. 26, **VII.51**; no. 27,
 IV.11; no. 28, **V.38**; no. 34, **V.66**; no. 36, **V.67**; no. 38, **V.65**; no. 39, **II.26**; no. 42,
 V.58; no. 57, **V.59**; no. 65, **V.60**; no. 84, **V.61**; no. 115, **IV.9**; no. 116, **VII.43**; no.
 117, **I.102**; no. 121, **V.47**; no. 122, **V.48**; no. 123, **V.49**; no. 125, **IV.3**; no. 129,
 I.105; no. 144, **I.40**; no. 145, **III.46**; no. 146, **II.41**; no. 147, **IV.41**; no. 148, **III.49**;
 no. 149, **III.50**; no. 150, **III.51**; no. 153, **III.16**
IEJ 41 (1991), 270, **II.130**; 275, **II.129**
IG XII.1, no. 11, **I.34**
IGLS IV no. 1319, **II.62**; no. 1320, **III.84**; no. 1321, **II.66**; no. 1330, **I.87**; no. 1336,
 V.46
IK Ephesos V, no. 1676, **II.95**; no. 1677, **I.90**
IK Kalchedon no. 75, **II.25**
IK Smyrna no. 295, **VI.37**; no. 296, **I.109**
IOSPE II no. 446, **VII.56**; no. 450, **VII.55**
Le Bohec, no. 4, **II.54**; no. 12, **VI.45**; no. 13, **III.83**; no. 14, **II.59**; no. 28, **I.50**; no.
 71, **VI.46**; no. 74, **II.70**; no. 75, **VI.62**; no. 79, **VI.17**; no. 80, **III.88**
MAMA III no. 222, **V.5**; III no. 262, **V.10**; III no. 344, **I.89**; III no. 440, **V.69**; IV no.
 202, **I.27**; VI no. 316, **V.72**; VI no. 335, **V.70**
MPAT no. 68, **III.34**; no. 108, **III.16**; no. 132, **III.36b**
New Docs. I no. 5(i), **VII.45**; I no. 5(ii), **VII.46**; II no. 114, **I.96**
Noy I no. 5, **II.73**; I no. 6, **IV.43**; I no. 8, **VI.63**; I no. 9, **VII.39**; I no. 11, **VI.40**; I no.
 12, **II.91**; I no. 13, **IV.21**; I no. 14, **II.57**; I no. 15, **VI.21**; I no. 17, **II.42**; I no. 18,
 VI.36; I no. 22, **III.89**; I no. 23, **II.19**; I no. 26, **I.14**; I no. 53, **VI.30**; I no. 145,
 III.80; I no. 159, **VII.50**; I no. 163, **II.53**; I no. 180, **I.112**; I no. 181, **II.51**; II no.
 11, **II.97**; II no. 25, **V.62**; II no. 56, **II.136**; II no. 60, **I.48**; II no. 62, **VI.39**; II no.
 68, **II.84**; II no. 69, **I.99**; II no. 85, **II.48**; II no. 96, **VI.33**; II no. 100, **VI.28**; II no.
 103, **VI.49**; II no. 106, **II.36**; II no. 110, **II.34**; II no. 112, **V.43**; II no. 113, **I.46**;
 II no. 117, **II.58**; II no. 121, **II.38**; II no. 124, **II.96**; II no. 127, **II.108**; II no. 163,
 VI.35; II no. 164, **VI.24**; II no. 165, **II.33**; II no. 170, **II.24**; II no. 171, **II.102**; II
 no. 179, **II.28**; II no. 183, **I.45**; II no. 189, **II.20**; II no. 193, **II.32**; II no. 194, **II.35**;
 II no. 207, **VII.35**; II no. 212, **II.92**; II no. 217, **VI.42**; II no. 218, **VI.38**; II no.
 223, **II.45**; II no. 224, **VII.33**; II no. 231, **II.43**; II no. 238, **I.43**; II no. 240, **II.104**;
 II no. 251, **II.72**; II no. 253, **II.49**; II no. 254, **V.64**; II no. 255, **VI.26**; II no. 256,
 II.46; II no. 257, **II.44**; II no. 258, **VI.43**; II no. 259, **II.37**; II no. 276, **V.44**; II no.
 277, **I.98**; II no. 279, **VI.10**; II no. 281, **II.93**; II no. 284, **VI.9**; II no. 288, **I.63**; II
 no. 290, **II.65**; II no. 307, **V.42**; II no. 322, **VI.23**; II no. 325, **VI.8**; II no. 328,
 II.88; II no. 337, **VI.29**; II no. 338, **II.29**; II no. 343, **I.97**; II no. 344, **II.107**; II
 no. 354, **V.63**; II no. 360, **I.25**; II no. 373, **II.23**; II no. 374, **II.86**; II no. 378, **VI.41**;
 II no. 390, **II.87**; II no. 402, **II.31**; II no. 414, **II.106**; II no. 451, **I.61**; II no. 459,
 I.47; II no. 486, **VI.14**; II no. 487, **II.21**; II no. 489, **VII.31**; II no. 491, **VII.32**; II
 no. 502, **II.5**; II no. 503, **I.44**; II no. 508, **I.41**; II no. 515, **I.42**; II no. 516, **II.90**;
 II no. 521, **II.81**; II no. 530, **VI.64**; II no. 535, **II.131**; II no. 540, **VI.25**; II no. 542,
 II.71; II no. 544, **II.89**; II no. 547, **VI.27**; II no. 549, **VI.34**; II no. 560, **II.68**; II
 no. 561, **I.49**; II no. 564, **II.94**; II no. 575, **II.47**; II no. 576, **II.100**; II no. 577,
 VII.30; II no. 584, **II.69**; II no. 585, **II.30**; II no. 601, **IV.25a-b**; II no. 602, **I.60**;
 II no. 603, **IV.65**; II no. 608, **VI.47**; II no. 618, **II.82**; II no. 626(iii), **VII.38**; II no.
 627(i), **VII.36**
OGIS I no. 428, **VI.4**; II no. 573, **VII.52**
Puech no. 26, **III.35**; no. 27, **III.40**

Rahmani no. 99, **III.44b**; no. 404, **III.39**; no. 789, **III.28**
REJ 101 (1937) 85-6, **V.22**
Reynolds and Tannenbaum, p. 5, Face a, **VII.11**; pp. 6-7, Face b, **VII.12**
RivAC 51 (1975) 362, **II.47**
Roueché no. 180.iii, **V.30**
Scheiber no. 3, **IV.42**; no. 7, **VI.44**; no. 8, **IV.22**; no. 10, **VI.18**
SCI 11 (1991/2), 150, **III.37a-c**
SEG 15 (1958) no. 873, **IV.32**; 26 (1976-77) no. 1162, **II.5**; 26 (1976-77) no. 1163,
   I.44; 26 (1976-77) no. 1167, **I.41**; 26 (1976-77) no. 1173, **I.42**; 26 (1976-77) no.
   1178, **II.81**; 26 (1976-77) no. 1183, **II.106**; 27 (1977) no. 1201, **II.54**; 29 (1979)
   no. 537, **I.95**; 33 (1983) no. 1277, **III.17**; 36 (1986) no. 970, **VII.11**; **VII.12**; 37
   (1987) no. 846, **V.30**; 41 (1991) no. 1558, **III.37a**; 41 (1991) no. 1738, **I.100**
Syria 5 (1924) 324, **VI.5**
TAM II.2, no. 612, **V.39**; IV.1, no. 374, **II.4**; IV.1, no. 376, **I.108**; V.2, no. 1142,
   VII.47
Trebilco, *Jewish Communities* 2.4.5, **V.7**; 3.2, **VII.17**; 3.3.2, **V.70**; 3.6.1, **V.68**; 4.5.1,
   V.71; 6.4.4, **VII.44**

3. Papyri

CPJ I no. 9a, **I.67**; I no. 10, **II.111**; I no. 14, **I.70**; I no. 20, **V.56**; I no. 21, **IV.5**; I no.
   23, **V.57**; I no. 24, **IV.6**; I no. 25, **IV.12**; I no. 28, **I.73**; I no. 38, **I.68**; I no. 43, **I.69**;
   I no. 46, **I.71**; I no. 69, **IV.18**; I no. 95, **I.72**; I no. 100, **IV.16**; I no. 101, **IV.17**; I
   no. 107, **IV.19**; I no. 127a, **IV.13**; I no. 127d, **V.51**; I no. 129, **II.64**; I no. 132,
   IV.14; I no. 137, **IV.15**; I no. 138, **II.6**; I no. 139, **II.8**; II no. 143, **II.83**; II no. 151,
   V.3; II no. 152, **I.76**; II no. 153, **V.80**; II no. 157, **V.82**; II no. 162, **IV.54**; II no.
   167, **IV.55**; II no. 178, **IV.56**; II no. 179, **IV.57**; II no. 181, **IV.53**; II no. 182,
   IV.58; II no. 183, **IV.59**; II no. 186, **III.13**; II no. 192, **IV.60**; II no. 195, **IV.61**;
   II no. 203, **IV.62**; II no. 209, **I.58**; II no. 228, **IV.63**; II no. 240, **IV.36**; II no. 272,
   I.81; II no. 282, **I.82**; II no. 418b, **IV.34**; II no. 419d, **I.78**; II no. 421, **IV.52**; II
   no. 428, **IV.37**; II no. 432, **II.39**; II no. 437, **V.85**; II no. 443, **V.86**; III no.452a,
   II.135; III no. 460, **IV.64**; III no. 473, **VI.6**; III no. 477, **IV.38**
New Docs. VI no. 24, **IV.7**
P.Köln III no. 144, **IV.7**

4. Legal texts

Codex Iustinianus 1.9.1, **I.113**
Codex Theodosianus 3.7.2, **IV.72**; 12.1.158, **VI.16**; 16.8.3, **VI.15**; 16.8.9, **V.93**;
   16.8.12, **VI.60**; 16.8.14, **III.78**; 16.8.17, **III.79**; 16.8.18, **II.138**; 16.8.19, **VII.58**;
   16.8.20, **IV.29**; 16.8.22, **II.121**; 16.8.24, **IV.73**; 16.8.25, **V.94**; 16.9.2, **IV.71**
Constitutio Sirmondiana 4, **II.147**
Digest 48.8.11, **II.119**; 50.2.3.3, **V.8**
Paulus, *Sententiae* 5.22.3-4, **II.120**

5. Coins

Goodenough III, fig. 700, **V.17**
RIC II, 227-8, nos. 58, 72 and 82, **IV.67**

6. Modern collections of ancient legal and literary texts

Linder no. 1, **II.119**; no. 2, **V.8**; no. 3, **I.113**; no. 6, **II.120**; no. 7, **VI.15**; no. 10, **II.147**; no. 11, **IV.71**; no. 18, **IV.72**; no. 21, **V.93**; no. 25, **VI.60**; no. 29, **VI.16**; no. 30, **III.78**; no. 34, **III.79**; no. 36, **II.138**; no. 39, **VII.58**; no. 40, **IV.29**; no. 41, **II.121**; no. 45, **IV.73**; no. 47, **V.94**

Stern I no. 11, **II.109**; I no. 68 (extracts only), **II.99**, **III.9**; I no. 105, **I.4**; I no. 115, **VII.1**; I no. 129, **VII.3**; I no. 143, **II.112**; I no. 147a, **IV.44b**; I no. 147b, **IV.44a**; I no. 186, **II.113**; I no. 188, **II.116**; I no. 189, **II.125**; I no. 190, **II.115**; I no. 194, **II.118**; I no. 262, **I.10**; II no. 281, **VII.2**; II no. 284, **I.54**; II no. 292, **IV.31**; II no. 293, **VII.41**; II no. 296, **I.62**; II no. 297, **II.11**; II no.301, **VII.20**; II no. 302, **VI.31**; II no. 303, **II.117**; II no. 306, **IV.45**; II no. 307, **II.144**; II no. 320, **IV.66**; II no. 333, **II.10**; II no. 334, **II.126**; II no. 419, **IV.46**; II no. 422, **IV.47**; II no. 430, **III.22**; II no. 430 (final section), **IV.50**; II no. 435, **VII.40**; II no. 437, **V.84**; II no. 482, **II.105**; II no. 495a, **I.86**; II no. 501, **VI.32**; II no. 504, **II.80**; II no. 538, **IV.48**; II no. 543, **II.123**

Indices

References are to the source numbers used in this book.

1. People

A. Jews and converts to Judaism

Agrippa I, I.5; I.74; VI.4

Agrippa II, IV.35; VI.5

Alexander, Hasmonaean son of Herod, I.28

Alexander (impostor), I.28

Alexander the *alabarch*, I.74; III.15; IV.30

Ananel, High Priest under Herod, III.32

Ananias, Jewish general in Egypt, IV.8

Andreas, rebel leader in Cyrene, V.84

Antipater, father of Herod the Great, VI.1

Apollos, early Christian convert, I.32; II.146

Aquila, early Christian convert, I.21; I.94 (intro.)

Aquila, translator of the Bible, V.40 (intro.); V.42 (intro.); VII.25

Archelaus, Judaean ethnarch, I.52

Aristoboulos II, I.10

Aristoboulos, Hasmonaean son of Herod, I.28

Artemion, rebel leader in Cyprus, V.84

Asabinos, Jew of Antioch, V.9; V.29

Bar-Jesus, Jewish sorcerer, II.127

Berenice, daughter of Agrippa I, V.77 (note); VI.4

Chelkias, Jewish general in Egypt, IV.8

Cypros, wife of Agrippa I, I.74

Demetrios, the *alabarch*, IV.35

Dositheos, son of Drimylos, IV.13 (note); V.51

Fulvia, Roman proselyte, VII.21

Gamaliel, son or grandson of Hillel the Elder, III.30

Gamaliel VI, Jewish Patriarch, II.121

Helena, Queen of Adiabene, III.6; III.18; III.20; III.36a; III.36b (note); VII.22

Herod the Great, I.19; I.28; II.123; III.17; III.32; V.78

Herod the tetrarch, I.30

Hillel the Elder, III.29

Izates, King of Adiabene, III.6; III.20; III.31 (with note); III.36a; VII.22-3

Jason, Hellenising High Priest, III.65; V.20

Josephus, the historian (personal experiences), I.23; I.26; VI.2

Judah I ha-Nasi, Jewish Patriarch, III.26; III.76 (intro.)

Judah IV, Jewish Patriarch, III.76 (note)

Judas Maccabaeus, III.64

Monobazus II, king of Adiabene, III.18; III.36a; VII.23

Nikanor, benefactor of the Temple, III.16

Onias, founder of Temple at Leontopolis, I.20

Paul, the Apostle, I.21; I.30; I.31; I.94; II.17; II.56; II.127; II.145-6; III.19; III.30; III.70-1; V.4; V.75; VI.3; VI.12; VII.9; VII.19

Philo (personal experiences), III.4; V.25; V.27

Priscilla, early Christian convert, I.21; I.94 (intro.)

Rabban Gamaliel, III.73

Rabbi Akiba, III.29; III.69; III.73

Rabbi Eleazer ben Azariah, III.73-4

Rabbi Mattiah ben Heresh, III.74

Saul, *see* Paul, the Apostle

Sceva, sons of, Jewish exorcists, II.128

Simon Maccabaeus, I.3

Simon, son of Boethus, High Priest under Herod, III.17; III.33

4. Jewish occupations

A. In the private sector

B. In Ptolemaic and Seleucid government service